INTRODUCTION TO LEGAL METHOD

AUSTRALIA
The Law Book Company Ltd.
Sydney : Melbourne : Brisbane

CANADA AND U.S.A.
The Carswell Company Ltd.
Agincourt, Ontario

INDIA
N. M. Tripathi Private Ltd.
Bombay

ISRAEL
Steimatzky's Agency Ltd.
Jerusalem : Tel Aviv : Haifa

MALAYSIA : SINGAPORE : BRUNEI
Malayan Law Journal
Singapore

NEW ZEALAND
Sweet & Maxwell (N.Z.) Ltd.
Wellington

PAKISTAN
Pakistan Law House
Karachi

INTRODUCTION
TO
LEGAL METHOD

by

JOHN H. FARRAR, LL.M.

Solicitor of the Supreme Court,
Senior Lecturer in Law at the University of Bristol

LONDON
SWEET & MAXWELL
1977

First edition 1977
Second impression 1978

*Published by Sweet & Maxwell
Ltd. of 11 New Fetter Lane,
London and printed in Great
Britain by J. W. Arrowsmith
Ltd., Bristol.*

ISBN Hardback 0 421 21170 9
Paperback 0 421 21190 3

PREFACE

THE aim of this book is to introduce the reader to law and legal method and to stimulate thought about law and society. Part I of the book introduces law by discussing the nature and functions of law, the classification of law and the basic techniques of social control used in the legal system. Part II introduces legal method more specifically by discussing the general problems of law and fact, legal categorisation and reasoning, the particular data and ground rules relating to case law, legislation, codification, legal literature and the impact of membership of the EEC. This Part is supplemented by three appendices which set out specimen legal sources, give instruction in legal bibliography and provide a detailed study of the case law process. Throughout Parts I and II there is an attempt to relate law to its social background and this is the special focus of Part II of the book which deals with socio-economic change, the limits of law and the underlying questions of policy and values. The book does not deal in any detail with the institutions of the legal system which are already adequately dealt with elsewhere and it is hoped that, together with works on the institutions, it can be used in a first-year course on the legal system in the universities and polytechnics. I have used the bulk of the material for that purpose in the LL.B. course at the University of Bristol. The main problem I encountered was the lack of a suitable accompanying text on legal method—a gap which this book attempts to fill. It is hoped that it will, therefore, be of some use to first-year law students in helping them to acquire a basic knowledge of legal rules, an understanding of the relationship of law to the social and economic environment in which it operates and the ability to handle facts and apply abstract concepts to them, which the Ormrod Report identified as the objectives of the academic stage of legal education. At the same time it is hoped that it will assist others (such as social scientists) who are keen to learn something of the lawyer's viewpoint and some basic detail about legal sources. Lastly it is hoped that it might be of some use to continental lawyers who need to be familiar with English legal method. The book reflects some experience which I have had in teaching EEC officials on courses held at the University of Bath from which, in all honesty, I probably learned as much as I taught about the differences between the various systems.

Although footnotes are used in the text I have tried to keep them to a minimum, and have added a bibliography of further reading at the end. I apologise for the table which appears on pages 205 *et seq.* Ideally, I would have liked to have inserted details of abbreviations, but there was insufficient space. As it is, there is a lot of detail crammed into a relatively small space. I only hope its utility will outweigh its unattractiveness.

The genesis of this book owes a great deal to Professor Glanville Williams' *Learning the Law.* It differs from that book, which is and will remain a guide, philosopher and friend to the aspiring law student, in the following respects. It is less didactic in style. It concentrates on legal method in more detail, and it attempts to give a prologue to a social view of law in the way described above. It makes frequent comparisons with Scots law and other systems. In some of these respects it owes something to Pollock's *A First Book of Jurisprudence*; Derham, Maher and Waller's *Introduction to Law*; and Levi's *Introduction to Legal Reasoning.* The late Professor Friedmann's *Law in a Changing Society*, Sir Rupert Cross, *Precedent in English Law* and Professor Robert Summers' *Law : its Nature, Functions and Limits* and his recent articles on legal techniques and process values have all been drawn upon for useful comment and examples. I have also profited from attending a seminar given by Professor Summers on the limits of law.

Despite its relative brevity this has not been an easy book to write. Whatever merit (if any) it has is due in some measure to students and colleagues who have discussed things with me. Amongst these I would particularly thank Neil Johnson, Dorothy Nelson, Hugh Beale, Stephen Jones, Brenda Sufrin, Tony Dugdale, and David and Carolyn Yates.

Last, for those sceptical academics who might think that to use this kind of material at the beginning of the first year is expecting too much too soon—all I can say is that it has been shown to work in the past with what I think was a moderate degree of success. I found student response on the whole to be enthusiastic. They seemed to use the training to advantage in other subjects, and jurisprudence was not such an alien subject to them in the third year.

JOHN FARRAR

January 1977.

ACKNOWLEDGMENTS

THE extract from *Essays in Jurisprudence and the Common Law* is reproduced by kind permission of Professor A. L. Goodhart and Cambridge University Press (© Cambridge University Press 1931).

The extract from pages 8 and 9 of *An Introduction to Legal Reasoning* by Edward Levi is reproduced by kind permission of the University of Chicago (© The University of Chicago. All rights reserved. Published 1948. Twelfth Impression 1968).

Extracts from "The Ratio of the Ratio Decidendi" (1959) 22 M.L.R. 597 are reproduced by kind permission of Professor Julius Stone and The Modern Law Review Ltd.

Extracts from *Law: its Nature, Functions and Limits* (2nd ed.), are reproduced by kind permission of Professor Robert S. Summers and Prentice-Hall Inc., Englewood Cliffs, N.J., U.S.A. (© 1972, 1965 Prentice-Hall Inc. All rights reserved).

The extract from [1975] C.M.L.R. is reproduced by kind permission of Common Law Reports Ltd.

The Education Act 1975 and Statutory Instrument 1974 No. 654 are reproduced by kind permission of Her Majesty's Stationery Office.

The extract from [1976] 1 Q.B. is reproduced by kind permission of The Incorporated Council of Law Reporting for England and Wales.

CONTENTS

BOOK II
SOURCES OF LAW AND METHODS OF LEGAL REASONING

BOOK III

PROBLEMS OF THE LAW AND LEGAL METHOD

APPENDICES

TABLE OF CASES

BOOK I

Introduction to Law

Chapter 1

THE NATURE AND FUNCTIONS OF LAW

It is customary to preface a discussion about law with one or two broad generalisations about the nature of man. Yet it is sometimes said that one cannot or should not generalise. This is patent nonsense. One can generalise but the generalisation must be supported by evidence, and the danger arises in generalising beyond the particular evidence available. Certain generalisations about man are universally valid, such as "all men are mortal" and that "from a global point of view there are limited resources." Some would go further and make other general comments about the human condition, about man being basically good or evil. Clearly there are dangers in generalisations of this latter order, and they often hide a particular ideological bias. It is probably better to view human nature as many-sided and contradictory and in any event not as a property inherent in man so much as a relation between men.

"Truisms" about Human Nature

Professor H. L. A. Hart in his book *The Concept of Law* [1] put forward certain generalisations about mankind which he says are truisms, and which, given survival as an aim, afford a reason (or more precisely a set of reasons) why morality and law endure and possess a specific content. The facts are

  (i) human vulnerability,
 (ii) approximate equality,
(iii) limited altruism,
 (iv) limited resources, and
  (v) limited understanding and strength of will.

These are of course vague, and some, such as approximate equality and limited understanding, are perhaps inherently controversial. Also, their status as truisms is ambiguous—since it is not clear whether their self-evidence is to be regarded as apparent on the face of them or only in the light of extraneous considerations which are to be assumed. Hart himself acknowledges that his truisms are based on the philosophical writings of Hobbes and Hume rather than empirical research. [2]

There is some research which has been done by psychologists, indicating a human need for order and predictability in life.[3] Clearly the scientific standing of such research findings may be a matter of controversy—controversy which sometimes challenges the basic claim of social science to be scientific. There are problems of clinical testing, coping with value considerations, and in the scope of the generalisations put forward. It may be that out of considerations such as these Hart relies on truisms and says that the relationship of his truisms to the existence of a common content of morality and law is not a matter of causation (cause and effect) but " natural necessity," by which he seems to mean that they afford practical reasons for such content.[4]

Social Order and Law

To a social scientist they afford reasons for social order in the sense of restraint, predictability, consistency, reciprocity and persistence in human behaviour.[5] A solitary individual—a hermit living in complete isolation from other human beings—probably requires nothing more than habits. Habits, according to some scientists, arise because of our limited supplies of mental and physical energy. It is debatable whether the individual family needs anything more than habits, although some families do in fact have rules. When one gets socialisation consisting at least of a number of families the habits, or at least some of them, seem to begin to crystallise into customs and then into rules.

The existence of such rules used to be explained by reference to a social contract, but the evidence for such a pact in early or present-day primitive communities is not forthcoming. Hume instead explained the existence of social order in terms of habit and self interest [6]; Durkheim in terms of solidarity.[7] Others more recently have emphasised particular factors such as a consensus of values, inertia, or conflict and coercion.[8] All of these are themes to which we shall return. Modern industrialised societies are complex systems with many variables operating. The social contract idea, although it has recently been resuscitated, is at best a simplistic artificial construction useful perhaps to *justify* the existing order or a better one, but not to explain it.[9] The factors which modern writers identify are useful (perhaps necessary) in an account of social order but they are not individually sufficient to explain it.

In primitive societies when rules are broken and the breach is not the subject-matter of feud, social order is often maintained by a series of unorganised sanctions such as ostracism, ridicule, avoidance and denial of favours. In some societies, such as the Yurok Indians, these were supplemented by go-betweens who acted in a positive but non-judicial way in disputes. Their role was primarily that of diplomats. Amongst the Luhya tribe of western Kenya, the elders intervene and perform a similar role. In such societies the emphasis is on reconciliation of the parties as much as resolution of a particular dispute, since there is a need for continuing contact between the parties.

Eventually some of the rules become recognised as laws. In England this was largely a result of adjudication and assimilation by the King's judges. From this you might infer that law in general is a set of particular laws recognised by the judges. This idea of law is a reasonable one but inadequate. It fails to indicate that people often talk of law not so much in terms of particular laws but in terms of a system. Law is sometimes equated with government and a legal system. In this sense law in our society would include Parliament, the courts, the judiciary, the legal profession and the police and bureaucracy who service the system. Again, some equate law with the legal process, which refers primarily to the legislative and judicial processes—the making of Acts of Parliament and delegated legislation, and the adjudication by judges. This book is principally about law in the sense of a set of laws and the legal process. It refers to the institutions but does not purport to give a detailed treatment of them. The sense in which we refer to law from time to time will, however, be clear from the context.

Law in all three senses of laws, system and process [10] is one of a number of means of social control fostering social order in modern society. The term " social control " was used by an American writer, Ross,[11] as a broad term to cover not only law but also public opinion, religion, education, custom and other less obvious things, such as art. In this broad sense it would cover the unorganised sanctions referred to above. Some recent writers have tended to limit its application to control of deviance.

In what ways does law as an instrument of social control help to foster social order? What are its social functions? [12] First, it maintains *public order*. Sometimes this is expressed in the cliché " law and order." This is a woolly term often used for emotive purposes by the less reputable species of policitian and is better avoided. Historically, law has evolved as an alternative to private feud and vengeance, and as a supplement to the informal social processes by which men and groups deal with disputes. Law has the advantage over both feud and the more informal alternatives, in that it provides a rationalised and conclusive settlement to disputes which is subject to public scrutiny.

Another aspect of maintenance of public order is the suppression of deviant behaviour. What is regarded as deviant differs as society changes. In an open society this is a matter of public debate and controversy. How far should the area of the law extend and for what reasons? We shall return to this topic later.

Secondly, law fosters social order by *facilitating co-operative action*. Law recognises certain basic underlying interests and provides a framework of rules for giving effect to them. Thus, for instance, it recognises a person's right to freedom from physical injury, and protects his property. It provides systems for transfer and inheritance of property and formation of groups for peaceful purposes.

Thirdly, it *constitutes and regulates the principal organs of power*. It provides for succession to power and defines who has the right to exercise what kind of power in society. The United Kingdom is peculiar in that it does not have a written constitution. It does, however, have a constitution consisting of a body of particular laws, conventions and traditions which regulate its political life.

Finally, law *communicates and reinforces social values*. Law has always enforced some morality. Clearly even the most primitive legal order seeks to regulate matters such as homicide and theft. Bentham [13] and John Stuart Mill [14] discussed the limits within which law should be used to enforce morality. Both favoured a rationalistic approach, and Mill put the emphasis on the value of the maximum freedom for the individual being compatible with the freedom of others. At the same time they both sought to reform the law so that it reflected their brand of morality, *utility*, the greatest happiness of the greatest number. Mill at least perceived a possible contradiction in these attitudes in that utility could lead to the tyranny of the majority and he sought to justify himself by modifying the rigours of utility. More recently the debate has continued between Lord Devlin [15] and Professor Hart [16] and others [17] over the identification of moral standards and the extent of the law's need and right to enforce them. Again, we shall return to this later.

With the growth of collectivism and the welfare state, a wide range of matters formerly left to the individual conscience has been made the subject of state control through law. At other times Parliament has legislated to regulate behaviour in advance of public opinion and has used the law partly as an educative medium on such issues as capital punishment, homosexuality, race relations and sex equality.

The relationship then between law and morality is a complex one. Analytically the relationship can be crudely represented thus:

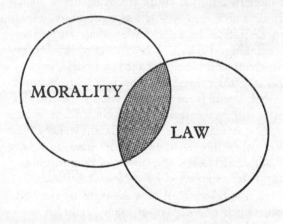

The shaded area represents the area of common ground where law enforces morality. The size of the shaded area is constantly changing. The one great danger with this simplification is that it perhaps suggests a commonly accepted morality in the sense of specific, ascertainable moral rules. In other words, it presupposes the existence of common morality and some consensus on its content. With the growth of relativism in moral beliefs it is becoming more and more difficult to identify a consensus morality. The areas of consensus are yielding ground to opinion and controversy. Any comprehensive view of a legal system must reflect both this tension and the underlying interests represented by existing institutions and pressure groups of varying kinds seeking either the maintenance or reform of the status quo. We shall explore this theme in the third part of this book.

The Normative Character of Law and Morality

We have seen the close analytical and causal relationship between law and morality. We are using the word law here in the sense of a set of particular laws. Perhaps it would be better to be even more explicit. The set of laws comprehends *legal rules, principles, standards and concepts*. How can one distinguish between these? [18]

An American writer, Dean Roscoe Pound, defines *rule* as a precept attaching a definite detailed consequence to a definite detailed state of facts. He gave as an example a provision in the ancient Code of Hammurabi " If a free man strike a free man, he shall pay ten shekels of silver," and made the point that primitive codes and modern criminal codes are made up of such rules.

His definition of a *principle* is less satisfactory. He adopted the Aristotelian definition of a principle as an authoritative starting point for reasoning. Perhaps a better definition for our purposes would be in terms of a precept of the same basic form as a rule, but expressed at a greater level of generality. An example might be " No man shall profit from his own wrong." Principles often, but do not necessarily have, some ethical content. It is arguable that principles are not made into law in a single judgment and that they evolve rather like custom.[19] They tend to emerge from a number of authorities often as a means of circumscribing a number of particular rules established by those authorities.

A *standard*, Pound defined as a measure of conduct prescribed by law from which one departs at one's peril. An example would be the standard of due care to avoid unreasonable risk of injury to others. Standards are perhaps of a greater level of generality than either rules and principles. Standards usually have some element of *ad hoc* evaluation in terms of fairness or reasonableness. In the case of *Knuller (Publishing, Printing and Promotions) Ltd.* v. *D.P.P.* [1973] A.C. 435, 487A–B (H.L.) Lord Simon of Glaisdale described the operation of standards as follows:

" They depend finally for their juridical classification not upon proof of the existence of some particular fact, but upon proof of the attainment of some degree. The law cannot always say that if fact X and fact Y are proved . . . legal result Z will ensue. Often the law can only say that if conduct of a stipulated standard is attained (or, more often, is not attained) legal result Z will ensue; and whether that standard has been attained cannot be with certainty known in advance by the persons involved, but has to await the evaluation of the tribunal of fact."

A *concept*, broadly speaking, is a class of things into which the facts of cases can be fitted. Sometimes in legal usage the word category is used instead of concept. Some concepts are ingredients of rules and principles such as the concepts of intention and good faith. Others such as ownership are of wider scope and are used in a broad generic way to embrace a number of rules, principles and standards. To a certain extent conceptual questions are questions about meaning and classification, *e.g.* is a bicycle a vehicle? In law, however, this is frequently complicated by the fact that the law has to make a decision in *borderline* cases for the purposes of social control. We shall examine this problem in more detail later.

Law is not unique in using rules, principles, standards and concepts. Morality also uses them together with attitudes. Morality, however, obviously differs from modern law in that it lacks a legislature and courts to adjudicate on disputes. Nevertheless, in so far as law and morality set out rules, principles and standards they are both said to have a normative character. Normative is derived from the Latin word "norma" which literally means a carpenter's measuring instrument, and the term norm [20] is used here to express the notion of a social standard applicable to fact as opposed to the fact to which the standard is applied. The application of a standard involves regulation or evaluation of fact. Law *in the sense of system and process* can be described in factual statements but the *structure of particular laws* and of morals (other than moral attitudes) is of a different grammatical form from factual statements. It is sometimes said that laws and morals are "ought" rather than "is"; that although their exact wording may differ their structure is ultimately reducible to the form "You ought (or you ought not) to do X." "Ought" is used here in an extended sense, but is perhaps suggestive of something which is or is to be justified in some way. Both law (as a set of laws) and morality can perhaps be justified on rational grounds, but law always falls back on the notion of authority and internal consistency in the use of authority, which is called *legality*. An appeal to authority to clinch an argument in strict terms constitutes a logical fallacy and *proves* nothing, but law as a practical system proceeds on this basis. It is strongly arguable that in its nature as the instrument of organised social control, law has to have recognised authoritative sources and that there has to be a background of coercion and force for it to resort to, to ensure compliance. These are then the most crucial differences between law and morality in our society, that law has clearly recognised authoritative sources and can fall back on institutionalised coercion and force.[21]

The Legitimacy of Law

However, even a legal system does not limit itself to force to guarantee its continuance. It seeks in addition to establish and cultivate a belief in its *legitimacy*.[22] Legitimacy according to its Latin origin meant conforming with law, or legality. However it has since acquired a more extended meaning which covers not only conformity with valid reasoning but also the possession of some extra quality of authenticity or genuineness. In the early period of a legal system, legitimacy may be based on *charismatic qualities* of particular rulers or judges. Later it may rest on the sanctity of *immemorial tradition*. Later still this may be in terms of the *impersonal rational authority* of the law—the rule of law not men—accepted both by those who administer the system and by the population at large. The common law shows traces of each of these—particularly tradition—although the emphasis in modern law is now shifting to the third. A general rationality is crucial to the legitimacy of the modern law and it may be, as we shall see in later chapters, that people are now coming to require that every law and legal practice should be justifiable on rational rather than traditional grounds. Rationality, according to the German lawyer and sociologist Max Weber, has two aspects—one a formal logical aspect based on intellectual consistency between the legal rules, principles, standards and concepts, and the other a substantive ideological or value aspect in the sense of conformity with the changing values of society.[23] The first is relatively static and the second dynamic. These represent a conflict or, more precisely, an antinomy which is constantly being resolved in the course of legal development.[24] Law must be stable, yet it cannot stand still.[25]

Notes

[1] H. L. A. Hart, *The Concept of Law*, pp. 189 *et seq.*

[2] *Ibid.* p. 254.

[3] See Edgar Bodenheimer, *Jurisprudence*, rev. ed., Chap. X.

[4] Hart, *op. cit.* p. 195.

[5] See Percy Cohen, *Modern Social Theory*, Chap. 2, and Hart, *op. cit.*

[6] *Treatise of Human Nature.*

[7] *The Division of Labour in Society.*

[8] See Cohen, *op. cit.*

[9] See the reference to John Rawls' use of the concept in his *Theory of Justice* in Chap. 14, *infra.*

[10] This is based on Roscoe Pound, *Social Control through Law*, p. 40.

[11] E. A. Ross, *Social Control.* For a useful modern discussion, see C. K. Watkins, *Social Control.*

[12] What follows is based on L. Broom and P. Selznick, *Sociology*, Chap. XII. See also M. D. A. Freeman, *The Legal Structure*, Part One.

[13] See Jeremy Bentham, *An Introduction to the Principles of Morals and Legislation*, ed. by J. H. Burns and H. L. A. Hart, pp. 281 *et seq.*

[14] *Essays on Liberty and Utilitarianism.*

[15] *The Enforcement of Morals.*

[16] *Law, Liberty and Morality.*

[17] See generally a very useful summary of the debate in Basil Mitchell, *Law, Morality and Religion in a Secular Society.*

[18] What follows is based on Roscoe Pound, *Social Control through Law*, pp. 45 *et seq.*, with obvious modifications. The soundest approach to ascertaining the meaning of such terms is to look and see how they are used in legal and moral language. Pound based his views on his familiarity with legal materials although he is a little dogmatic at times. For further discussion of rules and principles, see the materials referred to in the Bibliography.

[19] See Joseph Raz, "Legal Principles and the Limits of Law," 81 Yale L.J. 823, 848 (1972).

[20] Sociologists use norm in a different sense. They use it to describe a pattern of regularity in behaviour.

[21] See generally Dennis Lloyd, *The Idea of Law*, Chaps. 2 and 3.

[22] This is based on Max Weber, *Law in Economy and Society*, translated by Max Rheinstein.

[23] *Op. cit.* p. 6. Weber thought that the common law was substantively irrational since it was based too much on reaction to the particular case. See his views criticised by Rheinstein at pp. xlvii *et seq.*

[24] See Benjamin Cardozo, *The Paradoxes of Legal Science*, p. 7.

[25] R. Pound, *Interpretations of Legal History*, p. 13.

Chapter 2

THE TRADITIONAL GENERAL CLASSIFICATION OF LAW [1]

In Chapter 1, we saw something of the broad field covered by the law. We attempted some rough and ready classification based on the social functions carried out by the law. In Chapter 3, we shall have a look at particular basic techniques which the modern law has developed to carry out those functions.

In the meantime, let us pause a while and look at some traditional general classifications which lawyers have adopted and which you need to know early on in your studies. The reasons for the classifications are either historical or analytical.

Common Law and Civil Law

The term "common law" is a slippery one. Its meaning often changes with the company it keeps. In the broadest sense, it covers the legal tradition of developing law by judicial decisions. This grew up in England in the courts of common law and equity and was exported to much of the British Empire and Commonwealth. Thus England and Wales, Ireland, the United States (except Louisiana), Canada (except Québec), Australia, New Zealand and many African countries are all described as common law jurisdictions.

The term "civil law" is also somewhat slippery. Contrasted with the common law, it refers to the continental legal tradition based on Roman law, the writings of civilian jurists and the codes of the nineteenth and early twentieth centuries. The dominant approach here is sometimes said to be deductive—to look to the code as a set of rules and principles from which all else follows. Decided cases carry little weight as authorities. This broad generalisation involves a certain amount of simplification which we shall attempt to put right later. The laws of the original six members of the Common Market were all built up in the civil law tradition.

Scotland stands in an interesting intermediate position. Historically, Scotland had an autonomous common law built up on feudal custom. By the sixteenth century, although there was no formal adoption of Roman law there was a steady infiltration of its influence, and from then until the Napoleonic Wars, it was the practice of some Scots lawyers to pursue their studies of the civil law in continental law faculties. From the eighteenth century, however, a number of factors operated against this mainstream civilian influence. First, there was the political and commercial domination by England. Secondly, there was the gradual infiltration of English legal ideas, particularly via the House of Lords sitting on appeals from Scotland. Thirdly, there was the growth of really outstanding Scottish legal writings from the seventeenth century onwards which led to the development of a tradition which was more distinctly Scottish than civilian. We shall return to these writings in Chapter 10. Last, the practical difficulties of attending the continental faculties in unsettled times and the gradual growth of the Scots law schools eventually led to a severance of this link.[2]

Common Law and Equity

English law, unlike Scots law, developed a binary system. The common law here refers to the general customs of England which were adopted, shaped and formalised by judges of the King's Council. In the early period, the King's Council was a mixed body performing administrative, legislative and judicial functions. Eventually, the courts of Common Pleas, Exchequer and King's Bench became distinct courts performing an exclusively legal function.

To achieve greater consistency, the judges placed reliance on previous decisions in similar cases—a practice which eventually gave rise to a sophisticated cluster of rules or practices known now as the *doctrine of precedent* which we shall consider in detail in Chapter 7.

The common law alternated between periods of growth and periods of stagnation, but by the later Middle Ages, it suffered from a number of defects. It did not cover the whole field of social obligations. It had no means of eliciting the truth since it relied on documents rather than the evidence of the parties themselves. The process in the course of a legal action was often ineffective for various practical reasons and the common law was limited in the redress which it gave.

Some people, denied effective redress in the common law courts, petitioned the King or his Council. These petitions for extraordinary relief came to be handled by the Chancellor—in the early period always a cleric who was regarded as the Keeper of the King's Conscience.

The system of extraordinary relief gradually became institutionalised in the Court of Chancery and the principles became formalised in what is known as equity. In some cases, equity enforced rights not recognised at common law, such as the trust whereby one person (the trustee) held property for the benefit of another. In other matters such as contract, fraud and partnerships, it gave alternative and more efficient remedies. It developed special, more flexible procedures, many of which were extended by statute to the common law courts in the nineteenth century.

By the Judicature Acts of 1873 and 1875, the common law courts and the Court of Chancery were merged into a single High Court whose task it was to apply both common law and equity.

Nevertheless, the binary system still haunts the legal system, and we shall have to return to this again.

Before we pass from this topic, however, we must again refer to Scots law. As we have seen, it did not adopt the common law/equity distinction. Nevertheless, it did recognise principles based on equity in the broad sense. Lord Kames in his *Principles of Equity* at p. 17 described in 1760 how defences and remedies based on equity and in many cases similar to those developed in the Court of Chancery in England had long been administered in the Scots courts as part of their ordinary jurisdiction. " In England," he stated,

> " where the courts of equity and common law are different, the boundary between equity and common law, where the legislature did not interfere, will remain always the same. But in Scotland and other countries where equity and common law are united in one court, the boundary varies imperceptibly; for what originally is a rule in equity, loses its character when it is fully established in practice; and then it is considered as common law. . . ."

Thus Scotland had no need for the Judicature Acts.

Common Law and Legislation

Once again the term common law is used here in an extended sense to refer to case law generally and to cover equity.

The earliest examples of enacted laws are perhaps the decrees of the King's Council. Law-making in Parliament did not begin until the thirteenth century, and it was not until the sixteenth century that Acts of Parliament took the form in which they appear today. Until the nineteenth century, the volume of legislation was small. The change began after the Reform Act 1832 and legislation has now superseded the common law as the most fertile source of law. Some think that the fertility has become promiscuity.

The Queen in Parliament is the supreme legislative body in the United Kingdom, subject to the restrictions on the exercise of that sovereignty imposed or entailed by our membership of the Common Market.

Public and Private Law

The eighteenth-century Scottish institutional writer, John Erskine, stated this distinction neatly. He wrote: " The public law is that which hath more immediately in view the public weal and the preservation and good order of society; as laws concerning the constitution of the State, the administration of the government, the police of the country, public revenue, . . . the punishment of crimes, etc. Private law is that which is chiefly intended for ascertaining the civil rights of individuals." (*Institute of the Law of Scotland* I, 1, 29.) By civil rights, he refers to rights under the civil law as opposed to the criminal law, a distinction we shall examine in a moment. Today we would include under government the law relating to local authorities.

In many countries public law is an important division of the law. It has special constitutional significance and gives rise to separate systems of courts. This is not generally so in the United Kingdom. Our nearest approach to it is to have separate courts for the more serious criminal cases, and tribunals for various specialist matters, but there are procedures for bringing matters from the latter before the ordinary courts. Other public law matters are handled as a matter of course in the ordinary courts.

Nevertheless, as we shall see, public law is expanding at the expense of private law.

Civil and Criminal Law

This particular distinction has long been recognised by English and Scots law. Civil law here refers to the law which defines the rights and duties of persons to one another and provides a system of remedies. The main areas of civil law are the law of contract, the law of torts (which relates to civil wrongs such as trespass, libel and slander and negligence), family law and the law of property.

Criminal law is, generally speaking, concerned with acts or omissions which are contrary to public order and society as a whole and which render the guilty person liable to punishment.

Usually, criminal law requires proof of a particular intention but there are some modern laws such as some traffic offences or food and drugs offences, which are offences of strict liability where proof of the guilty act is sufficient.

Further classification of crimes is done either on the basis of the mode of trial—serious offences usually being tried on indictment before judge and jury and less serious or summary offences before magistrates—or on the basis of the harm done. Thus, there are crimes against the person, against property and against public rights such as the nebulous entities of public morality and decency.

Substantive Law and Procedure

Substantive law refers to the rules and principles defining the rights, powers and privileges possessed by persons whose status is recognised by law, and the corresponding duties, liabilities and disabilities to which others are subject under the law. The rules of procedure deal with the practical enforcement of those duties and liabilities, and the recognition of such disabilities.

Sometimes the term "adjective" or "adjectival" law is used in juxtaposition to substantive law. Adjective law is a wider term than procedure and procedural law. Professor D. M. Walker in *The Scottish Legal System*, 4th ed., p. 308, makes the point that adjective law differs with its context. Thus, in criminal law, it refers to the jurisdiction of the various criminal courts, their procedure, evidence, punishment and rights of appeal. In administrative law, it deals with the constitution and powers of administrative bodies and tribunals, procedure, and the awards they can make. In private law, it covers the jurisdiction of the courts, rules for the enforcement of rights, the remedies available and the procedure before and during the trial, evidence, and the rights of appeal.

Although these distinctions are made, substantive law, procedure and the other aspects of adjective law are closely linked in practice.

Notes

[1] For a number of alternative schemes of classification of the law, see *The Division and Classification of the Law*, ed. by J. A. Jolowicz. In Chap. 2, the author has adhered to traditional classifications simply because they introduce terms of art which students will find useful.

[2] See Lord Macmillan, " Scots Law a Subject of Comparative Study " in *Law and Other Things*, pp. 102 *et seq*. and T. B. Smith, *Scotland—the Development of its Laws and Constitution*, Chap. 1.

Chapter 3

METHODS OF SOCIAL CONTROL THROUGH LAW

WE saw in Chapter 1 how law is an instrument of social control, helping to maintain social order in a number of ways. Thus it serves to maintain public order, to facilitate co-operation, to regulate the exercise of power and to communicate and reinforce social values.

In this chapter we shall look at the methods of social control through law, at the basic techniques used by the modern law and the areas where they are used. But first, what precisely do we mean when we talk about such methods or techniques? We are thinking here not about sources of law and legal reasoning as such but about the various systems that a legislator can adopt to achieve social ends through law. Each general technique really involves a set of particular techniques.

In an essay published in 1971 [1] Professor Robert S. Summers identified these as the five basic techniques used in modern law: penal, grievance-remedial, private arranging, administrative-regulatory and public benefit conferral.

In this chapter we shall adopt his analysis but add two more techniques—the constitutive and fiscal techniques—and rename his last technique the conferral of social benefits. The scheme then is as shown on the diagram on p. 19. It is hoped that by studying that diagram and following this analysis you will appreciate more of the breadth and diversity of the law. At the same time we shall examine in relation to each technique what legal or other social alternatives are open to deal with problems in particular areas.

Let us now examine each of the techniques in the following order:

1. The Penal Technique
2. The Grievance-Remedial Technique
3. The Private Arranging Technique
4. The Constitutive Technique
5. The Administrative-Regulatory Technique
6. The Fiscal Technique
7. The Conferral of Social Benefits Technique.

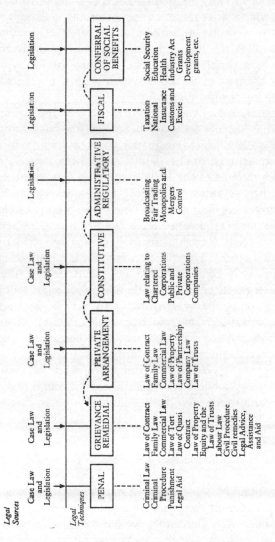

METHODS OF SOCIAL CONTROL THROUGH LAW
THE BASIC LEGAL TECHNIQUES

Legal Sources

Legal Techniques

PENAL	GRIEVANCE REMEDIAL	PRIVATE ARRANGEMENT	CONSTITUTIVE	ADMINISTRATIVE REGULATORY	FISCAL	CONFERRAL OF SOCIAL BENEFITS
Case Law and Legislation	Case Law and Legislation	Case Law and Legislation	Case Law and Legislation	Legislation	Legislation	Legislation
Criminal Law Criminal Procedure Punishment Legal Aid	Law of Contract Family Law Commercial Law Law of Tort Law of Quasi Contract Law of Property Equity and the Law of Trusts Labour Law Civil Procedure Civil remedies Legal Advice, Assistance and Aid	Law of Contract Family Law Commercial Law Law of Property Law of Partnership Company Law Law of Trusts	Law relating to Chartered Corporations Public and Private Corporations Companies	Broadcasting Fair Trading Monopolies and Mergers Control	Taxation National Insurance Customs and Excise	Social Security Education Health Industry Act Grants Development grants, etc.

1. *The Penal Technique* [2]

The first is an obvious one. It involves rules prohibiting certain deviant behaviour, the maintenance of a police force and other enforcement agencies to detect and prosecute violations, together with a system of courts to adjudicate questions of criminal liability. It also involves the maintenance of prisons, borstals and other such places as a penal system. The criminal justice system is in fact merely the part of the legal system created for the specific purpose of applying the penal technique.

There are some who argue that the very application of the penal technique is made necessary because of the basic injustices inherent in our society which create the tensions leading to anti-social behaviour. If a person is denied reasonable outlets for his or her energies then he or she is likely to react in a manner which society stigmatises as anti-social. Penal techniques are then regarded as involving a labelling process. Those who propound such views often premise their arguments on a conflict model of society, whereas the traditional " establishment " view tends to base itself on a consensus model. The question of what is a just society is obviously an immensely complex value judgment. It is easier to condemn particular practices as unjust than to produce an articulate and convincing conception of the just. This may be because our reaction against injustice is a " gut reaction," a matter of emotion rather than reason. Also, what appears just to one society may seem unjust to another. Unfortunately, criminal laws, once they are part of the legal system, gather a life and momentum of their own and it needs strong public pressure channelled through organised pressure groups and exerted on the legislature to effect change.

Alternatives

What viable alternatives are there to the application of the penal technique in dealing with deviant behaviour? First there is non-intervention. In some areas of behaviour it may be thought that the application of the penal technique is not morally justified or not practicable. An illustration would be private sexual behaviour. Again it might be felt that particular categories of offenders might be better dealt with by a simple warning. This is often done with child offenders. A second alternative which is the symptom of an underdeveloped system is to leave the injured party to obtain his own appropriate redress on the basis of reciprocity—an eye for an eye and a tooth for a tooth. This is a dangerous system and can lead to violence and anarchy. As society develops, matters which relate to public order are taken out of this category. In many societies a third social alternative is censure by public opinion in various ways, which range from the unorganised to organised forms which approximate to modern law. In some societies deviants are treated as mentally ill and dealt with accordingly. Illustrations of this are the treatment of homosexuals in some Indian tribes and the treatment of " liberals " in the U.S.S.R. Another social alternative to the application of the penal technique is the use of the fiscal technique. Behaviour which is regarded as anti-social in some way might be taxed heavily. An example of this is the practice of dividend-stripping whereby transactions in shares were carried out by financial manipulators to enable a tax refund to be obtained from the Inland Revenue when no tax had in fact been paid. Parliament introduced sweeping and complex tax legislation to penalise this particular form of deviance.

Effects of the penal technique

What are the particular effects of the application of the penal technique? [3]

First, the existence of the penal system deters some people from committing crimes. Some are deterred by the public enactment of penal prohibitions as such; others by the public announcement by law enforcement agencies that offenders will be brought to trial and punished; others by the physical presence of the police.

Perhaps a larger group accept penal prohibitions as part of the general mores of the society in which they live. Living honestly is a life-style. The existence of penal restrictions as such is almost peripheral to the totality of social factors producing conformity.

Thirdly, there is the effect of the penal technique on law-breakers. Clearly the existence of penal prohibitions and the enforcement agencies have been insufficient to inhibit them. Neither have they been inhibited by the general mores of society at large. Clearly their actual motivation may differ widely; often it will be unknown to the police and the courts even at the end of the day; sometimes it will be unknown to the people themselves. The latter is a characteristic not limited to law-breakers. The devil himself knoweth not the mind of a man.

To the police and other law enforcement agencies the application of penal technique is a job, the efficacy of which is measured in terms of crimes prevented or criminals apprehended.

To the lawyers and the courts the question is first one of proof of fact, the application of legal rules and then one of handling. Has the crime been proved beyond all reasonable doubt? What is the appropriate punishment? How best can the convicted person be dealt with to ensure that he does not break the law again? Or, if that seems a lost hope, how best can society be protected against him?

To those who work in the penal institutions the job is how to maintain discipline in an institution with these potentially conflicting goals of punishment, rehabilitation of the offender and deterrence from future crimes.

Example. One Saturday afternoon Mr. Brown, an old age pensioner, is " mugged " outside a Bristol football ground. His wallet containing £10 is stolen and he himself suffers cuts and bruises to his head. Witnesses describe two men who were seen to make the attack and Tom and Dave are subsequently arrested by the police. In an identification parade they are picked out by the witnesses and Mr. Brown as being the men responsible. Tom and Dave are charged with robbery. They are kept in custody overnight and the next morning they appear before magistrates. The case is adjourned for a week but Tom and Dave are refused bail so they are remanded in custody to the local prison.

A week later, they appear again before the magistrates and this time the committal proceedings commence. These proceedings are required for all serious charges to determine whether there is sufficient evidence for the case to go to trial at the Crown Court. At this stage, however, Tom and Dave are not on trial. The magistrates, having heard or read the evidence, decide that there is a case for the two men to answer, and they are committed in custody to the Crown Court. Both are granted legal aid.

After several weeks, the case comes up at the Crown Court. By this time, both men have seen their solicitors and barristers and have outlined their defence, which is that, although they had been to the match and were near the scene of the robbery at the time it took place, they were not the people who did it. At the trial Tom and Dave plead not guilty and the jury is sworn in. The prosecution counsel opens the case, stating the main facts on which the prosecution rely and the evidence which they intend to call. This evidence consists of the testimony of the witnesses, including Mr. Brown himself, who identify Tom and Dave as the men who committed the robbery. Each witness is called in turn and takes the oath. He is examined by prosecuting counsel, cross-examined by the respective counsel for Tom and Dave and then re-examined by prosecuting counsel. At the close of the prosecution evidence, counsel for Tom and Dave in turn present their case. Tom's counsel makes an opening speech and then calls Tom who gives evidence that he did not commit the robbery. Tom is cross-examined by prosecuting counsel and then re-examined by his own counsel. Tom's counsel then calls his employer, Mr. Jones, who gives evidence that Tom is a man of sound character who has, to his knowledge, never been in any trouble before. There is no cross-examination. Dave's counsel then addresses the court and calls Dave who testifies that he was with Tom at the relevant time and that he too was not involved in the robbery. Dave is cross-examined by prosecuting counsel but there is no re-examination. The prosecution sums up the case against the two men and their counsel reply.

At the conclusion of the evidence and speeches, the judge sums up the case to the jury. He tells them that there is no doubt that Mr. Brown was robbed and that the question is purely one of identity. He warns them of the special need for caution in dealing with identification evidence which he analyses. He then adds that the jury should only return verdicts of guilty against either man if they are satisfied that the prosecution has proved his guilt beyond reasonable doubt. He tells the jury to retire and try to reach a unanimous verdict. After an hour the jury returns and the foreman announces that they have found both men guilty of robbery.

The prosecution then call a police officer who gives evidence that Dave who is 27, has a number of previous convictions: two for theft, one for burglary and one for causing grievous bodily harm. For this last conviction he has spent a year in prison and was only released six months ago. On the other hand Tom, who is 18, has no previous convictions. The court receives social reports on the two men. These indicate that Dave has experienced a certain amount of difficulty in re-adjusting to normal life since coming out of prison and has also had financial problems. Concerning Tom, the report indicates that he has recently been troubled by the threat of redundancy and that his girl friend has left him. Counsel for Tom and Dave make pleas in mitigation, emphasising many of the points made in the reports. Tom's advocate stresses that the offence is completely out of character; that Tom has recently fallen into bad company, and it appears that his girl friend is ready to come back to him. Dave's counsel points out that Dave has only just come out of prison, has no job and is desperately short of money.

The judge tells the two men that this sort of conduct is far too common and that decent citizens are becoming scared to go out on the streets on Saturday afternoons. He adds that, by any standard, this is a serious offence and one that calls for stern measures. However, having heard the antecedents of both men, he is prepared to be lenient. He sentences Tom to borstal training, on the grounds of his youth and previous good record. Dave is sentenced to two years' imprisonment. Both men are advised that nothing in the judge's summing-up gives any cause to appeal against conviction and that there is no point in appealing to the Court of Appeal Criminal Division against the sentences which are certainly on the lenient side for this type of offence.

Thus you can see the existence of criminal law and criminal procedure. The matter goes before two courts, the magistrates' court for a preliminary hearing and the Crown Court for the full trial. There is also the possibility of further appeal. The case was investigated and brought by the police. Solicitors and barristers are involved in the process of representation. This involves ascertaining the facts, considering the charge, researching the law and then representing the client in court as an advocate in what is an adversary proceeding. In other words it is a contest rather than an inquisition. In this kind of case, which is pretty serious, the solicitor, having ascertained the facts and considered the charge, instructs (or briefs) a barrister who acts as the advocate in the Crown Court. Barristers have a monopoly of rights of audience in the higher courts, which include the Crown Court, handling the more serious kind of offence. Whether this division of the English and Scottish legal professions can be justified any longer is a matter of controversy which you will consider in the legal system part of your studies. Social workers are involved in producing reports on the two men. Then finally there are the borstal and prison institutions. I have given you a rather detailed example to enable you to get the feel of an actual case. The facts have been built up from practical experience. The procedures and terminology in Scotland are different in a number of respects.

2. *The Grievance-Remedial Technique* [4]

Professor Summers explains this technique as one which " defines remediable grievances, specifies remedies ... and provides for enforcement of remedial awards." [5]

This particular general technique involves the statement of substantive legal rules, principles and standards which create rights and duties and remedies to back up those rights. It involves the existence of civil courts to process claims for the establishment of particular rights, and machinery for the enforcement of remedies.

This technique is used throughout the civil law. What alternatives to it exist? First, as we have seen, matters which relate to public order are taken out of the category of grievance-remedial and involve the application of the penal technique. Secondly, individuals may seek to provide their own private systems to deal with disputes. They might for example insert a liquidated damages clause in a contract, stipulating precisely how much a defaulting party is to pay to the injured party. Again the parties might decide to deal with the matter solely in terms of insurance cover. An example here would be a crash between two motor vehicles. Many drivers prefer to handle the matter outside court by referring it to their insurance companies who tend to handle the infinite range of motor " accidents " on a " knock-for-knock " basis. Some traders deal on the basis of standard form conditions of Trade Associations, which provide their own mechanisms for dealing with disputes. Often such contracts and indeed commercial contracts generally provide for arbitration which usually but not always avoids adjudication, by the courts. An arbitration has the advantage of secrecy, informality and the possible use of a technical expert as arbitrator. It is not necessarily a cheaper procedure. Some contracts are now regulated by the application of the administrative regulatory technique which we shall consider later. Last, some disputes are dealt with by collective bargaining by trade unions and other representative bodies, and some by direct political action either in the form of pressure in Parliament or intervention by the Government. Obviously the latter are unusual cases.

Example. The classic case of the application of the grievance-remedial technique is a personal injuries claim in the law of tort.

Let us take an example. Mrs. Smith, a large old lady, is walking down the street in Bath, when she slips on a banana skin which Jim, a student, had just dropped in front of her. She breaks her leg and suffers nervous shock. What can she do? She goes along to Messrs. Whyte & Co., solicitors. Mr. Whyte advises her that she may have a claim in negligence against Jim under the law of tort.[6] The first thing he does is to write a letter to Jim making a claim with the hope of settlement out of court. Jim writes back a letter suggesting that Mrs. Smith should have looked where she was going. He then gets scared and goes along to see a solicitor, Sebastian Black. Messrs. Whyte & Co. consider whether they should sue in the High Court or county court and finally decide to sue for £1,000 damages in the county court since this will be cheaper and more convenient. They take out a summons (which is similar to a writ in the High Court) on which is endorsed a statement of claim alleging negligence. Sebastian Black enters a defence for Jim denying that Jim owed a duty of care to Mrs. Smith in the circumstances. A duty of care is one of the important ingredients in negligence. Sebastian Black also pleads in the alternative contributory negligence by Mrs. Smith. This means that even if Jim is held to be at fault Mrs. Smith was also careless to some degree in not looking where she was going. Various requests for information are made by both sides and then the parties come before the Registrar of the court for a pre-trial review. The purpose of this is to arrange matters with a view to shortening the hearing before the judge and giving the court officials an idea of how long the case will take. The Registrar asks if the parties have considered settlement out of court. They have, but the negotiations fell through.

The case is later heard before Judge Thomas. Mrs. Smith is represented by a barrister, Mr. Briggs. He outlines the facts of the case and calls his client and two witnesses to give evidence. Jim is represented by Sebastian Black since he is an experienced solicitor, and solicitors are allowed to appear in the county court, though not in the High Court. Mr. Black cross-examines Mrs. Smith and the witnesses. These are re-examined by Mr. Briggs. Mr. Black then presents the case for the defence and calls Jim to give evidence.

There is some legal argument on the issue of contributory negligence and whether one can recover damages for nervous shock in such circumstances.

The judge then delivers his judgment holding (1) that Jim was liable in negligence, and (2) that Mrs. Smith was not herself negligent, but that she cannot recover damages for nervous shock. He awards her damages of £450 plus costs.

After the trial, Jim fails to pay and Mrs. Smith consults Mr. Whyte as to enforcement of the judgment. Mr. Whyte advises her that as Jim is a student he is unlikely to have much money or many assets. She could theoretically apply to the court to levy execution on his assets but this is unlikely to be worthwhile. He then manages to negotiate with Mr. Black for Jim to pay by monthly instalments of £15.

You can see from this case that there was a set of substantive laws applicable—the rules, principles and standards of negligence in the law of tort. To enforce her right, Mrs. Smith went to a solicitor who handled the claim first of all informally, later formally by means of court proceedings. The court processed the paperwork, dealt formally with pre-trial matters and provided the forum for rational presentation of the evidence and the law. It then made a decision and provided some machinery for enforcement which in the end the parties did not use. The aggregate of these techniques we call collectively the grievance-remedial technique. It differs at almost every stage from the penal technique. Consider how.

Many writers have suggested that these are the only techniques used by the law. Professor Summers has usefully drawn our attention to the others mentioned above. One which closely relates to the grievance-remedial is the private arranging technique. By providing mechanisms for the private creation of rights which are legally recognised, the law enlarges the scope of matters covered by the grievance-remedial technique. Thus contracts and property transactions effected by people can be the subject of the grievance-remedial technique.

3. The Private Arranging Technique [7]

It is useful to think of the choice of the private arranging technique as one pole and direct governmental action as the other.[8] In between them are many possibilities involving some characteristics of both extremes. Examples of purely private arranging are perhaps marriage, purchase and sale, gifts, making a will, the creation of leases and rights of way and the formation of a club. All of these are left to individual initiative. What the law does here is to provide a framework of rules which primarily determine the validity of the transaction. For example, an Englishman living in Bristol makes a will on the back of a letter from the Inland Revenue and fails to have it witnessed. Is the will valid to transfer his property on death to the people he names, or must the matter be treated as one of intestacy? The law answers such a question by providing detailed legislation and case law which can be consulted. The answer is that the form of will does not matter but it must be in writing and signed in the presence of two witnesses. The will is therefore invalid and the property goes to his next-of-kin under the law of intestacy.

The law also provides a system for the determination of rights and duties and other liabilities. The latter, one can subsume under the grievance-remedial technique although there are sometimes situations where people want to have the legal position authoritatively determined without there being a grievance as such. As society becomes more and more collectivist, there is a movement towards direct government intervention in the private arranging area. Dicey's *Law and Opinion in the Nineteenth Century* traced this movement in nineteenth-century England. Thus the law interferes more today in the care and welfare of children, in the regulation of consumer transactions to achieve fair trading, and in order to establish some measure of social control of land. The two principal methods used are state control by direct or indirect ownership, or the application of the administrative-regulatory technique.

Example. Let us take an example of a consumer transaction.[9] Fred buys a tin of baked beans from his local supermarket. Clearly a private arrangement of purchase and sale of goods governed by the provisions of the Sale of Goods Act 1893 (as amended) and the general law of contract. This is a transaction to which the law sensibly attaches few formalities. Fred verbally indicates his offer to purchase the beans which the girl on the cash desk accepts on behalf of the supermarket company. He pays for it and the property in it passes to him. He chose it from a stack under a notice which said "2p off our normal price." He was a regular customer at the supermarket and thought that that meant that the cost was 10p since the beans had been 12p for some time, but he is charged

12p. He complains to the shop about misrepresentation but the manager denies his claim. He does not feel that he should go to a solicitor for such a trivial thing but, being a man of principle, investigates his legal position at a Citizens' Advice Bureau. They inform him that he has a possible claim for misrepresentation and that, theoretically, he could use the new arbitration procedure in the county court,[10] but that in practice the Registrar will think the matter too trivial to deal with. They also advise him that he should report the matter to his local Weights and Measures Inspector, since this probably involves a breach of the Trade Descriptions Act 1968 which imposes a criminal sanction. He does so but the Inspector ascertains that 12p involves a reduction from 14p which is the supermarket company's normal price throughout the rest of the country. Since the company, despite its numerous branches, is regarded in law as one single person there is no offence committed. Fred is finally advised to write to the Director-General of Fair Trading, a public official whose office was established by the Fair Trading Act 1973, which among other things, safeguards the consumer against unfair consumer practices. He receives a letter from the Director's staff saying that the Director-General has referred the matter to a committee. Fred eats the baked beans muttering something about the law being an ass.

As you can see, the law is developing in this area. Consumer protection is moving into the area of direct governmental intervention in the form of criminal sanctions and a government agency exercising wide powers in relation to such sales. The trouble is it all seems a little remote to people like Fred. There are limits to effective legal action as we shall see in more detail in a later chapter.

4. *The Constitutive Technique*

This technique is one which is closely related to the private arranging technique. Here the law recognises a group of people as *constituting a legal person*, for example a company, separate from the individuals comprised in the group. This is advantageous in a number of ways. Thus the corporation has perpetual succession—it does not die; the members can generally escape personal bankruptcy on its business failure and the corporation enables management to be separated from ownership of capital. The investors in most large companies play a very passive role. Management of the companies' affairs is in the hands of salaried professionals. The earliest forms of incorporation in this country were the chartered corporations which were incorporated by royal grant. Such corporations were responsible for organising a variety of social activities notable amongst which was the development of overseas trade and the colonisation of America. Later corporations were also created by specific Acts of Parliament but both methods were extremely expensive and by the middle of the nineteenth century Parliament eventually provided for an easier system of incorporation. This was incorporation by registration of certain documents with a public official and the payment of fees and duties. The most common form of corporation today is the limited liability company incorporated in this way. Over the last century a complex system of statute law, case law and informal regulation of corporations has developed.

The institution of a trust whereby one person declares himself a trustee for another, or transfers property to someone else to hold as trustee for the benefit of the transferor or a third person is akin to the constitutive technique, except that no new separate legal person results. Creation of a new legal person is the distinctive characteristic of the constitutive technique.

The trust is therefore better regarded as an example of the private arranging technique although in some other countries such like funds are sometimes regarded as legal persons.

5. The Administrative-Regulatory Technique [11]

Professor Summers distinguishes this technique from the penal in that it basically exists to regulate wholesome activity rather than prohibiting anti-social forms of behaviour. He distinguishes it from the grievance-remedial mainly on the ground that it is designed to operate preventively before a grievance has arisen. Under this technique, officials adopt regulatory standards, communicate thereon with those subject to them and take steps to ensure compliance. The steps will usually include a system of licensing, inspection and warning letters, often with some further step such as revocation of a licence or the bringing of administrative proceedings, civil litigation or a criminal prosecution as a last resort. This technique has been used much more in the past in the United States than in this country but is increasingly being used here.

Example. A striking example is the setting up of the Office of Fair Trading which we referred to above. Under the Fair Trading Act 1973 the Director-General of Fair Trading has duties in respect of protection of consumers, restrictive trade practices and monopolies. The Act also provides for the establishment of a Consumer Protection Advisory Committee and empowers the Secretary of State on the recommendation of the Director-General to make orders prohibiting or regulating practices in connection with consumer transactions which the Advisory Committee have found to have particular adverse effects upon the economic interests of consumers. The Director-General is empowered to institute action against suppliers and traders and other persons in business who persist in a course of conduct which is unfair to consumers and detrimental to their interests. Thus the Act creates a sophisticated set of techniques for regulating trade in the interests of the public.

Another example is the Prevention of Fraud (Investments) Act 1958 which aims at regulating the business of dealing in securities. The Act does this by prohibiting the carrying on of that business except by persons who are licensed by the Department of Trade or who fall within the class of dealers not required to obtain a licence. The latter are mainly City institutions. By section 3 of that Act any one can apply to the Department for a licence which must be renewed each year. The Act gives the Department power to demand deposits or guarantees as security in case of bankruptcy or liquidation of the licensee. The Department is given power to refuse a licence or to revoke a licence already granted, on various grounds. These include the commission of offences specified in the Act and the breach of rules which are known as the Licensed Dealers (Conduct of Business) Rules which are made under powers given by the Act. There is an elaborate procedure governing the way in which the Department exercises its powers and there is a right of appeal by the applicant to an independent tribunal of inquiry.

It is in fact very common in this country to have special tribunals of some sort or other as part of an administrative-regulatory mechanism. This is much less common in the United States where such matters generally go before the ordinary courts.

6. *The Fiscal Technique*

The Government raises money to finance its spending by legislation which imposes a variety of levies. Some taxes such as income tax, corporation tax and National Insurance contributions are direct and fall on natural and legal persons. Some are direct and fall on property such as the old death duties and the proposed wealth tax. Others are indirect and are based on consumption of goods and services. VAT is an example.

Behind the application of the fiscal technique is a complex structure of administration centred on the Commissioners of Inland Revenue and Customs and Excise. National Insurance administration is handled by the Department of Health and Social Security save that the Inland Revenue are now in practice the collectors. Some of the more indirect taxes are collected by the Post Office, *e.g.* TV licences.

7. *The Conferral of Social Benefits Technique* [12]

Modern government spends money raised by the application of the fiscal technique on a wide range of benefits and services which in earlier times were left to the individual, to the local community or in some cases to the Church. Examples are education, roads, the National Health Service and Social Security. In the past, such matters were categorised as being outside " lawyer's law." However, this is a somewhat nebulous category which we will consider in more detail later. Increasingly in public law and in so-called poverty law lawyers are rightly turning their attention to them.

Usually these benefits are regulated by statute so there is the basic legal task of construing the statute. Who administers the scheme? How? Is a particular person entitled to benefit? Is the conferral of a particular benefit a matter of right or the administrator's discretion? Is the discretion regulated in any way? Is there a system of appeal? These are all matters which can be regarded as within the legitimate province of law.

The main legal sources of social security law, for example, are a number of consolidating statutes with regulations made thereunder. A number of different government departments are concerned with various aspects—the Department of Employment, the Inland Revenue and the Department of Health and Social Security. The latter is the most important from a claimant's point of view.

As far as supplementary benefits, which are aimed at relieving poverty, are concerned there is a separate administrative agency, the Supplementary Benefits Commission. Appeals from the Commission's officers lie to independent tribunals, the Supplementary Benefits Appeals Tribunals. Family allowances and national insurance benefits are handled by local insurance officers with an elaborate system of appeals to tribunals. Points of law can, however, come before the High Court.

You can see that there are some similarities between this and the administrative-regulatory technique. The main difference lies in the nature of the business dealt with. The member of the public is in the role of a claimant against the state.

Example. Let us take an example of Jill, a deserted wife who has three children. Her husband is out of work and drawing unemployment benefit. She goes along to the local D.H.S.S. office and obtains supplementary benefit. She may in addition be advised to claim further discretionary benefits and also a rate rebate from her local authority. If she is dissatisfied with the benefits paid to her by the local office she may be advised to appeal in writing to the local Supplementary Benefits Tribunal. There is little formality involved and at present legal aid is not available although she may get legal advice and assistance short of representation from a solicitor, under what is popularly known as the £25 scheme. She would probably be better advised to try to obtain assistance from a voluntary group such as the Child Poverty Action Group who specialise in such matters.

Combinations of Techniques

As we saw in our " baked bean " example, it is possible for the law to use more than one technique to serve in a particular area. Sometimes, as we saw, such an overlap can be unfortunate with none of the techniques adequately dealing with the matter. Clearly when new legislation is being considered, the Government must choose which technique or combination of techniques will best achieve its legislative purpose.

The Legal Techniques and the Sources of Law

In the early history of English law, Parliament was not a very active source of law. Thus, until the nineteenth century, the use of the penal, grievance-remedial and private arranging techniques was largely the result of judge-made law. The development of the great departments of state and the increasing role of government has largely taken place over the last 100 years. The use of the administrative-regulatory, fiscal and social benefit conferral techniques has been through the medium of legislation. The courts still operate to create law in their traditional areas, but more and more innovation, particularly of a general kind, is now the result of legislative intervention.

Notes

[1] "The Technique Element in Law," 59 California L.R. 733 (1971). Also reproduced in *Essays in Honor of Hans Kelsen*, ed. by the *California Law Review* with a Preface by Albert A. Ehrenzweig (hereinafter called " the Essay "). Professor Summers applies his technique analysis to the legal system as a whole in his anthology *Law, Its Nature, Function and Limits* (2nd ed., 1972) (hereinafter called " Functions ").

[2] "The Essay," p. 736.

[3] See "Functions," p. 122.

[4] "Essay," p. 736; "Functions," Chap. 1.

[5] "Essay," p. 736.

[6] The law of torts is concerned with civil wrongs which basically do not involve a breach of contract or trust.

[7] "Essay," p. 741; "Functions," Chap. 5.

[8] Dahl and Lindblom, *Politics, Economics and Welfare*, Chap. 1; "Functions," p. 432.

[9] This is based on an actual case which was the subject-matter of an article in the *New Statesman*, March 8, 1975.

[10] This was introduced to deal with small claims and to avoid the paraphernalia of a full court hearing. See *Practice Direction* [1973] 3 All E.R. 448 for the new procedure.

[11] "Essay," p. 737; "Functions," Chap. 3.

[12] "Essay," p. 739; "Functions," Chap. 4.

BOOK II

Sources of Law and Methods of Legal Reasoning

CHAPTER 4

LAW AND FACT

LAW is applied to facts. This seems simple enough yet it is not. Lawyers constantly distinguish between what they regard as law and what they regard as fact. Anything which is not a question of law is treated as a question of fact. However, both these are slippery terms and are used in a number of different senses. This obviously can be very confusing. Nonetheless we will attempt to grasp the nettle. The distinction is important with regard to the division of function between judge and jury and crucial as regards the question of appeals, since the opportunities for appeal on questions of fact are very limited. Also from an educational point of view it is important to appreciate how lawyers approach the problems of fact-finding, description and categorisation.

A Question of Law

The term, question of law, is used in at least three different senses.[1] It can refer to a question which has already been answered by the law—on which there is clear law. On this basis, everything else is treated as a question of fact. Secondly, it can refer to a question as to what the law is. This arises out of uncertainty in the law. Thus the interpretation of a new ambiguous section in an Act of Parliament would, in the first sense, be a question of fact whereas in this second sense it is a question of law. Once the decision has been made, however, even in the first sense it becomes a question of law. A third sense arises out of the distinction between judge and jury. Questions of law in the first and second senses are questions for the judge. Other questions are questions of fact for the jury. However, this neat picture is obscured because even some issues which could be fact on this basis are regarded as within the area of the judge. Thus whether there is any evidence on which a reasonable man could find that a defendant was activated by malice in a defamation case is decided by the judge, although the actual question whether the defendant was activated by malice is a question of fact for the jury. The significance of this is that if there was malice the defendant cannot rely on any defence of privilege. Lawyers rather illogically call the first question a question of law simply because it is determined by the judge.

So far we have adopted a negative approach to fact. Can one be more specific by approaching the distinction from the point of view of fact?

Fact

Most people think they know what facts are. As J. R. Lucas, a philosopher, pointed out, to most people facts are " good, simple souls; there is no guile in them, nor any room for subjective bias." This popular opinion is, however, far from true. Facts are not the simple solid elements out of which the fabric of our knowledge is constructed. They rely on human perception and interpretation and description in language. These are not wholly passive and neutral activities. It is difficult to exclude value considerations. So much perception, interpretation and description involves tacit evaluations.

Mr. Lucas makes the very telling point that the basic word " fact " is *systematically ambiguous*. Its meaning varies with the particular context. Consequently one must be wary of philosophical discussions on the nature of fact which are carried on at a high level of abstraction, since there is too little context for any determinate meaning to survive. What are the facts will depend on the context of a particular dialogue, discussion or dispute. Also, within any particular context distinctions can perhaps be made between unquestioned facts, accepted facts and established facts. A further distinction can perhaps be made between unquestioned and unquestionable facts.

Facts for legal purposes usually cover making and doing things, the existence of objects, states of affairs and events in general. What they actually do cover will depend on the context of a particular dispute. Generally the courts have judicial notice of certain facts,[2] others will be presumed,[3] others accepted by both sides but the remainder will have to be established before the court by calling witnesses, producing documents and so on.

Primary and Secondary Facts

A distinction is often drawn by lawyers between primary and secondary facts. The importance of this distinction is that appellate courts do not usually interfere with findings of primary facts but may do so in relation to findings of secondary facts. In *British Launderers' Research Association* v. *Hendon Rating Authority*[4] in 1949, Denning L.J., as he then was, expressed the distinction in this way—

> " Primary facts are facts which are observed by witnesses and proved by oral testimony, or facts proved by the production of a thing itself, such as original documents. Their determination is essentially a question of fact for the tribunal of fact, and the only question of law that can arise on them is whether there was any evidence to support the finding. The conclusions from primary facts are, however, inferences deduced by a process of reasoning from them. If, and in so far as, those conclusions can as well be drawn by a layman (properly instructed on the law) as by a lawyer, they are conclusions of fact for the tribunal of fact, and the only questions of law which can arise on them are whether there was a proper direction in point of law; and whether the conclusion is one which could reasonably be drawn from the primary facts ... If, and in so far, however, as the correct conclusion to be drawn from primary facts requires, for its correctness, determination by a trained lawyer—as for instance because it involves the interpretation of documents or because the law and the facts cannot be separated, or because the law on the point cannot properly be understood or applied except by a trained lawyer— the conclusion is a conclusion of law on which an appellate tribunal is as competent to form an opinion as the tribunal of first instance."

Thus the distinction between primary and secondary facts seems tolerably clear, although the distinction between law and fact for legal purposes is still a little blurred. Sometimes the primary and secondary fact distinction is explained in terms of perception of facts and their evaluation.

Truth, Probability and Description

In an article in the *Modern Law Review*, Professor W. A. Wilson[5] classifies questions into three basic categories, namely, questions of truth, probability and description, a classification which is more helpful than that between primary and secondary facts. Truth questions turn on the credibility and reliability of witnesses. Probability questions involve an inference drawn from circumstantial evidence. Truth and probability questions are generally treated as questions of fact. Description questions are of a different type and turn on methods of interpretation and argumentation based on language and logic. Some description questions can be answered by the use of a universal—all Xs are Ys. Often in law this rests on legal dogmatism in a particular statute, e.g. all pigs are cattle for the purpose of the particular statute. At other times we proceed on the basis that some Xs are Ys. An example would be the case of a parked car constituting an obstruction on the highway. Not all parked cars constitute an obstruction. It depends on the circumstances. Also, obstructions can consist of things other than parked cars. Such matters have sometimes been regarded as questions of law. This is not quite correct, according to recent authorities.[6] The meaning of an ordinary word in the English language is not a question of law, but the proper construction of a statute is a question of law. If a word is used in its ordinary meaning it is for the tribunal which decides the case to consider not as law but as fact whether in the whole circumstances the words of a statute do or do not as a matter of ordinary usage of the English language cover or apply to the facts which have been proved. If the context shows that a word is being used in an unusual sense the court will determine what the unusual sense is. If it is alleged that the tribunal of fact reached a wrong decision then this is a question of law of a limited character. The question then is usually whether their decision was unreasonable in the sense that no tribunal acquainted with the ordinary use of language could reasonably reach that decision.[7]

There is some sense in this, since the meaning of words changes as social attitudes change, and it is undesirable for the law to fix a word from ordinary usage in a straitjacket of meaning which has grown archaic.[8]

To sum up this rather complicated position, *the overall assessment* whether a particular word is used in a statute in its ordinary sense, an unusual sense or as a legal term of art is a question of law. Where a word is thus found to be used in its ordinary sense, its meaning and the application to a particular set of facts is a question of fact, save that an appellate court will interfere if the finding is unreasonable, in the sense that no tribunal could reasonably have come to that conclusion.

There is a further kind of method used in relation to description questions, which is sometimes called a question of degree, and, when applied to words *in ordinary usage* (*i.e.* not legal terms of art), is generally regarded as a matter of fact. This usually involves weighing statements pointing one way against statements pointing another. Professor Wilson gives the example of whether a tea-break is too long.

Another question involving description which can either be subsumed under questions of degree or treated as an independent question arises out of the open texture of most language. Words arguably have a core of certainty and a penumbra of uncertainty or indeterminacy *in their usage*. Borderline cases crop up. Can the word aeroplane, for example, cover a flying-boat? In this kind of case the question will often not be purely a semantic one. Evaluation is frequently to the forefront rather than description as such.

Problems of description are a crucial part of the legal process and the particular description though often treated technically as a question of fact will have a particular legal significance in that legal consequences will ensue from it. Legal rules, principles and standards usually contain references to *general* classes of things (*i.e.* concepts or categories) and often involve questions of degree, open texture and evaluation in their structure.

To conclude then, although the distinction between primary and secondary facts is the orthodox distinction, it is suggested that you will have a clearer picture in your mind of the various approaches to fact if you distinguish between the following questions:

(1) truth
(2) probability
(3) description/evaluation
(4) legal categories.

Bear in mind that (3) and (4) are closely connected in practice. We shall return to legal categorisation in a moment.

Facts and Opinions

Questions of fact are sometimes distinguished by lawyers from questions of opinion. By opinion here one is referring to a layman's opinion rather than that of a judge in a case. Salmond puts the distinction neatly—" A question of fact is one capable of being answered by way of demonstration—a question of opinion is one

that cannot be so answered. The answer to it is a matter of specula-
tion which cannot be proved by any available evidence to be right
or wrong." [9] To say that a painting of Sir Thomas More is by
Holbein is to make a representation of fact—it either is or is not
true. To say that it is a beautiful painting is a matter of opinion.
Obviously, too much can be made of this distinction. Sometimes
we do not know and cannot know for certain that a particular
painter painted the particular picture and we rely on the opinion of
an expert as almost equivalent to fact. Again there may be a wide
or general consensus of opinion on a particular matter, *e.g.* Hitler
was a bad man. Technically, this is opinion although the *existence*
of the consensus is a fact.

Presumptions

Some matters which start off as questions of fact become treated as
questions of law as the legal system develops. One of the main
ways in which this happens is by means of the establishment of
legal presumptions. These are of two kinds—conclusive and rebuttable. The latter can be rebutted by sufficient evidence to the contrary. Thus before 1973, a person was presumed to have notice of
all public documents in a company's file at the Companies Registry
whether or not he knew of them. This was a conclusive presumption of law. An example of a rebuttable presumption is the presumption of innocence in criminal trials. A person is presumed
innocent until he is proved guilty.

Facts and their Legal Significance

So far we have considered facts largely from the point of view of
the law and fact distinction. Another extremely important question
with regard to facts is their significance amongst themselves. This
is regulated by the particular context and there are detailed rules of
evidence as to relevance which it would be premature to consider
here. Nevertheless one or two useful general things may be said
and they are best stated in the context of an example.

In his book mischievously entitled *The Bramble Bush* Karl
Llewellyn gives the following case by way of illustration at p. 48:

   " What are *the* facts? The plaintiff's name is Atkinson and
   the defendant's Walpole. The defendant, despite his name, is
   an Italian by extraction, but the plaintiff's ancestors came over

with the Pilgrims. The defendant has a schnautzer-dog named
Walter, red hair and $30,000 of life insurance. All these are
facts. The case, however, does not deal with life insurance. It
is about an auto accident. The defendant's auto was a Buick
painted pale magenta. He is married. His wife was in the back
seat, an irritable, somewhat faded blonde. She was attempting
back-seat driving when the accident occurred. He had turned
around to make objection. In the process the car swerved and
hit the plaintiff. The sun was shining; there was a rather
lovely dappled sky low to the West. The time was late Octo-
ber on a Tuesday. The road was smooth, concrete. It had been
put in by the McCarthy Road Work Company. How many of
these facts are important to the decision? How many of these
facts are, as we say, legally relevant? Is it relevant that the road
was in the country or the city; that it was concrete or tarmac
or of dirt; that it was a private or a public way? Is it relevant
that the defendant was driving a Buick, or a motor car, or a
vehicle? Is it important that he looked around as the car
swerved. Is it crucial? Would it have been the same if he had
been drunk, or had swerved for fun, to see how close he could
run by the plaintiff, but had missed his guess? "

Of these facts, Llewellyn states that you must discard some as
of no interest whatsoever, and treat others as dramatic, but legal
nothings. This overstates the case somewhat. Potentially every fact
may be relevant as regards proof of the facts of the case. For
example the fact that the person observed by a witness to have
caused the crash was said to have red hair and to be driving a pale
magenta Buick may be relevant in ascertaining whether that person
is the defendant in the particular case—a bare fact which is a
primary fact in Lord Denning's language and a truth question in
Professor Wilson's language.

When you look at the facts which are left, you then cease to
deal with them in the concrete and deal with them instead in *categories*, which you, for one reason or another, deem significant.
Llewellyn continues

"It is not the road between Pottsville and Arlington; it is a
' Highway.' It is not a particular pale magenta Buick eight, by
number 732507, but ' a motor car,' and perhaps even ' a vehicle.'
It is not a turning around to look at Adoree Walpole, but a

lapse from the supposedly proper procedure of careful drivers with which you are concerned. Each concrete fact of the case arranges itself, I say, as the *representative* of a much wider abstract *category* of facts, and it is not in itself but as a member of the category that you attribute significance to it."

The important thing then is the attribution of significance. The process at this last stage is no longer descriptive but ascriptive.[10] On the basis of certain facts which have been described we are applying legal rules, principles or standards, and ascribing legal responsibility and liability. The legal concepts or categories, which are integral parts of legal rules, principles and standards whereby liability is ascribed, are defeasible [11] in the sense that the law may recognise certain defences. In this respect the condition of the road for example might be a material factor.

In your studies, if your legal education follows the usual pattern, the basic facts will usually be given to you and your job will simply be to apply legal categories to them. If you go on to practise law, one of your most difficult tasks will be to ascertain the facts for categorisation. This is certainly true of practice as a solicitor, but a little less true of the Bar where some of the spadework should have been done by your instructing solicitor.

Notes

[1] See Salmond, *Jurisprudence* (12th ed. by P. J. Fitzgerald), pp. 66 *et seq.*

[2] " On Not Worshipping Facts " (1958) 8 *Philosophical Quarterly* 144.

[3] See Cross and Wilkins, *An Outline of the Law of Evidence* (4th ed.), Chap. 3.

[4] [1949] 1 K.B. 462, 471.

[5] " A Note on Fact and Law " (1963) 26 M.L.R. 609.

[6] *Cozens* v. *Brutus* [1973] A.C. 854 and *Dyson Holdings Ltd.* v. *Fox* [1976] Q.B. 503.

[7] This is based on a passage of Lord Reid's judgment in *Cozens* v. *Brutus* [1973] A.C. 854, 861c–e.

[8] See Bridge L.J. in *Dyson Holdings Ltd*. v. *Fox* [1976] Q.B. 503, 512H–513D. It is, however, difficult to reconcile this sensible approach with the idea of ascertaining the intention of the legislature at the time of the passing of an Act. *Vide infra*, Chap. 8.

[9] Salmond, *op. cit.* p. 69.

[10] See H. L. A. Hart, " The Ascription of Responsibility and Rights," in *Essays on Logic and Language*, Series 1 (Flew ed.), p. 144.

[11] *Ibid.* p. 148.

CHAPTER 5

LAW, AUTHORITY AND REASONING

KNOWLEDGE of the law and of the facts of a case are a prerequisite of legal reasoning. There is obviously a close relationship between reasoning and one's conception of reason. In a striking phrase, Coke in his *Commentary upon Littleton* (f. 97b) states " . . . reason is the life of the law, nay the common law itselfe is nothing else but reason, which is to be understood of an artificiall perfection of reason, gotten by long study, observation and experience; and not of every man's naturall reason; for, *Nemo nascitur artifex* " (No-one is born a craftsman).

According to modern dictionaries, to reason means to talk, to argue persuasively or to think in a connected, sensible or logical manner. Legal reasoning involves all three in the context of making law, administering laws, arguing cases in court, deciding cases and negotiating legal transactions. In this chapter we are concerned with the more general aspects of legal reasoning before we settle down to examine the sources of law and particular methods of reasoning in detail.

Distinctive Characteristics of Law

It is sometimes said in connection with legal reasoning that law has its own kind of discourse, its own kind of rhetoric and its own kind of logic.[1] There are certain dangers in thinking this about law. One is that it perhaps implies that the approach to law is the same the world over, and another is that it somehow isolates law as something completely autonomous and separate from everyday life. With regard to the first, this clearly is not so. Quite apart from individual constitutions and particular laws being different, some systems of law, such as Moslem and Judaic law, purport to be based on divine revelation; others, such as the laws of some Communist societies, are sometimes regarded as little more than an economic reflex where the authority of laws dissolves in an economic and political debate. This is not to say, however, that law is independent of economics and politics. As we shall see in Chapter 12, there is a close causal interaction between all three in Western societies but this does not amount to a complete equation.

There are nevertheless certain characteristics of legal language, rhetoric and logic which though possibly not unique to law are certainly distinctive features.

Legal Language

As regards legal language [2] there is a tendency, as we have seen, to categorise people and events, to think in terms of rules and principles and standards; to objectify. The law is usually expressed in generalities and the important problem, having established the existence of facts and described them, is to decide whether they fall under a general legal rule, principle or standard or within a general legal concept. This latter stage as we saw in the last chapter is ascription rather than description.

Another characteristic of legal language is its formality and precision. The basic wording used is a technical language despite its frequent appropriation of words from ordinary speech. Lawyers sometimes play Humpty Dumpty using words to mean what they want them to mean.

David Mellinkoff, an American writer, in his book *The Language of the Law* [3] in fact gives nine reasons for the distinctiveness of legal language. These are:

1. Frequent use of common words with uncommon meanings, *e.g.* action to refer to a law suit.
2. Frequent use of Old English and Middle English words, *e.g.* aforesaid.
3. Frequent use of Latin words, *e.g. mens rea*.
4. Use of Old French and Norman French words, *e.g.* choses in action.
5. Use of terms of art, *e.g.* fee simple.
6. Use of argot, by which he means a specialised legal vocabulary in which the words are not sufficiently technical as to qualify as terms of art, *e.g.* inferior court.
7. Frequent use of resonant formal words, *e.g.* " the truth, the whole truth and nothing but the truth."
8. Deliberate use of open-textured words, *i.e.* words with flexible meanings, *e.g.* just and equitable, reasonable.
9. Attempts at times at extreme precision.

Many of these reasons are due to historical origins and it is difficult to provide rational justification for them now. If one were to seek rational justification today for a distinctive legal language this would be, as Mellinkoff states,[4] in terms of its precision, brevity, intelligibility and durability. It goes without saying that much legal usage falls short of these ideals.

Quite apart from the language of the law itself lawyers and judges regard it as their role to *behave* formally in public hearings. Everything tends to be objectivised. " It is submitted that " is used by lawyers instead of " I say that." The judge often refers to himself as " the court." It is thought that the formalities of the hearing " help to secure its objectivity, that is, its impartiality, internal consistency, restraint and authority." [5] Whether this is so or, conversely, whether it is in fact a ground for alienation of the lay public is an open question.

Legal Rhetoric

Rhetoric [6] was defined by Aristotle in its most general sense as the faculty of persuasion.[7] Earlier Plato had put it in terms of " winning men's minds by words." To the Ancient Greeks it was an art to be practised in public places. Although the underlying method was the same, Aristotle distinguished between forensic rhetoric and deliberative rhetoric and thought that the pursuit of the latter was nobler and more worthy of the statesman.[8] Broadly speaking, lawyers use forensic rhetoric and judges deliberative rhetoric. Lawyers are representing the interests of their clients. Their function is to persuade the court. The judge on the other hand is seeking to arrive at and rationalise and justify his decision. The principal rhetorical device used in law is the appeal to authority. As we saw in Chapter 1 this is in strict terms a logical fallacy, but is used by law for reasons of convenience, indeed necessity. Law as organised, institutionalised social control needs recognised sources. In English law the appeal to authority is an appeal to the previous decisions of the courts and to legislation. In Roman law for a long period this was largely an appeal to the writings of particular jurists. In civil law jurisdictions it is primarily an appeal to the codes and other legislation. In civil law systems following the Roman law influence the writings of jurists—doctrine—has had great weight but traditionally the common law has treated such writings with caution and reserve—a practice which is changing, as we shall see in Chapter 10. In order to reason like an English lawyer then one has to know the sources of authority, the content of the particular authority and the set of ground rules for using authorities. You will learn something of this in the ensuing chapters of this part of the book.

Legal Logic

As for legal logic,[9] the term is fraught with ambiguity since some think it refers to the application of pure, theoretical logic to legal reasoning while others take it to refer to legal reasoning itself. The very notion that law is logical at all is sometimes criticised. " The life of the Law has not been logic; it has been experience," said Mr. Justice Holmes, a great American judge, at the beginning of his book *The Common Law*. Holmes had in mind *the syllogism*—the *deductive* line of argument that goes like this:

> All men are mortal.—Major premise
> Socrates is a man.—Minor premise
> ∴. Socrates is mortal.—Conclusion.

Now there is much in Holmes's point. Major premises are not given. They have to be chosen. Statutory provisions are reasonably straightforward but the formulation of a case law rule or principle as a major premise involves a process of abstraction from the facts of the earlier case and the choice of the level of abstraction may be conditioned by reaction to the facts of the case to be decided.

The minor premises—the facts—rest on perception, probability and description. This involves interpretation and evaluation in the broad sense as we have seen.

Finally, legal judgment, like any other piece of decision-making, ultimately involves an act of will. As Kant said, there is no rule for applying a rule. It is " the specific quality of so-called mother-wit." [10] Ultimately, it is the judge's decision primarily in the light of the facts and the law, but as we shall see other variables may also play a part.

This rejection of deductive logic as the prototype of legal reasoning does not mean that law does not use deduction at all. The point is it need not, and deductive logic often cannot easily be used for the reasons stated above.[11] Deductive logic only usually becomes relevant at all in the case of clearly expressed statutory rules or well established case law rules and principles.

Another branch of logic which was considered in an elementary form by Aristotle and later developed by Francis Bacon and John Stuart Mill is *inductive* logic. As Francis Bacon put it, induction leads the mind from fact to fact, like a working bee passing from flower to flower [12]; while deductive logic is like the spider drawing down thread from thread until it has produced a web. Induction thus involves the movement from the particular to the general as opposed to a movement from the general to the particular. As we shall see, the use of decided cases involves something like induction. The basic technique is argument by analogy—treating like cases as like. This often at some stage involves a consequential inductive movement from particular instances to a more generalised formulation as we shall see in the next chapter.

Another area of traditional logic is *classification per genus et differentiam*. This involves the use of categories—the genus—and the identification of members of the categories, the species. Genus involves possessing some essential quality but species have incidental differences (*differentiae*) amongst themselves. Now there is a distinction which has been drawn in the past between natural and artificial classes. Genera according to Aristotle are natural classes which are concerned with kind, *e.g.* mankind, and are not purely the result of the act of classing, whereas artificial classes obviously are, *e.g.* the class of all the things on my table. It is strongly arguable that natural classes are themselves a matter of convention and that there is only a difference of degree of acceptance between the natural and the artificial. Law is concerned with the act of classing—creating artificial classes—but often uses something like a *genus et differentia* approach. It is not, however, stuck to a fixed set of genera and species, and the classification scheme is constantly changing.

I have dealt with deduction, induction and classification rather briefly because I intend to come back to them in greater depth in the context of the particular sources of laws. Other methods of reasoning which are sometimes encountered in law and which are variations on the themes of deduction, induction and classification are the arguments of *inversion*, *a fortiori*, and *ad absurdum*. The first goes like this—

> If A then B
> ∴ if not A then not B.

This is in fact a dangerous kind of logical argument which can easily be fallacious. It is fallacious if a term in a premise is used in a particular sense and in the conclusion is treated in a general sense. Inversion arguments are sometimes used in law and so one must be on one's guard against fallacy.

The argument *a fortiori* is very common. If something is prohibited then it is assumed that anything more obvious is prohibited, *e.g.* it is forbidden to tread on the cricket pitch, then *a fortiori* it is forbidden to tear up the cricket pitch. This is a common kind of argument in general use, but in our example it presupposes that both may be subsumed under a more general rule prohibiting any damage to a cricket pitch in any way whatsoever.

Arguments *ad absurdum* are often expressed in deductive form. The aim is to make the conclusion of another's argument demonstrate an absurdity (*e.g.* if you say that, the logical conclusion of your argument is X and surely that is not so). There is no such thing as a *logical* absurdity, only logical *contradiction and invalidity*. Legal arguments *ad absurdum* are, therefore, rhetorical rather than logical devices unless they expose a contradiction in another's argument.

In the recent case of *Rugby Water Board* v. *Shaw-Fox* [1973] A.C. 202, 228D (H.L.) Lord Simon of Glaisdale said that " the purpose and value of logic to the law is to ensure that persons whose relevant circumstances are similar receive similar treatment. It is in other words to promote equity: to use it to defeat equity is to misuse it." He was referring to equity in the broad ethical sense of a species of justice and arguing against too technical an approach. Logic is concerned with *formal validity* of argumentation, not truth and justice. Law is interested in truth but primarily concerned with justice.

Legal Reasoning as Practical Reasoning

Having said all this, however, it must be admitted that practical reasoning in all walks of life departs from formal logic in precisely the same manner. It is not tied to deduction and induction; it makes frequent use of analogy; and is primarily concerned with *weighing various considerations* and *supporting conclusions with reasons*.[13] The link between reasons and conclusion need not be one of logical necessity and the adequacy and weight of reasons is a matter of convention. There are good reasons and bad reasons and their goodness and badness is determined by the prevailing value system of the culture of the time and place—a verdict which may be revised by posterity. Professor John Wisdom, a philosopher, put the matter in this way: A lawyer's argument is " not a *chain* of demonstrative reasoning. It is a presenting and representing of those features of the case which *severally co-operate* in favour of the conclusion, in favour of calling the situation by the name by which he wishes to call it. The reasons are like the legs of a chair, not the links of a chain." [14] He, therefore, saw the process as one of weighing the accumulation of several inconclusive items on each side. He obviously had in mind as his basic model case law argument at common law.

David Mellinkoff [15] put the matter very well when he said " What has made the common law great is less reason than an endless succession of reasons." It is the constant process of supporting the application of legal rules and principles and standards by reasons and modifying or discarding them when their application can no longer be supported which has enabled the common law to keep pace with social change in the past. In all this it has resembled other aspects of practical reasoning in other walks of life. This became strikingly obvious when the common law adopted the standard of reasonableness as its yardstick in many areas. The standard has been criticised by some legal commentators as too ambiguous and by others as a complete begging of the question. [16] Nevertheless it resembles the technique of classical rhetoric of reasoning from opinions that are generally accepted—something which was easier to do in a small city state than in modern society. The resemblance between legal reasoning and rhetoric is so marked that the Belgian writer Chaim Perelman characterises " legal logic " as a species of the new rhetoric. [17] The main problem about identifying legal reasoning with rhetoric is that the latter presupposes influencing a public audience which legal reasoning does not necessarily involve. [18] A person such as a legal scholar can engage in legal reasoning in complete isolation although it is quite likely that at some stage he will communicate the result. It is probably better to see legal reasoning and rhetoric as species of practical reasoning which overlap but are not identical. The relationship is thus:

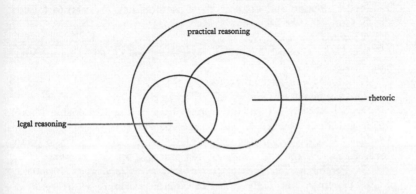

It is then the language and detailed ground rules about authority which are the most distinctive characteristics of legal reasoning. We shall pursue these in greater depth in the ensuing chapters.

Notes

[1] Cf. *International Encyclopedia of the Social Sciences*, Vol. 9, p. 197—" Legal Reasoning " (Harold J. Berman)—where he argues that this is the case although he acknowledges that the logic, rhetoric and discourse are similar to those of other social institutions and other scholarly disciplines.

[2] *Ibid*. pp. 201–202.

[3] Chap. II.

[4] *Ibid*. pp. 285 *et seq*.

[5] Berman, *op. cit*. p. 202.

[6] Berman, *op. cit*. pp. 200 *et seq*. The Belgian writer Chaim Perelman sees law and other aspects of practical reason as types of rhetoric. See *Justice*, Chap. IV and *The Idea of Justice and the Problem of Argument*.

[7] Aristotle, *The Art of Rhetoric* (Loeb ed. translated by J. H. Freese), Book I.

[8] *Ibid*. Book I, I.10.

[9] See Berman, *op. cit*. pp. 198 *et seq*.; Edward H. Levi, *An Introduction to Legal Reasoning*, pp. 1–8 and Windeyer J. in *Damjanovic & Sons Pty. Ltd*. v. *The Commonwealth* (1968) 42 A.L.J.R. 102, 109.

[10] Immanuel Kant's *Critique of Pure Reason* translated by Norman Kemp Smith, p. 177.

[11] See Lord Halsbury in *Quinn* v. *Leathem* [1901] A.C. 495, 506; D. Lloyd, " Reason and Logic in the Common Law " (1948) 64 L.Q.R. 468; G. Gottlieb, *The Logic of Choice*, Chap. II.

[12] *Novum Organum I*, 95.

[13] See D. P. Gauthier, *Practical Reasoning*, p. 17, and Chaim Perelman, *Justice*, p. 61.

[14] *Philosophy and Psycho-Analysis*, p. 157.

[15] *The Language of Law*, p. 454.

[16] See R. Powell, " The Unreasonableness of the Reasonable Man " [1957] C.L.P. 104 but *cf.* Lloyd, *op. cit.* p. 475.

[17] See " What is Legal Logic? " (1968) 3 Israel L.R. 1. See also Julius Stone, *Legal System and Lawyers' Reasonings*, pp. 325 *et seq*.

[18] *Cf.* Perelman, *The Idea of Justice and the Problem of Argument*, p. 138. Perelman constantly seems to equate reasoning with argumentation which he says is always developed in relation to an audience.

CHAPTER 6

HISTORICAL GROWTH AND THE SURVIVAL OF THE COMMON LAW AND EQUITY DISTINCTION

BRIEF reference was made in Chapter 2 to the distinction between common law and equity. In this chapter, we shall explore the distinction in more detail and consider how it affects modern case law.

The Philosophical Basis of the Distinction

Legal justice and equity are two species of the common genus, justice. Law as a body of rules and principles and standards is by its nature concerned with classes or sets of persons and events rather than individuals and individual instances. The result is, as Aristotle pointed out,[1] that sometimes it fails to achieve adequate justice in the particular case. Equity is a supplementary system of justice which caters more for the exigencies of a particular case. Gradually, law and equity coalesce in the normal course of legal development. As we have seen in Chapter 2, English law was peculiar—in fact retarded—in its development in this regard.

Historical Development

As we saw, the common law originally developed out of the recognition of general customs of the realm by the King's judges from the reign of Henry II onwards. Gradually, the judges' rulings were recorded and a system of substantive legal rules, principles, standards and concepts began to emerge. In Maine's striking phrase " So great is the ascendancy of the Law of Actions in the infancy of the Courts of Justice, that substantive law has at first the look of being gradually secreted in the interstices of procedure." [2] Practitioners knew that if they could bring the facts within an existing formula they would obtain redress for their clients. The law alternated between periods of creativity and periods of rigidity with regard to forms of action. The rigidity was mitigated to some extent by the use of fictions [3]—allegations of fictitious fact giving the court jurisdiction—to modern minds, an obnoxious method of reform but in their time a useful device for blending the old and the new. This was not always possible; the judges sometimes felt that the particular rule had been too long established to brook change. There was then a need for an auxiliary or supplemental agency to avoid injustice.

The practice grew of poor or disgruntled litigants petitioning the King or his Council for redress.[4] These petitions were handled by the Chancellor who, in the early period, was a cleric and the Keeper of the King's Conscience as well as the head of the office which issued the writs to start common law actions. At first the Chancellor simply made recommendations to the Council but later he made decisions on his own and eventually petitions were addressed to the Court of Chancery. In the early period the Chancellors did not consider " that they had to administer any body of substantive rules that differed from the ordinary law of the land. They were administering the law but they were administering it in cases which escaped the meshes of the ordinary courts." [5]

In this period equity was based on reason and conscience. John Selden, a writer of the seventeenth century, put it rather sarcastically as follows [6]:

"Equity is a roguish thing, for law we have a measure, know what to trust to. Equity is according to the conscience of him that is Chancellor, and as it is larger or narrower so is Equity. It is all one as if they should make the standard for the measure we call a foot to be the Chancellor's foot; what an uncertain measure would this be; one Chancellor has a long foot, another a short foot, a third an indifferent foot; it is the same thing in the Chancellor's conscience."

At the end of the Middle Ages the Chancellor ceased to be a cleric and later he was almost always a lawyer and often a common lawyer. This secularisation of administration led to a change in the development of equity. The jurisdiction began to be formalised. The writings of St. Germain [7] in the reign of Henry VIII gave a theoretical justification of equity, drawing on Aristotle, and a formulation of its rules and principles. These were used by later Chancellors to settle the jurisdiction. In the seventeenth century reports of cases in the Court of Chancery began to appear and by the beginning of the nineteenth century, when Lord Eldon was Lord Chancellor, equity had become a settled system as technical as the common law. Professors Keeton and Sheridan describe the position in this way—" In general, the merits of actual cases were subordinated to the intricacies of doctrine and the rules of equity assumed the shape of a second body of judge-made law, existing side by side with the common law and complementary to it." [8]

In the course of this development there was friction between the two systems but the practical issue of the validity of injunctions granted by the Court of Chancery was resolved in favour of equity in the reign of James I. The matter of principle, however, was not finally resolved until the Judicature Acts 1873 to 1875 to which we shall return later. There are still loose ends, as we shall see.

The Subject-Matter of Equity's Jurisdiction

Equity developed because of the rigours and inadequacies of the common law at various stages of the latter's development. The writ system was expensive, difficult and very technical. Also the common law failed to keep pace with social change at various times and occasionally the common law courts were unable to act against a powerful defendant who might intimidate juries and refuse to carry out the court's orders. These factors led to new doctrines and new procedures.

Equity's main area of intervention was in property transactions. It created and developed the trust whereby the enjoyment of property could be separated from the ownership of the legal title to the land. The trust was sometimes used as a tax avoidance device but it also enabled property to be left to persons in succession and later facilitated the early growth of the joint stock company. It has proved a singularly useful device for all manner of purposes ranging from charity to investment and the formation of social clubs.

Another area was the field of mortgages where the common law rules were cumbersome and harsh. Equity intervened to protect the borrower and the modern law is based mainly on the equitable rules.

Both trusts and mortgages are now partly covered by legislation but it is still necessary to refer to the old authorities on a number of points.

Equity intervened in the area of administration of the estates of deceased persons. It also developed an extensive jurisdiction to protect infants where there was property involved.

Equity developed a sophisticated jurisdiction in relation to fraud, a term to which it gave a wide interpretation. Its principal remedy here was rescission of the transaction, cancelling it out and restoring the parties to their original positions.

Another and crucially important area of equity's jurisdiction was the provision of auxiliary remedies. The Court of Chancery developed much more flexible procedures for commencing and pursuing an action than those which existed at common law. In the nineteenth century a number of these were extended to the common law courts by statute. At the end of the day the common law treated money compensation as the universal remedy for nearly all legal wrongs. Equity on the other hand granted injunctions— orders not to do or to do something—specific performance to compel the carrying out of a contract, and rectification of written documents in the case of mistake.

There are other less important areas of equity's jurisdiction which you will find discussed in specialist textbooks. Equity exercised no jurisdiction in the areas of tort and crime except possibly to grant an injunction and never concerned itself with the validity or termination of marriages.[9] In practice at the present time these areas constitute the bulk of litigation coming before the courts. This is not to say that equity is unimportant today since litigation tends to represent the pathology of a legal system. Many legal matters never come before the courts at all.

Equitable Approaches and the Maxims of Equity

Maxims are a very general kind of principle. The so-called rules or canons of construction to which we shall refer in Chapter 8 are examples. The role of the maxims of equity may have been to systematise the doctrine and practice for the purposes of legal training. Most of the maxims referred to below are taken from Francis' *Maxims of Equity* published in 1728.

Professors Keeton and Sheridan describe the equitable approaches as—natural justice, acting *in personam*, a preference for the substance rather than the form and discretionary remedies.[10]

As regards the first we have seen how equitable jurisdiction was accounted for on the basis of conscience and reason. This is particularly noticeable in equity's preference for equality which was an aspect of Aristotelian justice. "Equality is Equity." Further maxims illustrative of this approach are " Equity acts on the conscience " and " Equity looks upon that as done which ought to have been done."

The second approach means that equity would fine or imprison a person who failed to carry out its orders. This was a strong reason for the efficacy of the Court of Chancery. " Equity acts *in personam* " is the relevant maxim.

The third approach of preferring substance to form is also crystallised in an express maxim and was a strong reason for equity's moral superiority over the common law.

The fourth approach marks a crucial difference between equity and the common law. The remedies under the latter were and are available as of right. No relief was given in equity where there was an adequate common law remedy nor where the conduct of the applicant was disreputable. There are a number of maxims illustrative of this, the main being " Equity does nothing in vain," " He who comes to equity must come with clean hands," and " He who seeks equity must do equity."

Last, a note of caution must be given. The maxims are cited merely to illustrate the dominant approaches of equity. They are not universals.

The Effect of the Judicature Acts [11]

The Judicature Acts 1873–75 set up the basis of the modern English legal system. The objects of the Acts were threefold—to establish one Supreme Court of Judicature, to fuse the administration of common law and equity and to create new rules of procedure.

A single High Court was created in which the jurisdiction of the common courts and chancery were vested. Common law and equity were to be administered by all judges of all courts. Section 25 set out a list of specific cases of conflict and resolved them in favour of equity and section 25 (11) set out a general clause to the like effect. Section 25 (11) is now re-enacted in section 44 of the Supreme Court of Judicature (Consolidation) Act 1925 and prevents a conflict of common law and equitable remedies in most cases.[12]

The Present Position

With the creation of a single High Court in 1875 one might have expected that as well as a fusion of administration, there would

have been a fusion of the rules, principles, standards and concepts—
that the tenets of equity would have been released into the general
law. This has not generally happened. In most cases there is no real
conflict of principle or remedy—simply separate areas traditionally
covered by the two systems before 1875.[13]

The existence of the Chancery Division and judicial and textbook
terminology with its continual reference to the obsolete system of
courts help to preserve archaic distinctions. An American judge,
Judge Frank, once referred to these as the "traditional speech-
ways." In England, the problem is further perpetuated by the *de
facto* division of the Bar into common law and chancery
practitioners.

One of the main distinctions which remains is that between
specific equitable relief and common law damages. This gives rise
to a number of defects in the law.[14] The first is that equitable relief
will still only be given as an extraordinary remedy in cases where
no adequate remedy exists elsewhere. Historically, this is explicable
but it should not have survived in the modern law. Secondly, there
has not been a complete assimilation of the equitable principles of
relief from hardship due to equitable fraud, accident and mistake
with an action for damages in the law of contract. Thirdly, uncon-
scientious conduct of the plaintiff which will bar a claim for equitable relief will still not necessarily bar him from recovering damages
although it may affect the amount recovered.

The general effect of this conservative attitude on the part of
the majority of the judiciary has been inhibitive to the further
development of equity as a source of law and at best achieved
only limited and piecemeal assimilation of the two systems. Legislation has achieved some real fusion of principle in the property
law field and Lord Denning, the Master of the Rolls, has on a
number of occasions and with great ingenuity sought to resuscitate
equitable principles and extend them creatively,[15] but much remains
to be done in the law of contract.

Professors Keeton and Sheridan in their *Equity* describe the
present position as follows [16]:

> "The idea of Equity in English law is a gradually but con-
> stantly changing one. At present we are in a curious half-way
> stage where the division between common law and equity
> remains of vast practical importance and when at the same

time changes in doctrine are taking place as a result of the breaking down of this division. Fusion of administration is bringing about fusion of ideas and of method; but the process has a long way to go yet before it will be complete."

Elsewhere Professor Sheridan has summed up the state of equity today as " part eternal, part ephemeral and part nascent." [17]

Scotland has not suffered from this confusion. As we saw in Chapter 2, equity has been channelled into the mainstream of Scots law from the beginning.

Notes

[1] Aristotle, *Ethics*, Book V.

[2] See Sir Henry Maine, *Early Law and Customs*, p. 389. See further J. H. Baker, *An Introduction to English Legal History*, p. 78.

[3] See Baker, *op. cit.* pp. 290–292.

[4] For the development of the practice, see Baker, *op. cit.*, and G. W. Keeton and L. A. Sheridan, *Equity* (2nd ed.), Chaps. 1 and 2.

[5] F. W. Maitland, *Equity* (2nd ed., J. Brunyate), p. 5.

[6] *Table Talk* (ed. by Pollock), p. 43.

[7] *Doctor and Students* (Selden Soc.) (ed. T. F. T. Plucknett and J. L. Barton).

[8] *Op. cit.* p. 4.

[9] Keeton and Sheridan, *op. cit.* p. 5.

[10] *Op. cit.* pp. 5 *et seq.*

[11] See *e.g.* Keeton and Sheridan, *op. cit.*, Chap. III; P. H. Pettit, *Equity and the Law of Trusts* (3rd ed.), p. 7.

[12] See the interesting discussion by J. Tiley, *A Casebook on Equity and Succession*, pp. 20–21.

[13] See Tiley, *op. cit.*

[14] Keeton and Sheridan, *op. cit.* pp. 24 *et seq.*

[15] Keeton and Sheridan, *op. cit.* p. 37; Sheridan, " Equity Today " (1971) VI *Irish Jurist* 258.

[16] *Op. cit.* p. 29.

[17] (1971) VI *Irish Jurist* p. 270.

Chapter 7

CASE LAW

The Case Law Process and the Judge's Role

THE social world is in a constant state of flux. We have only got to reflect upon the events of our own lives to realise that this is so. At the same time, as we have seen, certain basic facts about human nature lead us to seek social order, and law is a useful device to facilitate this. Law tends towards the general, to reduce human behaviour to general rules and principles and concepts for the purposes of social control. At the same time every event is in a sense unique and there is a tension between the generality of the laws and the exigencies of the particular situation. Case law reflects this tension as we saw in the last chapter. Case law is the product of judicial reasoning in deciding cases in particular fact situations. As a source of law it is like a mosaic where the pattern emerges as the work develops. To those whose conceptions of rationality are rooted in logic this may seem intellectually imperfect. But, as we have seen, the great American judge Oliver Wendell Holmes, Jr. wrote[1] : " The life of the Law has not been logic; it has been experience." Indeed if one examines the oath taken by English judges one can see that the function of a judge is not to produce a system of rules or an institutional work possessing logical symmetry but " to do right to all manner of people after the laws and usages of this Realm without fear or favour, affection or ill-will."[2] The function of the judge is to apply the general legal rule or principle to the particular fact situation, which may at first sight appear to be a deductive process, but it is also to " do right " in that situation. This seems to imply an evaluation which goes beyond the law itself and which must be made in accordance with the " Law behind Law," *i.e.* the basic underlying values of the legal and ultimately the social system.[3] Obviously there are difficulties in the execution of this role—there is what a sociologist would call a role conflict.[4] Judges differ in their personalities and attitudes and this difference reflects itself in their interpretation of their role and the resolution of role conflict which comes to the fore in deciding borderline or difficult cases.

[In the early period as we saw, in the absence of a body of law, the judges had regard to customs and usages and assimilated them into a single set of rules, principles and standards. In this process notions of what was right played a crucial part. In the determination of what was right in this period men stressed the desirability of producing public order. It is only when this state of affairs is established that values can be given recognition.]

Analogy, Rules and Precedent

Once the decisions of the judges are remembered and recorded the system develops the eminently reasonable practice of treating like cases as like.[6] This produces convenience and consistency. The basic method of reasoning at this stage is by analogy.[7] Analogy, which is a common method of argument used by lawyer and layman alike, is an imperfect form of induction [8]; it proceeds on the basis of a number of *points of resemblance* of relations or attributes between cases. It rests not just on the number of attributes or relations which are found to exist in common, but also and more particularly on the relevance and importance of such attributes or relations. These are matters ultimately of practical judgment.[9] Further, unlike the use of analogy in the physical sciences which tends to proceed on the basis that because I know X and Y resemble each other in so many ways I believe them in fact *probably* to resemble them in every way, law being normative proceeds on the basis that because X and Y resemble each other in these ways they *ought* to resemble them in every way and thus be governed by the same legal rule or principle. John Stuart Mill pointed out that the use of analogies in the sciences served as " mere guideposts, pointing out the direction in which more rigorous investigations should be prosecuted." [10] In law on the other hand the process concludes not with an inference based on probabilities and further investigation but with the use of the resemblance as the basis of a *normative* step—the application of the old rule to the new case. The main debate thus takes place about the material similarities and dissimilarities in the facts but this is really only the tip of the iceberg. Underneath is the complex question of the *desirability and expediency* in extending the rule of the new fact situation. This is a question of policy and the values accepted by the legal system both in relation to the instant case and in relation to society at large.[11]

Formerly judges were reluctant to articulate such factors in their decision-making. Nowadays there is an increasing tendency for them to articulate them and to engage in a broader ranging justification of their decisions.[12] Clearly this is intellectually honest. Nevertheless some feel that by doing so the judges enter the political arena. The truth would seem, however, that they have always been there.

Thus case law involves reasoning by analogy. It also involves reasoning by rules.[13] In the formulation of rules the judges use normal classification techniques. They identify categories or concepts and species within them. Species are members rather than parts. Historically, however, the development tends to be an evolutionary movement from the particular to the general in the sense that the courts from case to case identify a number of particular species and later formulate a general concept or rule to embrace them all. The *categorisation* and rule formulation aspects of case law thus have a distinctly inductive character.[14]

Again as the law develops broad statements of principle are made which are pitched at a higher level of generality [15] and these often epitomise basic values or traditions of the legal system. Examples of this are the principle " No man shall profit from his own wrong " or some of the so-called maxims of equity such as " He who comes to equity must come with clean hands." As we have seen, usually but not necessarily they express some *ethical* value recognised by the law.

It is useful to contrast English and Scots law at this stage.[16] Scots law, as we have seen, developed out of an indigenous common law which was later influenced by Roman law and synthesised in institutional writings. After the Act of Union it naturally came under the influence of English law and superimposed a system of case law on a civilian and institutional foundation. In consequence of this tradition and certain specific legal procedures [17] in Scots law, the courts seem less concerned than English courts with the mere facts of a precedent. The emphasis is placed instead on legal principles, and the debate is often based on a choice between conflicting pronouncements of principle. Another way of putting this is that the Scots courts stress the rule aspect rather than the reasoning by analogy aspect of case law. This is less so, however, where a precedent of the House of Lords is concerned. Here the Scots courts seem to adhere more to the English pattern. Paradoxically, one can

nevertheless discern the former attitude reflected in the speeches
of Scottish Law Lords in English appeals.

Sometimes once a rule or principle has been established, it is
used in a manner that suggests deduction and the process of reasoning assumes a deductive form.[18] A classic example of this is
Lord Atkin's famous neighbour principle in *Donoghue* v. *Stevenson* [19] in 1932 which attempted to lay down a basic general test
of a duty of care in negligence. In this he formulated a principle
wide enough to cover the earlier cases. An extract from his speech
is set out in Appendix 3 which you will find useful to read when
you have finished this chapter. The principle which he laid down
has often been used as a starting point in subsequent cases.[20] The
residual elements involved in the process, however, prevent the
process from being a strictly logical one. There are elements of
discretion, as we have seen, first in the selection of the major premise and in its precise formulation. No case law rule or principle
is ever settled for all time. Secondly there is often some degree of
selection involved in the formulation of the minor premise. This
is at the level of fact.

Also, as we have seen in Chapter 5, conclusions do not follow
as a matter of logical necessity in legal cases but as a matter of
choice.[21] The process of choice is not thereby necessarily irrational.
The judge has heard the arguments on both sides and weighed
them up. Policy and value considerations enter into it to some
extent. *The decision-making process* is probably best described as
the interaction of a number of variables, as we shall see in Chapter 13. The judgment records the inferences drawn, but this may
be a rationalisation of the mental process involved. It will also be
concerned not only with rationalising the inference drawn, but
also justifying it. The two are inextricably joined in case law
reasoning.

English case law thus is the product of practical reasoning emerg-
ing from decision-making situations, and combining the attributes
of reasoning by analogy with those of reasoning by rules. With
regard to the ingredients of rules it adopts what might be described
as a shifting classification system which is anathema to traditional
logicians who see the world in a static, finite form. A rule or principle may be extended or contracted as the need arises. We examine
the underlying policy question in Chapters 13 and 14. To a certain
extent and within certain conventional limits, the judges are free

to choose the precise rules by which they are to be bound.⟧The limits are prescribed by the vague criteria of analogical reasoning and the more precise criteria of *stare decisis* or the doctrine of precedent.⟧In any event rules in any sphere of life never bind in an inexorable sense. There is flexibility inherent in their structure and often in their content. Language cannot attain the precision of the more abstract symbols used in mathematics and the use of standards such as reasonableness ensures a residual discretion in many cases. This is not to say that the process is entirely discretionary. It is rather pockets of discretion within a framework of rules.[22] ⟨Principles and standards, being pitched at a greater level of generality than rules, afford more scope for judicial discretion.⟩

The Formulation and Application of Case Law Rules [23]

Let us now consider the doctrine of precedent in more detail. What is it that is the binding element in a case? To what extent is a later court bound? Assuming that the later court can be bound, which courts bind which courts in the legal system? What we are mainly concerned with here is the aspect of case law which involves reasoning with rules, although it is impossible to separate this completely from the analogical aspect. You may find it useful at this stage to refer to Appendix 1 which sets out a specimen law report.

The Ratio Decidendi

⟨The actual decision on the facts of a case, which is often described by the Latin phrase *res judicata*,[24] is binding only on the parties to the action.⟩

⟨A distinction is made between this and the *ratio decidendi* which is something more abstract and which is absorbed into the general body of law.⟩ It is clearly an abstraction.[25] Can one define it any more precisely? ⟨There is no authoritative definition. Indeed the whole system of precedent, as opposed to the actual legal rules and principles and standards produced by that system, is probably a question of practice rather than law and consequently better approached as a matter of description rather than prescription.[26] *Ratio decidendi* has sometimes been defined or described as a reason or the reason for the decision or as the underlying principle of a case which forms its authoritative element.⟩ Sir Rupert Cross has described it as " Any rule of law expressly or impliedly treated by the judge as a necessary step in reaching his conclusion, having regard to the line of reasoning adopted by him, or a necessary part of his direction to the jury." [27] He is probably using rule there to cover principles and standards. These definitions and descriptions all contain question-begging elements, *e.g.* " authoritative," " impliedly," " necessary " and fail to recognise the role of a later court in relation to the *ratio*.

The courts in fact have not tied themselves down to any one definition. This is one problem. Another larger problem is that the concept of *ratio decidendi* is intrinsically difficult to comprehend since its *function* is to bridge the gap between reasoning by analogy and reasoning with rules.

Two jurists have thought that in the absence of an *authoritative* definition perhaps the solution is to establish a technique of identifying a *ratio* in a particular case rather on the basis of " I may not be able to define an elephant but I know one when I see one."

Wambaugh's test

The first of these was Professor Wambaugh's test of " inversion " set out in his book *The Study of Cases*. Assuming that *ratio decidendi* was basically *a general rule without which a case would have been decided otherwise* he then proceeds to instruct the novice and states his test in words which resemble a recipe in a cookery book :

" First frame carefully the supposed proposition of law. Let him then insert in the proposition a word reversing its meaning. Let him then inquire whether, if the court had conceived this new proposition to be good and had had it in mind, the decision would have been the same. If the answer be affirmative, then, however excellent the original proposition may be, the case is not a precedent for that proposition, if the answer be negative, the case is authority for the original proposition and possibly for other propositions also. In short, when a case turns only on one point, the proposition of the case, the reason of the decision, the *ratio decidendi*, must be a general rule without which the case must have been decided otherwise." [28]

As you can see, Wambaugh was thinking in the binary form of formal logic—that something is X or is not X. He is also thinking of legal reasoning being or at least resembling the logical process of deduction where conclusions necessarily follow from premises. Consequently his basic idea of inversion or negation is over-simple. Legal rules and principles are often of a complex form consisting of a number of concepts and have more than one contrary.[29] Also legal reasoning as we have seen does not proceed on a strictly logical basis. Ambiguity, openness and incompleteness in legal concepts, rules, principles and standards and the constant exercise of choice render this impossible.

Wambaugh's test is, therefore, ultimately impractical in all but the simplest type of case. Nevertheless it has proved fashionable in the past in American Law Schools [30] and you may find it a useful starting place until you have mastered the traditions of the common law and the matter has become second nature.

Goodhart's test

The second test is that of Professor Goodhart who, though American, has spent most of his professional life in England and was Professor of Jurisprudence at Oxford. His approach is perhaps more useful and is centred on the facts treated as material by the trial judge. He summarised his rules for finding the *ratio decidendi* of a case as follows [31]:

"(1) The principle of a case is not found in the reasons given in the opinion.

(2) The principle is not found in the rule of law set forth in the opinion.

(3) The principle is not necessarily found by a consideration of all the ascertainable facts of the case, and the judge's decision.

(4) *The principle of the case is found by taking account (a) of the facts treated by the judge as material, and (b) his decision as based on them.*

(5) In finding the principle it is also necessary to establish what facts were held to be immaterial by the judge, for the principle may depend as much on exclusion as it does on inclusion."

A conclusion based on a hypothetical fact is a *dictum*. By hypothetical fact is meant any fact the existence of which has not been determined or accepted by the judge.

The main reasons for these general rules were that as regards (1) the courts often state their reasons too widely and sometimes incorrectly—but the cases are nevertheless authoritative; as regards (2) sometimes there is no rule stated; as regards (3), (4) and (5) it is the facts which the trial judge regards as material which are important. In Goodhart's words " It is by his choice of material facts that the judge creates law." [32]

Professor Goodhart has subsequently explained that he was trying to provide a guide to the method which he believed most English courts followed when attempting to determine the *ratio decidendi* of a doubtful case.[33] His test seems useful [34] and yet it must be admitted that the courts do not always work in this way. As Sir Rupert Cross has put it neatly " . . . although it is always essential and sometimes sufficient in order to arrive at the *ratio decidendi* of a case to consider the facts treated as material by the court and the decision based on those facts, it is sometimes necessary to do a great deal more." [35] It is then, as he says, necessary to examine the way in which the case was argued and pleaded, the process of reasoning adopted by the judge and the relationship of the case to other decisions. It is also necessary to consider the status of the court itself since there is an increasing tendency by lower courts to adopt a more elastic view of what binds them when a matter has been fully argued before a higher court.

Stone's critique

In an article in the *Modern Law Review* in 1959 [36] Professor Julius Stone made some very convincing criticisms of Professor Goodhart's theory. He started from the premise that Goodhart is attempting to produce a prescriptive rather than a descriptive theory. This, Stone thinks, is his big mistake. *The process is basically one of choosing an appropriate level of generality. There is thus implicit in a decided case a number of potential rationes decidendi.* Stone analyses *Donoghue* v. *Stevenson* (the famous case of the alleged snail in the ginger beer bottle discussed in detail in Appendix 3) and shows how the range of facts could be stated at alternative levels. He lists them as follows:

(a) *Fact as to the agent of harm.* Dead snails, *or* any snails, *or* any noxious physical foreign body, *or* any noxious foreign element, physical or not, *or* any noxious element.

(b) *Fact as to vehicle of harm.* An opaque bottle of ginger beer, *or* an opaque bottle of beverage, *or* any bottle of beverage, *or* any container of commodities for human consumption, *or* any containers of any chattels for human use, *or* any chattel whatsoever, *or* any thing (including land or buildings).

(c) *Fact as to defendant's identity.* A manufacturer of goods nationally distributed through dispersed retailers, *or* any manufacturer, *or* any person working on the object for reward, *or* any person working on the object, *or* anyone dealing with the object.

(d) *Fact as to potential danger from vehicle of harm.* Object likely to become dangerous by negligence, *or* whether or not so.

(e) *Fact as to injury to plaintiff.* Physical personal injury, *or* nervous or physical personal injury, *or* any injury.

(f) *Fact as to plaintiff's identity.* A Scots widow, *or* a Scotswoman *or* a woman, *or* any adult, *or* any human being, *or* any legal person.

(g) *Fact as to plaintiff's relation to vehicle of harm.* Donee of purchaser, from retailer who bought directly from the defendant, *or* the purchaser from such retailer, *or* the purchaser from anyone, *or* any person related to such purchaser or other person, *or* any person into whose hands the object rightfully comes, *or* any person into whose hands it comes at all.

(h) *Fact as to discoverability of agent of harm.* The noxious element being not discoverable by inspection of any intermediate party, *or* not so discoverable without destroying the saleability of the commodity, *or* not so discoverable by any such party who had a duty to inspect, *or* not so discoverable by any such party who could reasonably be expected *by the defendant* to inspect, *or* not discoverable by any such party who could reasonably be expected *by the court or a jury* to inspect.

(j) *Fact as to time of litigation.* The facts complained of were litigated in 1932, *or* any time before 1932, *or* after 1932, *or* at any time.

Stone is convinced that Goodhart's neglect of this and his concentration on " material " facts has led him into error. Apart from some indication from the earlier case one starts off from the position that a *ratio* is only prescriptive for a later case whose facts are " on all fours " in every respect. Outside this range the question is always whether in the later court's view the presence in the instant case of *some* of the facts *at some* of their levels of generality is more relevant to its present decision than is the *absence* of the rest of them. To Stone this is not a question of the " materiality " of facts to the decision in the earlier case imposing itself on the later court. "It is rather a question of *the analogical relevance* of the prior holding to the later case, requiring the later court to choose between possibilities presented by the "earlier case."

It would seem that Professor Stone has made some convincing points and that it is a mistake to seek either for a prescriptive definition of the concept of *ratio decidendi* or to expect a case to yield up a single *ratio* in any event. It is more easily intelligible in terms of a *technique or process of abstraction and generalisation* which assumes its importance in later cases. The general point needs to be reiterated that ultimately it is the later court, considering the case in the light of the exigencies of the case before it, which is *in practical terms* the arbiter of the appropriate level of generality, at least until the latter case itself is reviewed in a subsequent case. Obviously in the meantime textbook writers can hazard *an opinion* as to the scope of the *ratio*. Perhaps this means at the end of the day that *ratio decidendi* is a flexible notion which is "fuzzy at the edges" [37] and purposely left so by the courts for policy reasons because *it itself* is not so much a rule as *an analogical technique used to create a rule*. [38] *Ratio decidendi* thus in ordinary, loose usage can refer to the technique and to a particular rule actually produced or likely to be produced by the technique.

Obiter Dicta

Orthodox legal thinking juxtaposes to *ratio decidendi* the concept of *obiter dictum* or *dicta*. An *obiter dictum* is something which is not *ratio decidendi*. Can one be more explicit than this?

Professor Patterson, another American jurist, has defined it as a "statement of law" in the judgment "which could not logically be a major premise of the selected facts of the decision." [39] Clearly he has been influenced by the Wambaugh conception of *ratio decidendi*. His definition, which does not make clear who is to select the facts, rests on two erroneous assumptions. First he assumes that the process is a logical one and secondly in any event he tries to turn logical deduction upside down. It is not possible from a conclusion and a middle premise to arrive at one single major premise or to put it in simpler terms one cannot logically start at the end and work back to the beginning. If one cannot identify what is logically *the* major premise by this process *a fortiori* one cannot identify what is *not* the major premise. All that one can do is to state *a range* of possible major premises or things incapable of being the major premise.

Professor Goodhart on the other hand, as we saw, approaches the matter from the point of view of the facts and says that an *obiter dictum* is " a conclusion based on a fact the existence of which has not been determined by the court." [40] Now as Sir Rupert Cross has pointed out there is a distinction which can be drawn between statements based on facts the existence of which is denied by the court and statements based on a fact the existence of which has not been determined by the court.[41] The latter may arise where the court gives a preliminary ruling on a point of law on assumed facts. Indeed such an event is common in Scots law, and the leading case in the law of torts, *Donoghue* v. *Stevenson* arose in this way.[42] In such cases the ruling can be regarded as *ratio decidendi* whereas in cases where the facts are denied by the court the statements are purely *obiter*.

Clearly the whole conception of *obiter dictum*, involving the negation of *ratio decidendi*, is affected by the fuzziness of *ratio*. Both *ratio* and *obiter* are analogical techniques. *Ratio* gives rise to a rule to follow; *obiter* to something of less force than a rule but which might be worth following. It has less force because the matter might not have been adequately thrashed out.

Within the category of *obiter dicta* there nevertheless seems to be a number of species with varying degrees of authority. Where the *dicta* are clearly irrelevant to the case in which they occur they are sometimes called mere *gratis dicta*.[43] Where they relate to a collateral issue in the case they are sometimes said to be *judicial dicta*.[44] Where the matter is heard on appeal, particularly in the House of Lords, the court sometimes in order to settle the state of the law in a particular field asks counsel to address them on the law and then makes general statements about the law. These are regarded as a superior species of *obiter dicta* and are likely to be followed in the High Court.[45]

Sometimes a later court faced with an inconvenient decision interprets the ruling as *obiter* in order to resist being bound by it. Mr. Dias has argued that " The distinction in such cases between *ratio* and *dicta* is but a device employed by subsequent courts for the adoption or rejection of doctrine expressed in previous cases according to the inclination of the judges."[46] This would amount to an overstatement of the case if we interpreted Mr. Dias's inclination as whim and regarded this as true of all *obiter dicta*. The process is a little more sophisticated than that, as we have seen.

Finding the Ratio of Decisions in Appellate Courts [47]

So far what we have said about *ratio decidendi* and *obiter dicta* has been built on the model of a decision by a single judge. Obviously it applies to first instance decisions in the High Court and county court. The Court of Appeal and House of Lords, however, sit with more than one judge. How does one extract a *ratio* if all the judges give separate judgments? One starts with a simple proposition—follow the majority. This proposition, however, begs a number of questions. First, while one can always discern their decision, their individual reasons may differ. There is authority for the view that if there are two grounds given for a decision by different judges or groups of judges, the narrower ground should prevail as the *ratio*. It cannot be said, however, that this is firmly established practice. Secondly the case may be fragmented into a number of different issues and there may be different majorities on different issues. It has recently been held by the Court of Appeal in an interlocutory appeal [48] that where there is no discernible *ratio decidendi* common to the majority in the House of Lords the Court of Appeal is not bound by the reasoning in those speeches and is free to adopt any reasoning which appears to be correct provided it supports the actual decision of the House. It is likely that a similar practice would be adopted in relation to decisions of the Court of Appeal, although there is no authority on the point.

Last, the above proposition assumes that the matter is one which is governed by strict rules, whereas the judges seem sometimes to treat it as tradition which can be discarded if it stands in the way of justice in the particular case.

Where the court is equally divided there is a clear practice in the House of Lords to dismiss the appeal on the principle *semper praesumitur pro negante* (" The presumption is always in favour of the negative ").[49] In other words the *ratio* of the court from which the appeal came becomes the *ratio* of the House of Lords when the House of Lords is evenly divided.

The position in the Court of Appeal is not so clear. In *The Vera Cruz* [50] in 1880 it was said that a subsequent Court of Appeal was not bound by a previous decision of that court when the earlier court was evenly divided. Brett M.R. said that the practice of following other courts of equal status was based on judicial comity and this did not exist where an earlier court was equally divided. This practice did not apply to the House of Lords. The reasoning is not very convincing and the practice laid down by him was not followed in *Hart* v. *The Riversdale Mill Co. Ltd.*[51] in 1928, where the Court of Appeal regarded itself as bound by the decision of an equally divided Court of Exchequer Chamber, the forerunner of the present Court of Appeal. *The Vera Cruz* case does not, however, appear to have been cited. The practice of *The Vera Cruz* was, however, followed in *Galloway* v. *Galloway*[52] in 1954 although neither *The Vera Cruz* nor *Hart's* case seems to have been considered.

The practice, therefore, is not well settled. The present state of the authorities is muddled, and a clear, rationally justified rule has still to be laid down. In practice, however, the problem is not likely to be acute since the Court of Appeal normally sits with three judges, except on interlocutory matters when there are two. The latter are pre-trial matters, which are usually of less importance, and the decisions are not often reported.

Exceptional Cases

You may from time to time come across two rather anomalous types of case. The first is a case which was the subject of a resolution of the judges meeting informally in the Exchequer Chamber to hear legal arguments. These often arose out of actual cases but were dealt with not as a species of appeal, rather as a moot. Once a point had been resolved in this way it was authoritative and could not be reopened before the courts. The Court of Exchequer Chamber has long since disappeared but there is a similar kind of procedure under section 36 of the Criminal Justice Act 1972 known as an Attorney-General's reference. The matter arises out of an actual case where an accused has been acquitted but the Crown wish a point of law to be resolved. The matter is referred by the Attorney-General to the Court of Appeal (Criminal Division) for a determination. The opinion is treated in practice as equivalent to a *ratio decidendi*.

Distinguishing Cases

Instead of following or refusing to follow an earlier case the court may distinguish it. This differs from a refusal to follow or overrule the previous case which are courses only open to a court which is not bound to follow a decision of the earlier court. In distinguishing, certain factual differences are found which justify the court not following the earlier case while still accepting that the earlier case is good law.

The recognition of similarity and difference between cases lies at the root of English legal reasoning, as we saw earlier in this chapter. Because of the vagueness surrounding the concept of *ratio* and the possibility of distinguishing cases, some argue that the courts are never really bound. To a certain extent this seems to arise out of a failure to appreciate what is meant by being bound in this context. The expression conjures up to some the idea of a person wrapped in chains and physically compelled to do a particular thing. Judges are clearly not bound (even metaphorically) in this way. Further there is always in the nature of things going to be some factual difference between cases. What is it that stops the judge from always using the difference to formulate a new rule? As we have seen, convenience and consistency play a large part. Distinguishing cases in fact involves more than just identifying a factual difference. It involves using it as a justification for departing from the ruling in the earlier case. The court's acceptance of the distinction as a basis for departing from the earlier ruling usually rests on some notion such as morality, social policy or common sense.[53] Often one hears these summed up in a general reference to justice or to public policy or just plain policy. We return to the questions of policy and values in Chapters 13 and 14.

Professor Glanville Williams in *Learning the Law* divides distinguishing into two types—restrictive and non-restrictive.[54] The latter, he says, occurs where the court accepts the expressed *ratio decidendi* of the earlier case and does not seek to curtail it, but finds that the case before it does not fall within it because of some material difference of fact. Restrictive distinguishing cuts down the *ratio decidendi* of the earlier case by treating as material to the earlier decision some fact which the earlier court regarded or appeared to regard as immaterial. It can be seen that this view is inconsistent with Professor Goodhart's view that the judge in a case is the arbiter of what are material facts. Professor Williams in fact rejects that view and also argues that the judge has not an unlimited discretion to jettison facts as immaterial.

Since two of the leading jurists differ on such a fundamental point

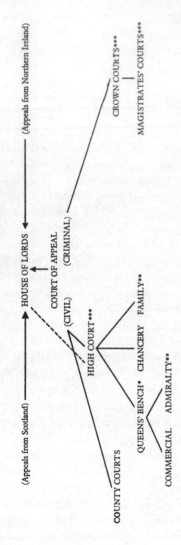

The Present Court Structure in England and Wales

(Appeals from Northern Ireland)

(Appeals from Scotland) → HOUSE OF LORDS ←

COURT OF APPEAL
(CIVIL)   (CRIMINAL)

HIGH COURT***

QUEENS' BENCH*   CHANCERY   FAMILY**

COMMERCIAL   ADMIRALTY**

COUNTY COURTS

CROWN COURTS***

MAGISTRATES' COURTS***

Notes

----Leapfrogging procedure.

*Under the Judicature Acts, there were also Common Pleas and Exchequer Divisions. These merged with the Queen's Bench Division in 1881.

**Under the Judicature Acts, there was a Probate Divorce and Admiralty Division. This was changed by the Administration of Justice Act 1970, which created the Family Division and transferred Admiralty to Queen's Bench and Contentious Probate to Chancery.

***Each Division of the High Court has a Divisional Court which exercises a species of appellate jurisdiction. Thus appeals from the Matrimonial jurisdiction of the magistrates' courts go to the Divisional Court of the Family Division. There can also be appeals by a procedure known as case stated from the magistrates' and Crown Courts to the Divisional Court of the Queen's Bench Division. This is irrational but historically explicable.

it might be asked how can we ascertain the true position? [55] The answer would seem to be that distinguishing cases is a complex process which cannot easily be reduced to one fixed formula. The best way to understand it is to examine the ways in which different judges approach their task. This involves reading the cases. It would seem that there is scope here for socio-legal research identifying the types of situations in which judges distinguished cases and the justification they used. The problems, of course, are the building of a comprehensive research framework and the fact that one would be effectively limited to reported cases, which in some respects represent the pathology of the legal system (the abnormal cases) and are thus not a true random sample of all cases before the courts.

Stare Decisis and the Hierarchy of Courts

The expression *stare decisis* is a Latin phrase sometimes used to describe the doctrine of precedent generally; at other times it refers to the detailed ground rules governing which courts bind which other courts in the legal system. In translation it means to stand by what has been decided. Strictly speaking the phrase should be *stare rationibus decidendis* since it is the *ratio decidendi* not the decision which binds.[56]

There is some debate in the legal literature as to when the system developed in its present form.[57] If one takes this to mean precisely in its modern form most of the development has necessarily taken place after the passing of the Judicature Acts.

On p. 76 you will see a diagram which gives the present court structure.

The House of Lords

This stands at the apex of the system and occupies an anomalous position if one thinks in terms of the classical conception of a separation of powers. The anomaly has been mitigated to a large extent by the fact that the lay peers have not participated in ordinary appeals since the *Trial of Daniel O'Connell* [58] in the nineteenth century.

From the middle of the nineteenth century the rule developed that the House of Lords was bound by its previous decisions.[59] This was finally clearly recognised by the House of Lords itself in *London Street Tramways Co.* v. *L.C.C.*[60] in 1898. Some argued that this was a rule of practice rather than law,[61] and in 1966, before the commencement of business, Lord Gardiner L.C. on behalf of himself and the Lords of Appeal read a statement to the effect that they proposed in future to depart from their own decisions where it appeared right to do so.[62] In certain areas where there was a greater need for certainty they would adhere strictly to their earlier decisions.

In practice the House of Lords has made sparing use of its newly assumed freedom.[63] In *Conway* v. *Rimmer* [64] in 1968 the majority preferred to distinguish rather than overrule an earlier House of Lords decision. In *Jones* v. *Secretary of State for Social Services* [65] in 1972 the majority followed an earlier decision although most of them thought it was wrong. Some of their Lordships justified their attitude on the basis that matters of statutory construction were generally not suitable cases in which to exercise this power.

Again in *Knuller Ltd.* v. *D.P.P.*[66] in 1972 the majority followed the earlier decision in *Shaw* v. *D.P.P.*[67] which established the offence of a conspiracy to corrupt public morals. This was despite the fact that the decision had been much criticised.[68]

In *British Railways Board* v. *Herrington* [69] in 1972 the House of Lords effectively overruled an earlier decision although they did not do so expressly in reliance on the *Practice Direction*. In *Miliangos* v. *George Frank (Textiles) Ltd.*[70] in 1975 the majority of the House of Lords clearly exercised their power and overruled a previous House of Lords decision which had confirmed that judgments should only be given in sterling. This change enabled the law to keep in step with commercial needs in times of floating currencies and with the approach of the majority of other countries facing similar problems.

In the *Jones* case [71] Lord Simon of Glaisdale raised the possibility of the House adopting the American practice of prospective over-ruling of cases, *i.e.* following an earlier authority in the case before them but stating that it will not be followed in future. The practice has not so far been adopted and there appear to be strong arguments against it.[72] The main arguments are that it distorts the public's expectation of the judicial role, and that it can lead to injustice in relation to particular cases.

Underlying the reluctance of the House of Lords to adopt a more activist role is the point made recently by Lord Simon in his dissenting judgment in the *Miliangos* case.[73] He said that: " The training and experience of a judge is unsuitable for this type of decision making unaided: his circumspection is too narrow; his very qualities of keen perception of his immediate problem tend to militate against sound judgment of the wider and more general issues involved." If they are to undertake legislative responsibilities, he said, official advice and a balanced executive view might be made available by a law officer or his counsel acting as *amicus curiae*.

The Court of Appeal

The Court of Appeal consists of two divisions—civil and criminal—and usually sits with three members.

Civil Division. The basic rule as regards the Civil Division was laid down by the court itself in 1944 in *Young* v. *Bristol Aeroplane Co. Ltd.*,[74] although its decision was later affirmed by the House of Lords. The court is bound by its previous decisions except in three situations. These are:

(1) Where there are two conflicting decisions, a later court can choose.
(2) Where the decision is inconsistent with a *subsequent* House of Lords decision.
(3) Where the decision was given *per incuriam*,[75] which means a failure to advert to an earlier inconsistent decision of itself or the House of Lords.

To these has been added a fourth by *Boys* v. *Chaplin*[76] in 1968. This provides that the decision of a court of two judges on an interlocutory matter does not bind a subsequent court.

Recently, since the 1966 statement by Lord Gardiner, Lord Denning M.R., who is the senior judge in the Civil Division, has attempted to break away from the basic rule laid down in *Young's* case. So far he has failed to persuade his brethren who prefer to distinguish rather than overrule inconvenient precedents.[77]

The issues involved can be illustrated by the recent Rent Act case of *Farrell* v. *Alexander* [1976] 1 Q.B. 167 where the majority held that they were bound by earlier authorities. Lord Denning argued that they should not be bound by earlier Court of Appeal decisions. The appellants were not legally aided and they would probably be deterred by the cost of going to the House of Lords. Thus an injustice would be perpetrated. Scarman L.J. said (at p. 371) that he had immense sympathy for Lord Denning's approach but thought that it was damaging to the law in the long run although it would produce justice in the instant case. Consistency is necessary to certainty—one of the great objectives of law. The Court of Appeal—at the very centre of our legal system—is responsible for its stability, its consistency and its predictability. The task of law reform, which calls for wide-ranging techniques of consultation and discussion that cannot be compressed into the forensic medium, is for others. However, the appellants did in fact take the case to the House of Lords where the majority of the Law Lords approved Lord Denning's dissenting judgment (see [1976] 2 All E.R. 721).

Lord Denning recently added a new dimension to the general debate by persuading his brethren in *Broome* v. *Cassell & Co.*[78] in 1971 that an earlier decision of the House of Lords was *per incuriam* and consequently the Court of Appeal was not bound to follow it. The House of Lords,[79] however, subsequently denied this power and Lord Hailsham delivered a magisterial rebuke.[80] Although one might object to the pompous manner in which the latter was delivered and feel an instinctive admiration for Lord Denning's audacity it would seem that the reasoning of the House of Lords in this matter was probably sound. Now that one can " leap frog " direct from the High Court to the House of Lords in suitable cases there is much less need for the Court of Appeal to adopt a role such as Lord Denning seeks for it. As for the comparative advantages of distinguishing and overruling, distinguishing, as we saw, leaves the earlier decision intact. It leaves to a later court the responsibility of overruling it.[81]

Criminal Division. The Criminal Division is in fact the successor to an earlier court, the Court of Criminal Appeal. In the latter it was laid down in *R.* v. *Taylor*[32] in 1950 that the court had to deal with the liberty of the subject, and where a full court, assembled for the purpose, considered that in an earlier case the law had been misapplied or misunderstood it could and should reconsider it. This rule applies to the Criminal Division[83] as it clearly should.

Divisional courts

These are an anomalous species of court whose jurisdiction could perhaps be conveniently merged with that of the Court of Appeal. In civil matters they are bound by decisions of the House of Lords and the Court of Appeal (Civil Division) as well as their own.[84] Logic would require that in criminal matters they should be governed by a rule similar to that in *R. v. Taylor* but this does not appear to be the case.[85]

High Court

High Court and Crown Court judges are bound by the decisions of superior courts but not bound by each other's rulings although in practice they generally follow them.[86]

Other courts

The county court and magistrates' courts are bound by decisions of the superior courts but their decisions do not bind each other.[87]

The Judicial Committee of the Privy Council

Although this is the Court of Appeal of the colonies and remnants of the British Commonwealth its decisions have never bound English courts and are merely persuasive.[88] Since, however, the committee customarily includes a majority of English Law Lords some of the recommendations have acquired considerable authority. A leading case in the law of torts, *The Wagon Mound*,[89] has effectively overruled the Court of Appeal decision in *Re Polemis*.[90]

The European Court of Justice

This is the ultimate interpreter of EEC sources of law and will be discussed in Chapter 11.

A Comparison with the Position of Case Law in French and German Law [91]

The role of case law in France and Germany can only be understood by considering its relationship with legislation. Both France and Germany are largely codified systems. There is a tradition in both countries of hiding judicial law-making behind the guise of interpretation. In fact article 5 of the French Civil Code expressly forbids the judges to lay down general rules.

Despite this theory and that provision, do the judges in fact make law? The answer would seem to be that they do but they do so within a basic framework established by the codes and legislation.[92] The scope of judicial law-making is thus more limited than in the common law world and Scotland. In French administrative law, however, the Conseil d'Etat engages in overt law-making.

Another important point is that the rules laid down by the courts do not have the same authority as the legal rules contained in the codes or legislation. The rules laid down by the courts can always be rejected or modified by a later court. They are not authoritative and are not legally binding although they are frequently followed in practice. David and Brierley describe the position thus: " The judicially created rule only exists and is only applied so long as the judges—that is each judge—consider it a good rule. Under these conditions it is understandable that one hesitates to speak of a truly legal rule (règle)." [93]

Conclusion

Case law is still an important source of English law and its authority is greater than in French and German law. Our case law is a form of practical reasoning, which is basically an amalgam of reasoning by analogy and reasoning with rules with a superstructure of techniques for identifying the scope of the ratio and detailed ground rules determining the relationship of courts in the legal system. Although English courts, unlike the French and German courts, accept a doctrine of binding precedent it does not bind in an inexorable sense and there is considerable scope for manoeuvre within the system. Judges by reason of their different personality attributes and the exigencies of the particular case oscillate between the two poles of certainty and flexibility. In the words of Lord Denning some are " timorous souls " and others are " bold spirits." [94]

Professor Julius Stone, with his usual learning and insight, sums up the position in slightly rhetorical English in this way [95]:

> " In short a ' rule ' or ' principle ' as it emerges from a precedent case is subject in its further elaboration to continual review, in the light of analogies and differences, not merely in the logical relations between legal concepts and propositions, not merely in the relations between fact situations, and the problems springing from these; but also in the light of the import of these analogies and differences for what is thought by the latter court to yield a tolerably acceptable result in terms of ' policy,' ' ethics,' ' justice,' ' expediency ' or whatever other norm of desirability the law may be thought to subserve. No ' ineluctable logic,' but *a composite of the logical relations seen*

between legal proposition, of observations of facts and conse-
quences, and of value judgments about the acceptability of
these consequences, is what finally comes to bear upon the
alternatives with which ' the rule of *stare decisis* ' confronts
the courts, and especially appellate courts. And this, it may be
supposed, is why finally we cannot assess the product of their
work in terms of any less complex quality than that of
wisdom." ⚓

In Appendix 1 we set out a specimen law report with explanatory
notes, in Appendix 2 we give details of the law reports and in
Appendix 3 we study a particular illustration of the case law process
at work, in the conceptual development of negligence. You will
probably find it useful to turn to these Appendices now.

Notes

[1] *The Common Law*, p. 1.

[2] See the wording of the oath discussed by Lord Denning in *The Road to Justice*, pp. 4 *et seq.* See also Lord Simon of Glaisdale in *Rugby Water Board* v. *Shaw-Fox* [1973] A.C. 228D.

[3] Denning, *op. cit.* p. 4.

[4] See the discussion of social roles in Vilhelm Aubert's *Elements of Sociology*, Chap. III and see also Robert B. Seidman, " The Judicial Process Reconsidered in the Light of Role-Theory " (1969) 32 M.L.R. 516, 520, where he argues that the courts should formulate rules of conduct for " trouble " cases.

[5] See P. Stein and J. Shand, *Legal Values in Western Society*, Chap. 2.

[6] The early writer and judge, Bracton, in his treatise on the laws of England stated the principle thus, " If like matters arise, let them be decided by like since the occasion is a good one for proceeding *a similibus ad similia.*" Bracton, *The Laws and Customs of England* (Thorne ed.), Vol. 2, p. 21.

[7] See Edward H. Levi, *An Introduction to Legal Reasoning*, p. 1.

[8] John Stuart Mill, *A System of Logic* (8th ed.), Chap. XX, pp. 364–368.

[9] See Irving M. Copi, *Introduction to Logic* (4th ed.), p. 360.

[10] See note 8 above.

[11] See Levi, *op. cit.* pp. 1–8 for a brilliant discussion of this process. Karl Llewellyn used the phrase " situation sense " in this context in *The Common Law Tradition.*

[12] See in connection with the law of tort, Clive Symmons' article, "The Duty of Care in Negligence: Recently Expressed Policy Elements" (1971) 34 M.L.R. 394 and 528.

[13] See Gidon Gottlieb, *The Logic of Choice*, Chap. VI.

[14] See Levi, *op. cit.*, for a description of the classification process involved in the development of negligence and see Appendix 3.

[15] See Lord Reid in *Home Office* v. *Dorset Yacht Co. Ltd.* [1970] A.C. 1004, 1026H–1027B.

[16] See Professor T. B. Smith in *Judicial Precedent in Scots Law*, pp. 106–107.

[17] The main procedure is that of "relevancy." In the quaint words of Professor David Walker in "The Theory of Relevancy," 63 *Juridical Review* 1, "The question is: do the averments of fact focused by the pleas-in-law support the conclusions of the summons? If not, the action is irrelevant." To test this the allegations of fact are accepted by the court. The leading case of *Donoghue* v. *Stevenson* [1932] A.C. 562 arose out of this procedure.

[18] See Lord Simon of Glaisdale's comments in the tax case of *Lupton* v. *F.A. & A.B. Ltd.* [1972] A.C. 634, 658–659.

[19] [1932] A.C. 562.

[20] See generally Appendix 3.

[21] See G. Gottlieb's *The Logic of Choice*, pp. 69 *et seq.* and esp. p. 87.

[22] See generally on this Julius Stone, "The Ratio of the Ratio Decidendi" in (1959) 22 M.L.R. 597, 610 *et seq.*

[23] Much of what follows is based on Sir Rupert Cross, *Precedent in English Law* (2nd ed.).

[24] Literally the thing has been adjudicated upon.

[25] *Cf.* Professor Glanville Williams, *Learning the Law* (9th ed.), Chap. 6. It is assumed that you have read this.

[26] See further on this, *Salmond on Jurisprudence* (11th ed. by Glanville Williams), p. 188. *Cf.* J. Stone, 69 Col.L.R. 1162 (1969). See also D. Lloyd, *Introduction to Jurisprudence* (3rd ed.), p. 709.

[27] *Ibid.* p. 77.

[28] See his *Study of Cases* (1894 ed.), pp. 17–18.

[29] See Cross, *op. cit.* p. 52.

[30] See *e.g.* Karl Llewellyn's *Bramble Bush*, p. 45. This may not, however, have represented his maturer view. See William Twining, *Karl Llewellyn and the Realist Movement*, p. 234.

[31] *Essays in Jurisprudence and the Common Law*, pp. 25–26 (my italics).

[32] *Ibid.* p. 10.

[33] See (1959) 22 M.L.R. 123–124. He states there that "there is no actual *uniform* operation of English courts concerning the application of precedents" (p. 123).

[34] He appears to receive some support from the recent judgment of Lord Simon of Glaisdale in the tax case of *Lupton* v. *F.A. & A.B. Ltd.* [1972] A.C. 634 at pp. 658–659. Lord Simon emphasises, however, that material facts found in the case need to be reassessed in the light of subsequent decisions.

[35] *Op. cit.* p. 76.

[36] See " The Ratio of the Ratio Decidendi " in (1959) 22 M.L.R. 597. See also 69 Col.L.R. 1162 (1969).

[37] The phrase is Lord Hailsham's used in relation to the common law generally in *English Law and its Future*, a broadcast talk reprinted in *The Listener* of August 29, 1974, p. 265.

[38] *Cf.*, however, Gidon Gottlieb's *The Logic of Choice*, pp. 84–85.

[39] *Jurisprudence*, p. 313. See Sir Rupert Cross' criticisms, *op. cit.* pp. 80–81.

[40] Goodhart, *op. cit.* p. 22.

[41] Cross, *op. cit.* p. 81.

[42] *Vide supra*, especially footnote 17.

[43] See Vaughan C.J. in *Bole* v. *Horton* (1673) Vaughan 360, 382.

[44] See R. E. Megarry in (1944) 60 L.Q.R. 222.

[45] See Cairns J. in *W. B. Anderson & Sons Ltd.* v. *Rhodes* [1967] 2 All E.R. 850.

[46] *Jurisprudence* (4th ed.), p. 192.

[47] For a more detailed discussion see Sir Rupert Cross, *Precedent in English Law* (2nd ed.), pp. 90 *et seq.*

[48] In *re Harper* v. *N.C.B.* [1974] Q.B. 614.

[49] *Beamish* v. *Beamish* (1861) 9 H.L.C. 274.

[50] (1880) 9 P.D. 96.

[51] [1928] 1 K.B. 176.

[52] [1954] P. 312.

[53] See A. W. B. Simpson, " The Ratio Decidendi of a case and the Doctrine of Binding Precedent " in *Oxford Essays in Jurisprudence* (1st series), ed. by A. G. Guest, p. 175.

[54] 9th ed., p. 76.

[55] Lord Simon in *Lupton* v. *F.A. & A.B. Ltd.* [1972] A.C. 634, 658–659 appears to support Professor Williams's view here.

[56] Cross, *op. cit.* p. 104.

[57] See Allen, *op. cit.* p. 219.

[58] *R.* v. *O'Connell* (1844) *Reports of State Trials* (N.S.) 2.

[59] *Beamish* v. *Beamish* (1859) 9 H.L.C. 274.

[60] [1898] A.C. 375.

[61] *Vide supra.*

[62] See [1966] 3 All E.R. 77.

[63] For an interesting general discussion of the factors involved see Lord Diplock in *Geelong Harbour Trust Comrs.* v. *Gibbs Bright & Co.* [1974] A.C. 810 (P.C.). See also Lord Reid, " The Judge as Lawmaker " in (1972) XII J.S.P.T.L. (N.S.) 22 at p. 25.

[64] [1968] A.C. 910.

[65] [1972] A.C. 944.

[66] [1973] A.C. 435.

[67] [1962] A.C. 220.

[68] See for instance H. L. A. Hart, *Law, Liberty and Morality,* pp. 6 *et seq.*

[69] [1972] A.C. 877.

[70] [1976] A.C. 443.

[71] [1972] A.C. 944, 1026.

[72] See M. D. A. Freeman, " Standards of Adjudication, Judicial Law Making and Prospective Overruling " in (1973) 26 C.L.P. 166. *Cf.* Wolfgang Friedmann, " Limits of Judicial Lawmaking and Prospective Overruling " (1966) 29 M.L.R. 593.

[73] [1976] A.C. 490G–491A. *Cf.* Lord Devlin, "The Judges and Lawmakers " (1976) 39 M.L.R. 1.

[74] [1944] K.B. 718. For a more detailed discussion see Cross, *op. cit.* p. 108.

[75] For a discussion of this phrase see Lord Denning M.R. in *Miliangos* v. *George Frank (Textiles) Ltd.* [1975] Q.B. 487, 503, and Lord Simon of Glaisdale in the House of Lords [1976] A.C. 477 *et seq.*

[76] [1968] 2 Q.B. 1.

[77] See *Boys* v. *Chaplin, supra; Gallie* v. *Lee* [1969] 2 Ch. 17, 37; *Hanning* v. *Maitland (No. 2)* [1970] 1 Q.B. 580, 587; *Barrington* v. *Lee* [1972] 1 Q.B. 326, 338; *Tiverton Estates Ltd.* v. *Wearwell Ltd.* [1975] Ch. 146; *Dyson Holdings Ltd.* v. *Fox* [1975] 3 W.L.R. 744, 748c and *Farrell* v. *Alexander* [1976] 1 Q.B. 345, 359G–H. In each of these cases read the statements of the other judges, especially Stephenson L.J. in *Barrington* v. *Lee* [1972] 1 Q.B. 326 at p. 345 and Scarman L.J. in the *Tiverton Estates* case [1975] Ch. 172–173 and *Farrell's* case [1976] 1 Q.B. 345, 371B–E. In *Miliangos* v. *George Frank (Textiles) Ltd.* [1975] 1 Q.B. 487, 503F, Lord Denning defers to the majority view.

[78] [1971] 2 All E.R. 187 (C.A.).

[79] *Cassell & Co.* v. *Broome* [1972] A.C. 1027. See generally Professor Julius Stone, " On the Liberation of Appellate Judges—How not to do it ! " in (1972) 35 M.L.R. 449.

[80] [1972] A.C. 1027, 1054E–F.

[81] See generally Julius Stone, *op. cit.*

[82] [1950] 2 K.B. 368.

[83] *R.* v. *Gould* [1968] 2 Q.B. 65. See G. Zellick, " Precedent in the Court of Appeal, Criminal Division " [1974] Crim.L.R. 222.

84 *Read* v. *Joannoa* (1890) 25 Q.B.D. 300 at pp. 302–303.

85 *Police Authority for Huddersfield* v. *Watson* [1947] K.B. 842. See generally Cross, *op. cit.* pp. 112 *et seq.*

86 See Lord Goddard C.J. in *Police Authority* v. *Watson* [1947] K.B. 842, 848.

87 See Cross, *op. cit.* p. 115.

88 Cross, *op. cit.* p. 105.

89 [1961] A.C. 388.

90 [1921] 3 K.B. 560.

91 See René David and John E. C. Brierley, *Major Legal Systems in the World Today*, pp. 103 *et seq.*; John H. Merryman, *The Civil Law Tradition*, Chap. VI; F. H. Lawson, *A Common Lawyer Looks at the Civil Law*, pp. 83 *et seq.*

92 David and Brierley, *op. cit.* p. 105.

93 *Op. cit.* p. 106.

94 *Candler* v. *Crane, Christmas & Co.* [1951] 2 K.B. 164, 178.

95 " The Ratio of the Ratio Decidendi " (1959) 22 M.L.R. 597, 618 (my italics). See the accounts, in the context of Stone's exposition of " the categories of illusory reference " in Stone, *The Province and Function of Law* (1946, repr. 1968, Wm. Hein), 186 *et seq.*, and Stone, *Legal System and Lawyers' Reasonings* (1964), 269 *et seq.*

Chapter 8

LEGISLATION

An Outline of the Legislative Process

UNTIL the nineteenth century Parliament was primarily a deliberative body and in practice legislation was not a very productive source of law. However, with the rapid changes in society created by the Industrial Revolution and with the growth of modern government, legislation has become the most productive source in fact, as well as the most important source in English legal theory. The crucial fact still remains, however, that Parliament has other tasks to perform apart from legislation. These political tasks limit the time it can spend on legislation and the effective control it can exert over its detailed provisions.

Although legislation is now the principal expression of public policy in legal form, the sources of that policy are the political parties, the departments of state with their permanent civil servants, and public opinion represented by the whole heterogeneous world of pressure groups and the views expressed and reported in the mass media.[1] The legislative process represents a constant interaction between these. Pressure groups are an essential part of the modern political scene. Added to these are the Law Commissions which on less controversial matters play an advisory role to Parliament and act as a major source of reform ideas. In the formulation of those ideas and in the consultative process pressure groups again exert influence. We will return to the broader problems involved in law reform in Chapter 14.

The actual mechanics involved in the enactment of the main legislation are as follows.[2] The civil servants who are responsible for formulating the principles behind a particular Act of Parliament brief the departmental lawyers who in turn draft instructions to the Parliamentary Counsel to the Treasury to prepare a draft Bill. The latter are a band of draftsmen recruited from the Bar and solicitors and trained in the mysteries of their art. They are nominally under the control of the Prime Minister but are very much a law unto themselves. They normally have to work to a pretty tight timetable and usually work in pairs. The senior of the two draftsmen takes full responsibility for the drafting of the Bill and any amendments and advises the ministers and parliamentary officials as to matters arising during the passage of the Bill through Parliament. The draft Bill is discussed in departmental committees but normally there is no outside scrutiny until the Bill is introduced into Parliament. In this latter respect there is a contrast with legislation resulting from recommendations of the Law Commission which often appends a draft Bill to its reports.

The main structure of a Bill is as follows:

> Long Title
> Preamble (if any)
> Enacting formula
> Short title
> Definitions (sometimes, perversely, this section appears in the middle or at the end)
> Principal provisions
> Administrative provisions
> Transitional provisions
> Repealing clauses
> The date of coming into effect
> Schedules.

(A copy of the Education Act 1975 (with annotations) is set out in Appendix 1. You may find it useful to refer to this now. Further details appear in Appendix 2.)

No special facilities are available to private members as regards the drafting of Bills although sometimes they are assisted by parliamentary counsel and sometimes the Government can be persuaded to adopt the private member's Bill as their own. Normally private members' Bills rank after Government Bills in the parliamentary timetable although a Standing Order allows for a limited amount of precedence. This is regulated amongst the members by ballot.

The procedure for a public (non-money) Bill is begun by a first reading in either the House of Commons or the House of Lords which consists of placing the title of the Bill before the House of Commons or House of Lords. After this the Bill is printed and a second reading follows in which the general principles of the Bill are discussed. The Bill is then normally sent to one of the Standing Committees for detailed discussion and amendment. Sometimes this takes place before a Committee of the whole House.

Next follows the Report stage before the House when further amendments can be made. The Bill then follows a similar routine in the other House and sometimes there is reference back on particular points between the Houses. The Bill is then read for a third time and given the Royal Assent.

There are differing procedures for the special types of legislation which we will mention later.

Problems of Language and Drafting [3]

Whereas case law emanates from the exigencies of a particular fact situation and the solution of a particular problem, legislation usually speaks in general terms and in the abstract. The problem then is to place the species within the genus and the facts of the particular case within a species. The classification used by a statute is a static not a shifting scheme. It does not change until it is expressly amended by subsequent legislation.

Ambiguity, Vagueness and Open Texture

The main problems here are the inherent ambiguity and vagueness of language. The three principal types of ambiguity are homonymy where the same word has two distinct meanings (e.g. conveyance which can mean a vehicle or a legal document), polysemy where a word has many senses attached to it (e.g. real) and amphiboly which arises out of uncertain grammatical construction, e.g. the definition of anthropology as " the science of man embracing woman." Some words are vague and as we have seen there is a distinct type of vagueness which is sometimes described as open texture. Words arguably have a core of certainty and a penumbra of uncertainty in their usage. The penumbral uncertainty or indeterminacy is open texture.[4] The use of words as ingredients in general classification schemes means that potentially the schemes have this characteristic of open texture. In fact the most common examples in law such as " fair," " just," " equitable " and " reasonable " involve value judgments. The law makes frequent use of these words to legitimise ad hoc but reasoned choice in a particular case. They constantly appear in standards. The tradition of using a particular word in the legal system regulates the discretion to some extent since there are many analogies to fall back on in the case law and previous statutes.

Semantic Levels

In an interesting dissenting judgment in *Maunsell* v. *Olins* [1975]
A.C. 373, 391E (with which Lord Diplock concurred) Lord Simon
of Glaisdale added the following points:

> "Statutory language, like all language, is capable of an almost
> infinite gradation of 'register'—*i.e.* it will be used at the
> semantic level appropriate to the subject matter and to the
> audience addressed (the man in the street, lawyers, merchants,
> etc.). It is the duty of a court of construction to tune in to
> such register and so to interpret the statutory language as to
> give to it the primary meaning which is appropriate in that
> register (unless it is clear that some other meaning must be
> given in order to carry out the statutory purpose or to avoid
> injustice, anomaly, absurdity or contradiction). In other words,
> statutory language must always be given presumptively the
> most natural and ordinary meaning which is appropriate in the
> circumstances."

Language and Social Control

These are general problems of language which confront the draftsman and the courts. The problem is exacerbated by the nature of
law itself. The role of language in lawmaking is not only communication of detail; it is also *delimitation of the scope of social
control*. This requires a degree of foresight of the patterns of social
behaviour and a forecast of future social behaviour, which is super-
human. In practice different legal systems employ different styles of
legislative drafting to attempt to cope with the problem. The French
often prefer to use general principles whereas in the past we have
tended to err on the side of excessive detail so that our statutes
sometimes emerge as labyrinths of definitions, amplifications and
cross-references. The result is often difficult for a lawyer to understand and almost completely unintelligible to a layman. Clearly
there are some areas of law such as tax and criminal law where
detail is required. It might, however, be argued that this style is
inappropriate to all areas of law.

Interpretation of Legislation by the Courts

The role of the judge in relation to legislation is that of interpreter.
Legislative categories can be interpreted and re-interpreted but, as

we have seen, unlike case law categories they cannot be reworked.[5] Under English law, unlike continental and American law, legislation cannot generally be used as the basis of argument by analogy.

Faced with the facts that statutes are the result of political debate and compromise which reflects itself in their intelligibility and that there are problems of language, the courts have developed a set of principles to be applied in the interpretation of legislation. I call them principles, some call them rules. The word principle is probably better as it emphasises their level of generality. They are more in the nature of canons or maxims than detailed rules.

Ascertaining the Legislature's Intention

In *Rugby Water Board* v. *Shaw-Fox* [1973] A.C. 202, 231-232 Lord Simon of Glaisdale described the position as follows:

" The task of the courts is to ascertain what was the intention of Parliament, actual or to be imputed, in relation to the facts as found by the court. There are a number of established canons of interpretation to assist the courts in ascertaining and applying the parliamentary intention. These canons have two aspects: first, as a code of communication whereby the draftsman signals the parliamentary intention to the courts; and secondly, as the quintessence of what experience has found to be the best guide to parliamentary intention. Different canons of interpretation will be more useful according as the first or second of these aspects is dominant. For example if it seems likely that the draftsman has envisaged the actual situation facing the court, it is the more likely that an intention as to the legal result has been formed and evinced; so that the aspect of the canons as a code of communication will be dominant, and such a rule as that the words of a statute dealing with ordinary affairs are used in their ordinary meaning and with normal grammatical sense will be particularly significant. If, on the other hand, it seems likely that the draftsman has not envisaged the actual situation facing the court, it may be necessary to impute an intention to Parliament, by trying to ascertain what in all the circumstances would have been the likely intention of Parliament in relation to the actual situation had it been envisaged; so that the aspect of the canons as the quintessence of what experience has found to be the best guide to parliamentary intention will be dominant, and such a rule as that Parliament is to be presumed to intend justice and avoid injustice or anomaly will be particularly significant."

The term "intention of the legislature" has its critics and it must be confessed that it suffers from a certain ambiguity.[8] Who is to be taken as the legislature for this purpose? Is it simply the majority of those present who voted for the whole of the Bill? Is it meaningful in any event to talk about their intention? Nevertheless, despite these ambiguities, as Lord Simon's speech indicates, it has found favour with the judges as a term of art. What they usually mean by it is the broad aims of the particular statute or the intended meaning or purpose of a particular provision. (A crucial ambiguity is whether the intention is to be ascertained at the date of the passing of the Act or whether it can be regarded as a continuing thing so that the words used can be understood in their current usage.) The orthodox view is the former but there are signs of a tendency towards the latter.[9]

General Approaches

There are three principles applied by the judges in construing an Act of Parliament, which indeed are of such a level of generality that they have sometimes been called "approaches to construction."[10] These are the so-called mischief, literal and golden rules. This is the order of their historical development. It is, however, better in order to analyse them to deal with the so-called literal rule first since ascertaining the ordinary meaning is obviously the beginning of any construction of words.

The literal rule

In the language of Bayley J.[11]: "It is very desirable in all cases to adhere to the words of an Act of Parliament, giving to them that sense which is their natural import in the order in which they are placed." Put in this way this approach corresponds to what the French call "L'interprétation grammaticale."[12] As can be seen, the literal rule seems to assume that there is generally a plain meaning and that it is the court's function to give effect to it even though the result is absurd or unjust.[13] The judges who adopt this approach emphasise that the remedy against such absurdity or injustice lies in the hands of the legislature. Clearly this is based on an oversimple understanding of the nature of language, the problems of draftsmanship [14] and the scope of the judicial function. It is because of these factors that the so-called golden rule developed.

The golden rule

This was clearly stated by Parke B. in *Becke* v. *Smith* [15] in 1836 when he said:

> " It is a very useful rule in the construction of a statute to adhere to the ordinary meaning of the words used, and to the grammatical construction, unless that is at variance with the intention of the legislature to be collected from the statute itself, or leads to any manifest absurdity or repugnance, in which case the language may be varied or modified so as to avoid such inconvenience, but no further."

Now there are a number of points which arise out of that statement. First, what is the relationship of this to the literal approach? The answer is that one applies the literal approach first and it is only if this results in a manifest or great absurdity that the courts will consider whether there is a secondary meaning possible which is to be preferred. Normally this is as far as the process goes. The courts for obvious reasons are reluctant to tamper with a legislative text. This can be seen from a classic statement of the so-called rule by Lord Blackburn in *River Wear Commissioners* v. *Adamson* [16] in 1877 when he said:

> " I believe that it is not disputed that what Lord Wensley-dale used to call the golden rule is right, *viz*. that we are to take the whole statute together, and construe it all together, giving the words their ordinary signification, unless when so applied they produce an inconsistency, or an absurdity or inconvenience so great as to convince the Court that the intention could not have been to use them in their ordinary significance, and to justify the Court in putting on them some other signification, which, though less proper, is one which the Court thinks the words will bear." [17]

The " golden rule " resembles the French " interprétation logique " in seeking to avoid absurdity but the French approach seems to take in a wider range of considerations including statutory analogies and general principles of law; in short reference is made to the whole " logic " of the French legal system.[18]

The mischief rule

The third approach is the so-called mischief rule laid down in *Heydon's Case* in 1584 by the Barons of the Exchequer. Coke reports their resolution as follows [19]:

> " And it was resolved by them, that for the sure and true interpretation of all statutes in general (be they penal or beneficial, restrictive or enlarging of the Common Law), four things are to be discerned and considered:
>
> 1st What was the Common Law before the making of the Act,
>
> 2nd What was the mischief and defect for which the Common Law did not provide,
>
> 3rd What remedy the Parliament hath resolved and appointed to cure the disease of the commonwealth,
>
> And, 4th The true reason of the remedy; and then the office of all the Judges is always to make such construction as shall suppress the mischief, and advance the remedy, and to suppress subtle inventions and evasions for continuance of the mischief, and pro privato commodo, and to add force and life to the cure and remedy, according to the true intent of the makers of the Act, pro bono publico."

This approach bears a close relationship to the equity of a statute idea which prevailed on the continent at the time and which owed its theoretical origins to Aristotle's discussion of equity in his *Ethics.*[20]

Coke in his Institutes states the latter idea as follows [21]:

> " Equity is a construction made by the judges, that cases out of the letter of a statute, yet being within the same mischief, or cause of the making of the same, shall be within the same remedy that the statute provideth; and the reason hereof is, for that the law-makers could not possibly set down all cases in express terms."

This is, however, to state the principles too narrowly since the full scope of the doctrine was also to exclude cases which were within the letter but outside the spirit of the statute.[22]

As can be seen the equity of the statute approach so stated goes beyond the four propositions laid down in *Heydon's Case*. The equity of the statute approach was somewhat discredited by the nineteenth century in England and although there have been some attempts to revive it in the common law world in recent years they have not been successful in England.[23] Meanwhile, however, the so-called mischief rule has continued as good law. Clearly there is an overlap between it and the golden rule and in its terms it seems inconsistent with the literal rule.

In his dissenting judgment in *Maunsell* v. *Olins* [1975] A.C. 373, 395A–c Lord Simon of Glaisdale explained the mischief rule in these terms:

" The rule in *Heydon's Case*, 3 Co.Rep. 7a itself is sometimes stated as a primary canon of construction, sometimes as secondary (*i.e.* available in the case of an ambiguity): *cf. Maxwell*, pp. 40, 96, with *Craies on Statute Law*, 7th ed. (1971), pp. 94, 96. We think that the explanation of this is that the rule is available at two stages. The first task of a court of construction is to put itself in the shoes of the draftsman—to consider what knowledge he had and, importantly, what statutory objective he had—if only as a guide to the linguistic register. Here is the first consideration of the mischief. Being thus placed in the shoes of the draftsman, the court proceeds to ascertain the meaning of the statutory language. In this task the first and most elementary rule of construction is to consider the plain and primary meaning, in their appropriate register, of the words used. If there is no such plain meaning (*i.e.* if there is an ambiguity), a number of secondary canons are available to resolve it. Of these one of the most important is the rule in *Heydon's Case*. Here, then, may be a second consideration of the mischief."

The mischief rule bears some resemblance to two different French approaches to interpretation, " l'interprétation historique " and " l'interpretation téléologique." [24] The first of these seeks primarily to ascertain the intention of the draftsmen by research into the legislative history of the statute. It is frequently used, except in criminal and tax law where it cannot be employed to produce an effect unfavourable to the accused or the taxpayer. The second approach, which is sometimes called " extensive " or " progressive " interpretation, shares the purposive approach of the mischief rule but is perhaps closer to the original equity of the statute idea in that it allows legislation to be applied to cases outside the strict letter of the original legislation but within its " but social " or contemporary social purpose. In this latter respect the teleological approach is the converse of the historical approach. In general the lower French courts seem to show a preference for the historical approach. The teleological approach is not adopted if its use would produce conclusions contrary to the grammatical or logical approaches. It is in fact mainly used in the higher courts which are more aware of their role as arbiters of conflicting interests.

The Law Commissions' Proposals

The Law Commissions in their Joint Report in 1969 recognised that the present state of affairs was unsatisfactory and recommended legislation to clarify the situation. Of the three rules they favoured the mischief rule but recognised that it suffered from certain defects.[25] Quite apart from the general archaism of its language the Report points out the rule reflected a different constitutional balance between the Executive, Parliament and the public than would now be acceptable. It is not clear on the face of the rule how much the judge should concentrate on the actual language used. The rule assumes that legislation is subordinate to the common law; and lastly it grew up before the so-called " extrinsic evidence exclusion rule."

The latter rule provides that the courts must focus on the actual language used in the statute and not venture outside to look at *Hansard* or reports of committees. Although this rule has never been applied to prevent the courts resorting to extrinsic materials when searching for the *mischief*, it has been rigorously applied generally.[26] In this latter respect the United Kingdom differs from continental countries and indeed certain common law jurisdictions which allow freer citation of " travaux préparatoires."

The Law Commissions recommended an updated version of the mischief rule, mandating the courts to adopt " a construction which would promote the general legislative purpose underlying the provision." [27] They did not favour allowing resort to *Hansard* but did favour considerable relaxation of the extrinsic evidence rule in respect of documents such as White Papers and Reports and the use on an experimental basis of explanatory memoranda written in layman's language which would pass through Parliament with the relevant Act. There was professional hostility to this and so far these recommendations have not been enacted.[28] To a certain extent the position has been modified by section 3 of the European Communities Act 1972 in relation to EEC matters as we shall see in a later chapter. Also there are indications in speeches in recent cases in the House of Lords that some at least of the Law Lords are prepared to adopt the purposive approach even in the absence of express legislation.[29] This seems eminently desirable but highlights the unsatisfactory status of the other so-called rules and their relationship with each other.

Specific Principles and Presumptions

There are in fact a whole host of specific principles and presumptions which you can find in such books as Maxwell on the Interpretation of Statutes, Craies' Statute Law and Odgers' Construction of Deeds and Statutes.

There is a set of principles which govern the extent to which you can resort to other parts of an Act when construing a specific provision.[30] Although basically you are entitled to read the Act as a whole you should only modify the primary meaning of a particular provision by reference to other parts of the Act if the primary meaning is ambiguous. There is some inconsistency between these principles and most words are open textured and capable at times of being construed as ambiguous.

There is also a set of principles which are based on grammar, syntax and logic.[31] Examples of these are the *expressio unius exclusio alterius* and *ejusdem generis* principles. The *expressio unius* principle means that the expression of one thing results in the exclusion of another. An old example of this will suffice. The Poor Relief Act 1601 imposed rates on occupiers of " lands, houses . . . and coalmines." It was held that this excluded mines other than coalmines. The word " land " might in its ordinary meaning have been wide enough to cover all mines but the specific reference to coalmines meant that land was not intended to cover mines in this case.[32] A useful example of the *ejusdem generis* principle is *Brownsea Haven Properties Ltd*. v. *Poole Corporation* [33] in 1958. The principle is based on the logician's approach to classification and definition by *genus et differentia*. As we have seen logicians divide the world into broad classes—genera—and into members of the classes, called species. The principle then provides that where there is a list of particular species which can be grouped into one genus and these are followed by general words the scope of those general words is to be cut down to make them fit into the genus. In the *Brownsea* case the Court of Appeal considered a statutory provision which authorised a local authority to make orders concerning road traffic " in all times of public processions, rejoicings, or illuminations, and in any case when the streets are thronged or liable to be obstructed. . . ." The local authority had made an order that certain streets should carry only one-way traffic for a period of six months. The court held that this order was invalid since " in any case " had to be read *ejusdem generis* with the earlier words and could not, therefore, cover dislocations due to ordinary traffic.

Now whereas principles such as these are not as binding as ordinary legal rules in that they yield in each case to the particular words used, there is a further set of presumptions of even weaker force.[34] These are pointers rather than rules or principles. Examples of these are the presumptions that Parliament did not intend to deprive a person of a vested right without compensation or to oust the jurisdiction of the courts.

Last, the Interpretation Act 1889 prescribes definitions of certain words and phrases which are commonly used in legislation. These general definitions are, however, displaced by a contrary intention, express or implied, in the particular Act.

Particular Species of Legislation

So far we have talked in fairly general terms and the outline of procedure at the beginning of this chapter was that applicable to the most important kind of Act, the public general Act.

A distinction is drawn between *public general Acts, local Acts* and *private Acts*.[35] In fact local Acts are a species of public Act which is limited in its scope to a particular locality. The important distinction is between public and private Acts. Private Acts, which are not to be confused with private members' Bills which lead to public Acts, confer a *privilegium*, that is an exception from the general law or a provision for something which cannot be obtained by means of the general law. They are also governed by different procedures, being drafted by parliamentary agents (specialist outside practitioners) and originating by petition. They are formally advertised and the procedure in Committee is quasi-judicial with the petitioners and their opponents being heard and evidence being given.

Sometimes a new statute is passed which re-enacts the contents of many earlier statutes with only such modifications as are necessary to produce a coherent whole.[36] This is called *a consolidating Act*. The Law Commission is actively engaged in work on consolidation which is a time-consuming but necessary process.

Where an Act attempts to sum up the existing legislation and common law and equity on a particular topic it is called *a code*. Codification is an important but controversial topic which will be dealt with in the next chapter.

Lastly we have *delegated legislation*. This is legislation by subordinate law-making bodies which has been sanctioned by Parliament. The relevant bodies must act within their powers which the courts scrutinise carefully. If the courts find that the powers have been exceeded the delegated legislation is invalid. Delegated legislation consists mainly of statutory instruments made by government departments. Statutory instruments are usually required to be laid before Parliament for a prescribed period and in the absence of a negative ruling they become law. Sometimes the converse applies in that they do not take effect unless approved. In the preparation of delegated legislation there is usually consultation with outside bodies such as the relevant interest groups.

Modernisation and Reform

Parliamentary procedures, the style of drafting and the methods of promulgation of legislation have all crystallised in a more leisurely age before Parliament sought to control so many aspects of life through the medium of legislation. All three have been the subject of mounting criticisms in recent years. In the United Kingdom and elsewhere lawyers are becoming more aware of the advantages which might ensue from the use of computers and computer techniques. Let us look briefly at the developing use of computers and then consider recent general proposals for reform of legislation.

Computers [37]

Recently the Government decided to produce the new edition of *Statutes in Force* using computer typesetting so that a statute is printed in a way in which it can be read by a computer. This has a number of advantages, principal among which is the possibility of improving the production of accurate versions of the statutes or parts of them.

Computers are also useful for storing legal information in a way which enables it to be quickly retrieved. They provide a useful tool for analysis of and search for legal materials. Clearly such use involves immense problems of programming legal data which are particularly difficult if one includes case law as well. There is also the problem of expense. These problems inhibit the widespread use of computers at present.

Reform of Legislation—the Renton Report

The Renton Committee on the Preparation of Legislation was set up under the Conservative Government on May 7, 1973, and reported in 1975. Its membership included parliamentarians, representatives of the Law Commissions, civil servants, legal practitioners and businessmen. Its terms of reference were to review the drafting of public Bills with a view to achieving greater simplicity and clarity. These terms of reference were, in fact, very similar to those of the last Committee which reported on the subject in 1875.[38] The present Report [39] is a useful statement and critique of the present system and proffers many more practical recommendations than did its predecessor which has been described as " a hurried and perfunctory performance." [40]

Criticisms of the present system

Draftsmen of British legislation have always been the butt of both professional and lay criticism except perhaps in the halcyon days when a judge such as Hengham C.J. could say to counsel " Ne glosez point le Statut; nous le savons menz de vous, qar nous les feimes." [41] The principal criticisms [42] have tended to be that the language used is obscure and circumlocutious; the structure illogical and over-elaborate; the methods of amendment confusing and the treatment of Scots law a mess. These criticisms are easily made and all of them can be supported by some examples. Nevertheless, parliamentary counsel labour under considerable difficulties—they are short-staffed and over-worked; Parliament legislates in a promiscuous manner; increasingly, legislative controls are used to supplement or replace self-regulation; areas such as tax and town planning have become notoriously complex; and lastly, a statute is in any event a single document operating at different levels catering for different needs. Thus a Bill and later an Act is catering for the legislators, the legal profession, and administrators as well as the general public. Their needs can and often do conflict. What therefore, would *Renton* do about it?

Reform proposals

First and foremost, the Report stresses the need for the recruitment and training of more parliamentary counsel. The manpower problem is constantly referred to in the Report.

With reference to drafting technique, the Committee emphasises the need for consideration of the ultimate " consumer." The Report sets out a host of sensible suggestions for improving drafting technique ranging from the inclusion in statutes of statements of general principle and purpose to the use of simple mathematical formulae where appropriate, *i.e.* in tax legislation. It favours textual amendment, whereby the amended wording can be reproduced, wherever possible, and sparing use of legislation by reference to other legislation.

The Report stresses the need for greater consideration to be given to legislation for Scotland. Separate provisions and indeed separate Acts may be desirable. Devolution might solve some of the present problems.

Progressive consolidation is regarded as obviously necessary although the Statute Law Society's suggestion of a " crash programme " is dismissed as impractical. Responsibility for consolidation should remain with the Law Commission which should have its depleted staff of draftsmen restored to its former strength. The Report is silent on the vexed question of codification.

The Committee favoured the increased use of computers as drafting and printing aids. The information retrieval system should be based on *Statutes in Force*, which should be continually updated, and the system should preferably include an historical file.

The Report recommends that the Statute Law Committee which has hitherto operated in secrecy should continue the work of the Renton Committee and publish periodic reports.

In some ways, the most disappointing part of the Renton Report is its consideration of the Law Commissions' Report on *Interpretation of Statutes*.[43] It accepted that the methods of interpretation influences the style of drafting and was of the view that ultimately the question boiled down to the degree of confidence which Parliament has in the courts. In order to assist the courts Renton thought that there should be a new and comprehensive Interpretation Act which should set out the guiding principles that constructions are to be preferred which (a) promoted the general legislative purpose; (b) were consistent with international obligations; and (c) excluded retrospective effect. Proposals (a) and (b) were the proposals of the Law Commissions. The Report accepted the Law Commissions' proposals that in construing an Act all parts of the Act and all relevant international agreements and treaties should be considered. To these it added (rather unnecessarily) EEC instruments and then adopted the vague formula drafted by the Law Commissions that the weight accorded to each of these factors should be no more than is appropriate in the circumstances—a positive discretion wrapped up in negative wording. Unlike the Law Commissions, the Renton Committee would exclude reference to White Papers and similar documents and reports of Royal Commissions and similar bodies. The latter is a retrograde step in the light of the existing law [44] which allows them to be considered to ascertain the mischief for the purposes of the application of the mischief rule and it is hoped that it will not be adopted. Royal Commission and Law Commission reports are easily accessible, fully reasoned, non-partisan documents and should continue to be admissible. Needless to say, the use of specially prepared explanatory memoranda was not in general favoured.

Conclusion

Clearly, much of the Renton Report is exhortative and its implimentation will depend on the goodwill of Government draftsmen. As James Fitzjames Stephen said in his evidence to the Select Committee in 1875, " ... drawing an Act of any importance is very much like writing a book : you must conceive the subject in your own mind and draw it accordingly. I do not think any rule will help you to do it." [45] However, the exhortations of the Renton Report will no doubt play the same role as the pamphlet [46] prepared in the nineteenth century by Sir Henry Thring who was appointed to take charge of the newly constituted office of Parliamentary Counsel to the Treasury in 1869. Thring's evidence to the 1875 Committee is worth recalling since in some ways it is more adventurous than the Renton Report. He said:

" ... I have a very strong opinion indeed that you ought to use the best popular language, and never use technical language at all unless it be absolutely necessary. My reason is that technical legal language is, in my judgment, the most imprecise of all technical language; and therefore by using it you do not get precision, and you do get words which are not familiar to ordinary persons; and my opinion is that, so far as is possible, an Act of Parliament ought to be understood by ordinary persons." [47]

His successors have often lost sight of this goal. At the very least, as Renton now recognises, there should be varied styles for different areas of law with emphasis on the ultimate " consumers." It is, however, difficult to think of this as progress. Membership of the EEC will probably have some effect on the form of our legislation in the long term. We shall consider this in Chapter 11.

Notes

[1] See generally my *Law Reform and the Law Commission*, Chaps. 4, 5 and 6.

[2] This is based on the Statute Law Society pamphlet, *Statute Law Deficiencies*, Part II.

[3] See further my *Law Reform and the Law Commission*, Chap. 5. On the different approaches of case law and statute see Windeyer J. in *Damjanovic & Sons Pty. Ltd.* v. *The Commonwealth* (1968) 42 A.L.J.R. 102, 109.

[4] See H. L. A. Hart, *The Concept of Law*, p. 125.

[5] See Edward Levi, *An Introduction to Legal Reasoning*, p. 30.

[6] See Dennis Lloyd, " Law and Public Policy " (1955) 8 C.L.P. 42 at p. 57.

[7] See Lord Reid in *Maunsell* v. *Olins* [1975] A.C. 373, 382E where he said " They are not rules in the ordinary sense of having binding force. They are our servants not our masters. They are aids to construction, presumptions or pointers. Not infrequently one ' rule ' points in one direction, another in a different direction. In each case we must look at all relevant circumstances and decide as a matter of judgment what weight to attach to any particular ' rule '."

[8] See the various dicta set out in Craies' *Statute Law* (7th ed.) by S. Edgar, pp. 64 *et seq.* and see also G. C. MacCallum, Jr., " Legislative Intent " in *Essays in Legal Philosophy*, ed. by R. S. Summers, 237.

[9] See *H. E. Green & Sons* v. *Minister of Health* (*No. 2*) [1948] 1 K.B. 575, and *Dyson Holdings Ltd.* v. *Fox* [1976] Q.B. 503, and *cf.* *Brutus* v. *Cozens* [1973] A.C. 854.

[10] See the Law Commissions' Report, *The Interpretation of Statutes* (Law Com. No. 21), p. 14.

[11] *R.* v. *Inhabitants of Ramsgate* (1827) 6 B. & C. 712.

[12] See R. David and H. P. De Vries, *The French Legal System*, p. 87.

[13] See *e.g.* Lord Esher M.R. in *R.* v. *The Judge of the City of London Court* [1892] 1 Q.B. 273 at p. 290.

[14] Law Com. No. 21, p. 17.

[15] (1836) 2 M. & W. at p. 195.

[16] (1877) 2 App.Cas. 743, 764–765.

[17] See further the Law Commissions' Report, *op. cit.* pp. 15–17.

[18] See further David and De Vries, *op. cit.* pp. 88–91.

[19] (1584) 3 Co.Rep. 7a.

[20] See Allen, *Law in the Making* (7th ed.), pp. 451 *et seq.* See also *supra*, Chap. 6.

[21] 1 Inst. 24 (b).

[22] See Plowden's note on *Eyston* v. *Studd* (1574) Plow. 459, 465.

[23] See my *Law Reform and the Law Commission*, p. 64, n. 37, for the materials.

[24] See David and De Vries, *op. cit.* pp. 91 *et seq.*

[25] See Law Com. No. 21, pp. 19 *et seq.*

[26] *Ibid.* pp. 27 *et seq.* See further n. 44, *infra*.

[27] *Ibid.* pp. 48 *et seq.*

[28] See further my *Law Reform and the Law Commission*, pp. 52 *et seq.* and the Renton Report discussed at the end of this chapter.

[29] See *e.g. Jones* v. *Secretary of State for Social Services* [1972] A.C. 944, 1005E–F, especially Lord Diplock's speech.

[30] The Law Commissions' Report contains a useful summary in Chap. V.

[31] See generally Odgers, *Construction of Deeds and Statutes* (5th ed. by G. Dworkin), Chap. 13.

[32] *Lead Smelting Co.* v. *Richardson* (1762) 3 Burr. 1341.

[33] [1958] Ch. 574.

[34] See the Law Commissions' Report, pp. 21 *et seq.*

[35] Sir Courtenay Ilbert, *Legislative Methods and Forms*, p. 26.

[36] See generally Lord Simon of Glaisdale in *Maunsell* v. *Olins* [1975] A.C. 373, 392c–F.

[37] See further Colin Tapper, *Computers and the Law*, Chap. 4.

[38] Report of the Select Committee on Acts of Parliament 1875 (280) (viii 213). For a survey of its work, see Sir C. Ilbert, *Legislative Methods and Forms*, pp. 67 *et seq.*

[39] Cmnd. 6053. See the notes by H. H. Marshall, Q.C. (1975) 24 I.C.L.Q. 572 and J. H. Farrar (1975) 38 M.L.R. 553.

[40] Sir William Graham-Harrison, "An Examination of the Main Criticisms of the Statute Book and the Possibility of Improvement" (1935) J.S.P.T.L. 9, 11.

[41] "Do not gloss the statute; we know it better than you because we make them." Y.B. 33 & 35 Edward I (Rolls Series) 83 (1305).

[42] See these usefully summarised in Chap. VI of the Renton Report. See also the Memorandum of the S.P.T.L. in (1974) 13 J.S.P.T.L.(N.S.) 96 and *Statute Law: A Radical Simplification*—a report by the Statute Law Society.

[43] Law Com. No. 21, discussed *supra*. See also H. Bloom's note in (1970) 33 M.L.R. 197; J. H. Farrar, *Law Reform and the Law Commission*, pp. 47 *et seq*.

[44] See the authorities cited in the Law Commissions' Report, p. 28. See also *Wachtel* v. *Wachtel* [1973] Fam. 72 (C.A.) and *Black-Clawson International Limited* v. *Papierwerke Waldhof-Aschaffenburg A.G.* [1975] A.C. 591. Such reports have been admitted to ascertain the mischief for the purposes of the mischief rule. The law as restated in the *Black-Clawson* case is still not very clear. All the Law Lords seem to support admissibility for the purposes of ascertaining the mischief. The majority appear to reject any more general use. It is submitted that the distinction is an artificial one which is inconsistent with the practice of the European court.

[45] *Minutes of Evidence*, p. 29, para. 357.

[46] Eventually published in 1877 under the title *Practical Legislation: or the Composition and Language of Acts of Parliament*.

[47] *Minutes of Evidence*, p. 121, para. 1633; *cf*. the Renton Report, para. 7.5.

CHAPTER 9

CODES AND CODIFICATION

Bentham and the History of Codification in England and Wales

WE have seen in the last chapter that in English law a code is a species of statute which attempts to sum up the existing legislation and common law and equity on a particular topic. In England we owe our main theories on codification to the legal philosopher, Jeremy Bentham, who wrote during the late eighteenth and early nineteenth centuries. Indeed we appear to owe to him the word " codification." [1]

According to Bentham in his *General View of a Complete Code of Laws*, the object of a code is to ensure that everyone may consult the law affecting him in the least possible time.[2] Whatever is not in the code ought not to have the force of law. The style should reflect force, harmony and nobleness.

> ' With this view, the legislator might sprinkle here and there moral sentences, provided they are very short, and in accordance with the subject, and he [the legislator] would do no ill if he were to allow marks of his paternal tenderness to flow down upon his paper, as proof of the benevolence which guides his pen." [3]

The code should speak a language familiar to everyone; it should be simple and clear.[5] The code having been prepared all unwritten law should be forbidden. Judges should merely interpret the code and if they see an error or omission they should notify the legislature and suggest a correction which should be adopted by legislation.[6] Once in a hundred years the code should be revised to remove obsolete terms.

Bentham's views, typical of his age, overrated the power of Government and underrated the difficulties involved.[7] His attitude to the past was that it was from the folly not the wisdom of our ancestors that we have so much to learn.[8] His plans aimed at finality and paid insufficient attention to legal development and social change.

He was not, however, the first English writer to favour a code. Bacon in the early seventeenth century had favoured drastic consolidation; James I toyed with codification and in the interregnum some lawyers favoured root and branch reform including codification. Indeed to the Parliament of Saints the Ten Commandments would suffice. Nothing came of these great plans.[9]

Bentham, however, for all his extremism or perhaps because of it, was more influential. The second part of the nineteenth century was a prolific period of law reform. The major reforms were, however, in procedure and the court structure not so much in the form of law.

In India there were successful experiments with codification but little came of the codification movement in England. Sir James Fitzjames Stephen who had drafted some of the Indian codes prepared drafts which were never enacted in this country. Eventually, however, Judge Chalmers' Bills of Exchange Bill and Sale of Goods Bill were enacted and put on the Statute Book in 1882 and 1893 respectively. Also Sir Frederick Pollock's Partnership Bill was eventually enacted in 1890 after 10 years of machinations in Parliament. These can be regarded as codes. So too in a loose sense can the property legislation of the 1920s but this was primarily consolidation and reform rather than restatement. More recently we have had the Theft Act 1968 which again was primarily reform.[9]

The Law Commissions have codification as a major item on their agenda being charged with the duty of (at least) considering it under the Law Commissions Act 1965.

Choosing an Appropriate Model

One of the most difficult questions facing English lawyers tackling codification is what form the code should take.[10] The two basic paradigms are the French and German civil codes respectively. The former is more in the form of a statement of general principles leaving the courts with a necessarily creative role in fact if not in theory. The German code, however, is more on the lines of Bentham's ideas and is more detailed. In fact the aim was to provide a complete answer to any legal problem within the conceptual framework of the code.

The codes drafted for India incorporated hypothetical factual examples so that the code is at once a statute and a collection of decided cases, the latter with the advantage that they were decided by the legislature.

Another idea, put forward in 1865, was that a code should be more elaborate and consist of the rules, examples of the application of the rules and then the reasons for the rules.

It would seem that there is and should be no single paradigm of a code and that differing forms and styles might be required by different legal traditions and even by different areas of law. In some areas of law such as crime there is a need for certainty; in others such as commercial law there is a need for flexibility.

Interpretation and the Role of the Judge

The courts start with a presumption in the case of a *consolidating* Act that no significant changes were intended. Indeed the Consolidation of Enactments (Procedure) Act 1949 lays down a special simplified procedure for such Acts provided that they do not effect changes in the existing law which in the opinion of a Joint Committee of both Houses, the Lord Chancellor and the Speaker ought to be the subject of a separate Act.[11]

The presumption and the procedure do not apply to a codifying Act.[12] The basic principle here was laid down by the House of Lords in *Bank of England* v. *Vagliano*[13] in 1891. In the words of Lord Herschell the principle is:

"... in the first instance to examine the language of the statute and to ask what is its natural meaning un-influenced by any considerations derived from the previous state of the law and not to start with enquiring how the law previously stood and then, assuming that it was probably intended to leave it unaltered, to see if the words of the enactment will bear an interpretation in conformity with this view.... I am of course far from asserting that resort may never be had to the previous state of the law for the purpose of aiding in the construction of the provisions of the code. If for example such a provision be of doubtful import, such resort will be perfectly legitimate."

Thus one can still look at the previous law in cases of ambiguity or where words have acquired a technical meaning.[14]

Clearly this is not what Bentham intended. Such is the conservative approach of English lawyers, it is thought, that even if the code expressly forbade resort to such materials lawyers would still in practice resort to them for guidance.

Sir Leslie Scarman, the first Chairman of the English Law Commission, has emphasised that if more and more of English law is codified the role of the judges will change. "They will lose their priestly character as oracles drawing from within upon the experience of themselves and their predecessors in office to declare the law; they will stand forth as the authoritative interpreters of the code." [15] Clearly much will depend on the form that future codification takes and the change in role need not necessarily result in a change in status.

The Pros and Cons of Codification

We saw earlier how codification is a matter of controversy. Let us now examine the controversy.[16]

The main argument traditionally used, and frequently used by the Law Commissions, is the great bulk or unwieldiness of the present law. It is argued that a code would produce in its place systematic, compact and accessible law. The law would be more accessible to the public, even if not necessarily completely intelligible to them. Case law produces gaps, uncertainties and irrational distinctions which a code would remove. Also it has been argued that the common law has not in recent times been able to adapt itself quickly enough to changing conditions. This has been particularly true in the field of contract. There is some substance in all these arguments.

Against these are a number of arguments which were put forward in the nineteenth century and have been reiterated recently. First it is said that a code is necessarily incomplete and cannot provide for all future cases. The easiest way of meeting this criticism is to recognise its partial truth and compare this with the gaps under the existing law. Then it is argued that a code is difficult to alter. In this country there is no reason why this should be so. Parliament will not abdicate its legislative functions once a code has been enacted, the judges will continue to interpret it and the Law Commissions will presumably continue in business.

Next, it is said that the common law is more malleable. Although there is some force in this criticism it is tempered to a certain extent by the doctrine of precedent. Again, it is said that a code is more likely to engender competition of conflicting rules and principles than the common law. This obviously depends on the quality of draftsmanship and might arise if the drafting of codes for different areas of law was in different hands and was not adequately supervised.

Another argument is that the legal textbooks perform the function of a code but these are clearly not authoritative unless and until they are archaic.

It is also argued that a code in order to approach completeness must consist of rules so minute and numerous that no man can learn or retain them, and that in any event, it is impossible to provide completely for particular future cases. The answer to this is that one has a choice as regards the subject-matter of a code and, as regards its form, it should not aim at a comprehensive specification of cases but at providing a series of rules applicable to cases.

More fundamental criticisms are those made by Savigny who attacked the codification movement in Germany in the nineteenth century and argued that a code will not adjust to the customs and experience of the community, the *Volksgeist*, and will destroy continuity in legal development. Apart from the inherent vagueness of the concept of the *Volksgeist*, there is no reason why a code which restates the English law developed over centuries and which is kept up to date by a body such as the Law Commission should not meet the changing needs of society.

Last, we have the brunt of Professor Hahlo's powerful criticism in an article in the *Modern Law Review* in 1967, dramatically entitled, "Here Lies the Common Law: Rest in Peace." [17] It did not seem unlikely to him (to employ his double negative) that as a result of codification the influence of English law outside the United Kingdom would decrease. It will suffer a loss of status from being the senior member of the Anglo-American common law family to becoming one of a large number of codified systems. He asked rhetorically "will America succeed England as the chief custodian of the common law?" Professor Gower, by way of rejoinder,[18] argued that America had nearly overtaken England in legal development already because of its use of Restatements of the law and the Model and Uniform codes. We could be more helpful to other members of the Anglo-American family by our work in law reform and codification than by leaving our law in its present form.

To sum up the debate the truth would appear to be that the arguments for and against codification are of such a high level of generality that they cannot be established or refuted scientifically. At the end of the day the choice seems to be one of policy both as to whether and what to codify and the form the code should take.

Although the Law Commission is obliged to consider codification by the terms of the Act which set it up it seems recently to have been having second thoughts, certainly as far as its projected code of the law of contract is concerned. It appears to be proceeding with its work on the criminal and landlord and tenant codes and on reform and consolidation of family law with a view to a family code. These are clearly desirable. Since Parliament remains the ultimate watershed it has to be convinced that the end-product is necessary. There are at present no special procedures for codification measures and therefore parliamentary control is an effective fetter on reforming zeal.

Notes

1 Murray's *Dictionary*.
2 See the Bowring edition of Bentham's *Works*, Vol. 3, p. 193.
3 *Ibid*. p. 205.
4 *Ibid*. p. 208.
5 *Ibid*. p. 209.
6 *Ibid*. p. 210.
7 See Sir C. Ilbert, *Legislative Methods and Forms*, p. 123.
8 *The Book of Fallacies* (Bowring ed.), Vol. 2, p. 401.
9 See my *Law Reform and the Law Commission*, Chap. 1.
10 *Ibid*. pp. 57 *et seq*. and pp. 97 *et seq*.
11 See Erskine May, *Parliamentary Practice* (19th ed. by Sir David Lidderdale), pp. 524–525. Greater latitude is allowed to Bills to consolidate with amendments to give effect to recommendations of the Law Commissions, *op. cit*. p. 525. See also Lord Simon of Glaisdale in *Maunsell* v. *Olins* [1975] A.C. 392c–e.
12 See Odgers, *Construction of Deeds and Statutes* (5th ed.) by G. Dworkin, p. 335.
13 [1891] A.C. 107, 144.
14 Odgers, p. 335.
15 *Codification and Judge Made Law*, p. 11.
16 The following summary of the arguments is taken from *Law Reform and the Law Commission*. See also Bruce Donald, " Codification in Common Law Systems " (1973) 47 A.L.J. 160.
17 (1967) 30 M.L.R. 241. See also Professor Aubrey Diamond's " Codification of the Law of Contract " in (1968) 31 M.L.R. 361.
18 (1967) 30 M.L.R. 262.

Chapter 10

DOCTRINE

General Comparisons of Approach

We have seen that the common law is largely the product of the judiciary. On the continent, until the codifications of the nineteenth century, learned writings (which are usually referred to as *doctrine*) were a fundamental source of law. In England learned writers have traditionally played a subordinate role and their writings have never enjoyed the status afforded to continental doctrinal writings before the codifications. The position on the continent since codification seems to be that doctrine still enjoys high prestige but is now really an important *secondary* source in areas governed by the codes and other legislation.[1] This latter role should not be underestimated since, as David and Brierley[2] point out, doctrine creates the legal vocabulary and ideas used by legislators, and influences the methods of statutory interpretation.

Scots law seems to invest certain learned writings with very high authority and it is possibly true to say that these enjoy something of the status of the pre-codification continental doctrine.[3] Not all the writings of such a writer are necessarily regarded as having this institutional status and the position of writings by subsequent authors varies according to the author's reputation. Scots lawyers are loath to invest them with institutional status.

The Position of Doctrine in English Law

The position of learned writings in English law has in fact varied at different periods of legal history.[4] Certain classical authors are recognised as authorities and there has gradually been a relaxation of the strange, necromantic rule allowing only the citation of dead authors.

In this chapter we shall look at four great writers who wrote at critical stages in the development of English law—Bracton, Coke, Blackstone and Pollock—assess their authority at the present day and then we shall attempt to describe the modern practice.

Bracton wrote at an early stage in English legal history when the common law was only just beginning to acquire autonomy as a system and there were distinct traces of a Roman law influence in his work. Coke marks the end of the early period and an attempt to preserve the learning of the past in the service of the future. Blackstone represents an accurate and elegant restatement of the common law as it had developed by the mid eighteenth century, prior to the movement for reform. Pollock manifests the preservation of the old learning blended with a wide general culture and an interest in the rational development of the law, while at the same time avoiding the excesses of Bentham. Let us now look at each of them in turn.

Bracton [5]

Bracton was an ecclesiastic who served as a judge in the thirteenth century. He is an important figure in the early common law. His principal treatise was an exposition of the laws and customs of England unrivalled either in literary style or completeness until Blackstone's *Commentaries* in the eighteenth century. His work was influenced to some extent by Roman law but the precise extent is a matter of conjecture. The book shows that even at this early date English law had become based on the forms of actions (*i.e.* specific formulae into which a cause of action must be fitted) and decided cases. Indeed Bracton states expressly " If like matters arise let them be decided by like, since the occasion is a good one for proceeding a similibus ad similia." [6] At this time there were no published reports so he had to rely on his knowledge of the plea rolls—the formal record. After his death Bracton's reputation fluctuated. With the growth of a legal profession centred around the Inns of Court, learned only in its own system, the common law eschewed general principle and became in Pollock and Maitland's words " an evasive commentary upon writs and statutes." [7] In the sixteenth century Bracton was known to and cited by Coke to liberalise the common law. Sir Matthew Hale in his *History of the Common Law* put the authority of Bracton's treatise on a level with that of the records of the courts [8] and Blackstone also recognised it as authoritative.[9]

Coke [10]

Sir Edward Coke was first a law officer of the crown, then a judge, then later a politician. During his lifetime he was an important figure in the constitutional struggles of the early seventeenth

century, but we are concerned here with his writings as a source
of law.

Coke was learned in the law and a skilful pleader although his
writings are often verbose and lacking in form. His most important
works are his *Reports* and his *Institutes*. In his day there was no
agreement as to the form a report should take. Coke's reports
come in all shapes and sizes—ranging from summaries of the law
to very detailed reports of important cases, all containing his own
comments. The *Institutes* met the need of the time for the old law
to be restated in modern form. There are four *Institutes*. The first
is his commentary on Littleton (an earlier writer of considerable
reputation) which deals with land law and some of the law of
obligations and procedure. The second deals with statutes, the third
with criminal law and the fourth with the jurisdiction of the
courts.

Parts of Coke's writings are unreliable from the point of view
of strict historical scholarship, but all of them have been influential. His knowledge of the ancient law has never been rivalled; he
communicated his research in English instead of the Latin and law
French of the original materials.

The authority of his writings can be judged from the following
judicial remarks:

(a) in *Garland* v. *Jekyll* (1824) 2 Bing. 296 Best C.J. said " The
fact is Lord Coke has no authority for what he states on the particular point, but I am afraid we should get rid of a good deal of
what is considered law in Westminster Hall if what Lord Coke
says without authority is not law."

(b) *Garland* v. *Jekyll* was referred to by Darling J. in *R.* v. *Case-
ment* [1917] 1 K.B. 98, 141 when he delivered the judgment of
the Court of Criminal Appeal. He said

> " It has been said to us that we should not follow Lord Coke
> because Stephen in his commentaries and other writers have
> spoken lightly of the authority and learning of Lord Coke.
> It may be that they have done so. Of course they have all the
> advantage. They are his successors. If Lord Coke were in a
> position to answer them, it may be that they would be sorry
> that they had entered into argument with him ... he has been
> recognised as a great authority in these courts for centuries."

Blackstone [11]

Blackstone was the first Professor of English Law at Oxford and published his lectures under the title of *Commentaries on the Laws of England* in 1761. In 1770 he was made a judge.

From the point of view of style the *Commentaries* are admirable. The books were aimed beyond the legal profession to the educated public at large. Blackstone's classification follows Roman law to some extent. Thus the order is the nature of law, rights of persons, rights of things, private wrongs and public wrongs.

From the point of view of substance the work has been criticised. There is a lack of profundity and critical acumen.[12] Bentham in particular resented its complacency.[13] Nevertheless the work was a success, particularly in the colonies and the United States where it was the only available source of the common law for many frontier lawyers and judges. Blackstone's *Commentaries* are regarded as authoritative because of their clear style, comprehensiveness and accuracy. Despite Bentham's strictures the *Commentaries* facilitated reform because of their clear statement of the existing law.

Pollock [14]

Sir Frederick Pollock lived from 1845 until 1937. He was an academic lawyer who came from a family of eminent practising lawyers. His knowledge was prodigious and his literary style was graceful. The writer of *The Times* obituary described him as " perhaps the last representative of the old broad culture." He was the author of leading textbooks on the law of contract, tort, possession and partnership and was the draftsman of the Bill which became the Partnership Act 1890. His principal contribution was to show students and practitioners that English law was no mere collection of precedents and statutes but a system of rules, principles and standards which was logically coherent and yet eminently practical because it was the product of long experience.[15]

Lord Wright wrote of him in the *Law Quarterly Review*—" the writings of a lawyer like Pollock, constantly cited in the courts and quoted by the judges, are entitled to claim a place under his category of unwritten law, even in a system like ours which does not normally seek its law from institutional writers." [16]

The Status of Classical Writers

We have mentioned above four leading writers. There are others such as Glanvil, Hale, Hawkins, Fry and Lindley who could also be mentioned. Can we make meaningful general remarks about them? It seems that unlike certain Roman jurists who enjoyed what is known as the *jus respondendi*,[17] they do not enjoy the status of a primary source of law and there is no English equivalent of the Roman law of citations to determine their standing amongst each other.[18] The earlier English writers are sometimes the only source of knowledge or information about the old law but even where this is not the case they are accepted as a valuable secondary source. Nevertheless as Lord Goddard C.J. said in *Bastin* v. *Davies* [1950] 2 K.B. 579, 582 the court " would never hesitate to disagree with a statement in a textbook, however authoritative or however long it has stood, if it thought it right to do so." [19]

The Citation of Modern Writers

The old rule of practice was that the works of living authors could not be cited but could be plagiarised by counsel by incorporation into their own submissions to the court.[20] Various reasons have been given for this [21]—the fear that living authors would change their minds and render the law uncertain; the growth of law reporting rendered it unnecessary to cite secondary sources; and the notion that the passage of time would result in the elimination of errors by subsequent editors. Sir Robert Megarry V.-C., who speaks with considerable knowledge and experience in these matters, in his *Miscellany-at-Law* (1955), p. 328, adds the further reason that

" there are a number of living authors whose appearance and demeanour do something to sap the confidence in their omniscience which the printed page may have instilled; the dead, on the other hand, so often leave little clue to what manner of men they were save the majestic skill with which they have arrayed the learning of centuries and exposed the failings of the bench."

The old rule has become honoured more in its breach than its observance. There is an interesting exchange between counsel and the Bench in *R.* v. *Ion* (1852) 2 Den. 475, 488.

" Metcalfe (counsel) . . . In the 11th edition of a work, formerly edited by one of your Lordships, *Archbold on Criminal Plead-*

ing by Welsby, Mr. Welsby, who may be cited as authority, comments on the words ' utter or publish ' . . .

Pollock C. B.—Not yet an authority.

Metcalfe.—It is no doubt a rule that a writer on law is not to be considered an authority in his lifetime. The only exception to the rule, perhaps, is the case of Justice Story.

Coleridge J.—Story is dead.

Cresswell J.—No doubt the cases are carefully abstracted by Mr. Welsby in the passage you refer to.

Lord Campbell C.J.—It is scarcely necessary to say that my opinion of Mr. Welsby is one of sincere respect."

The reporter, Denison, appends a footnote to the effect that the rule seemed to be more honoured in the breach than in its observance and he refers to a number of writers who had been cited in their lifetime.

There are numerous conflicting passages in the reports on the application of the rule [22] but certainly the practice has now developed of citing living authors. It may be as Hood Phillips maintains that the judges allow themselves more latitude than they do counsel.[23]

In 1947 Sir Alfred Denning (as he then was) wrote in the *Law Quarterly Review* [24] that " the notion that (academic lawyers') works are not of authority except after the author's death, has long been exploded. Indeed the more recent the work, the more persuasive it is." This view has not been universally accepted but there seems to be an increasing tendency to accept academic writings as a convenient secondary source of law or alternatively as a source of suggestions of what the law should be where there is a gap or the law is unclear.[25] As Lord Denning said such books " are written by men who have studied the law as a science with more detachment than is possible to men engaged in practice."

Sir Robert Megarry, who is both a writer and a judge, expressed the matter a little more cautiously in *Cordell* v. *Second Clanfield Properties Ltd.* [1968] 2 Ch. 9, 16 when he said:

" the process of authorship is entirely different from that of judicial decision. The author, no doubt, has the benefit of a broad and comprehensive survey of his chosen subject as a whole, together with a lengthy period of gestation and intermittent opportunities for reconsideration. But he is exposed to the peril of yielding to preconceptions, and he lacks the advantage of that impact and sharpening of focus which the detailed facts of a particular case bring to the judge. Above all, he has to form his ideas without the aid of the purifying ordeal of skilled argument on the specific facts of a contested case. Argued law is tough law. This is as true today as it was in 1409 when Hankford J. said: ' Homme ne scaveroit de quel metal un campane fuit, si ceo ne fuit bien batu, quasi diceret, le ley per bon disputacion serra bien conus '; [Just as it is said ' A man will not know of what metal a bell is made if it has not been well beaten (rung) ' so the law shall be well known by good disputation] and these words are none the less apt for a judge who sits, as I do, within earshot of the bells of St. Clements. I would therefore give credit to the words of any reputable author in a book or article as expressing tenable and arguable ideas, as fertilisers of thought, and as conveniently expressing the fruits of research in print, often in apt and persuasive language. But I would do no more than that; and in particular, I would expose those views to the testing and refining process of argument. Today, as of old, by good disputing shall the law be well known."

The current Scottish position appears to be that where there is a statement of the law in an institutional work which has not been contradicted the judges will look upon that statement as representing the law of Scotland.[26] The authority of such a statement has sometimes been said to be equivalent to that of a decision of the Inner House of the Court of Session to the same effect. There seems to be consensus between Lord Normand [27] (extrajudicially) and Professors Smith [28] and Walker [29] on this point although Professor Walker adds that the evaluation of any such statement depends largely on whether the legal context has changed, whether the passage has been approved of or criticised, and on its consistency with the law on related topics.

In conclusion, therefore, it must be admitted that even with the latest shift in practice we still seem to differ to some degree from continental systems in our treatment of learned writings. As with interpretation of legislation it would seem that we are likely to be influenced by the continental practices adopted by the European Court.

Details about legal literature appear in Appendix 2 at the end of this book.

Notes

[1] René David and John Brierley, *Major Legal Systems in the World Today*, p. 112.

[2] For the continental practice generally see David and Brierley, *op. cit.* pp. 112 *et seq.* and J. H. Merryman, *The Civil Law Tradition*, Chap. IX. It may, however, be dangerous to generalise as the amount of codification and legislation and the nature of legal literature differ from one civil law jurisdiction to another. These have some bearing on the *precise* weight to be afforded to doctrine.

[3] For Scots law see Lord Macmillan, " Scots Law as a Subject of Comparative Study " in *Law and Other Things*, p. 111; The British Commonwealth series Vol. II—Scotland by T. B. Smith, pp. 32–33; and *Principles of Scottish Private Law* (2nd ed.), Vol. I, by D. M. Walker, pp. 27–28.

[4] See Sir P. Winfield, *The Chief Sources of English Legal History*, p. 254. See also D. L. Carey Miller, " Legal Writings as a Source in English Law " (1975) 8 C.I.L.S.A. 236.

[5] See further Sir William Holdsworth, *Some Makers of English Law*, Lecture 1.

[6] See Bracton, *Laws and Customs of England* (Thorne ed.), Vol. 2, p. 21.

[7] Pollock and Maitland, *History of English Law*, Vol. 1, p. 204.

[8] *History of the Common Law*, p. 189.

[9] *Commentaries*, Vol. 1, 72.

[10] See Holdsworth, *op. cit.*, Lecture VI.

[11] *Ibid.* pp. 240 *et seq.*

[12] Max Radin, *Handbook of Anglo-American Legal History*, p. 287.

[13] See *Fragment on Government*.

[14] Holdsworth, *op. cit.* pp. 279 *et seq.*

[15] *Ibid.* p. 286.

[16] (1937) 53 L.Q.R. 152.

[17] *i.e.* the privilege of giving *responsa* with the Emperor's authority. See *Digest* 1.2.2,49 and Barry Nicholas, *An Introduction to Roman Law*, p. 31.

[18] See on this Carey Miller, *op. cit.* and Gray, *Nature and Sources of Law*.

[19] See also *Button* v. *D.P.P.* [1966] A.C. 591.

[20] See *e.g. Greenlands Ltd.* v. *Wilmshurst* (1913) 29 T.L.R. 685, 687, *per* Vaughan Williams L.J. and *Tichborne* v. *Weir* (1892) 67 L.T. 735, 736, *per* Lord Esher M.R.

[21] See Carey Miller, *op. cit.* and R. E. Megarry, *Miscellany-at-Law* (1955), p. 328.

[22] See *e.g.* the authorities cited by Megarry and Carey Miller, *op. cit.*

[23] *A First Book of English Law* (1970), p. 223.

[24] (1947) 63 L.Q.R. 516.

[25] For an interesting discussion of the influence of textbooks on the development of the law of contract see A. W. B. Simpson, " Innovation in Nineteenth Century Contract Law " (1975) 91 L.Q.R. 247.

[26] See Lord Benholme in *Drew* v. *Drew* (1870) 9 M. 163, 167 and Lord Inglis in *Kennedy* v. *Stewart* (1889) 16 R. 421, 430.

[27] *The Scottish Judicature and Legal Procedure,* p. 40.

[28] Smith, *op. cit.* p. 32.

[29] Walker, *op. cit.* p. 27.

Chapter 11

THE IMPACT OF THE EEC

EEC Sources of Law [1]

SINCE January 1, 1973, the United Kingdom has been a Member State of the European Economic Community. This was achieved by a Treaty of Accession followed by the European Communities Act 1972. By the former the United Kingdom government acceded to the Treaty of Rome and the other treaties constituting the EEC and by the latter it provided that EEC sources of law should take internal effect in the United Kingdom. The EEC as a whole is an autonomous legal system which is neither national nor international since it lacks many of the aspects of a national system and yet is something more than a mere international treaty-based institution. This apparently paradoxical status results from its function which is primarily economic, the Member States having limited their sovereignty to promote the establishment of a common market.

The institutional framework consists of the Council of Ministers from the Member States, the Commission which (*inter alia*) is the bureaucracy of the system, the European Parliament which has not power but influence, and last the European Court of Justice.

The reason why the European Parliament has influence rather than power is that so far the national governments have been reluctant to cede any of their sovereignty to such a body. It nevertheless provides a useful forum for discussing EEC projects. Both the Council of Ministers and the Commission are given prescribed legislative powers under the treaties.

The actual sources of EEC law are shown on the diagram on p. 123. From this you can see straight away that a basic distinction is drawn between primary and secondary law and that within this framework a further distinction is drawn between directly applicable and not directly applicable provisions.

Primary law means the law contained in the articles of the main treaties. This takes precedence over national law. This supremacy is recognised as far as the United Kingdom is concerned by section 2 (1) of the European Communities Act 1972 which provides:

SOURCES OF LAW AND LAW MAKING IN THE EEC

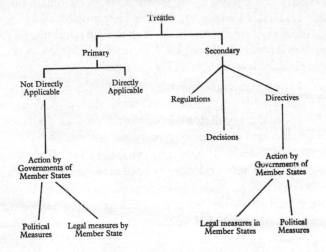

" All such rights, powers, liabilities, obligations and restrictions from time to time created or arising by or under the Treaties, and all such remedies and procedures from time to time provided for by or under the Treaties, as in accordance with the Treaties are without further enactment to be given legal effect or used in the United Kingdom shall be recognised and available in law, and be enforced, allowed and followed accordingly."

Sometimes, however, the primary law is not directly applicable, that is the Treaty is less explicit and requires further steps to be taken. These further steps are then taken either by the enactment of specific legislation in the individual Member States or by political action by the governments of the Member States.

Secondary law derives from instruments made under the treaties by the Council of Ministers or the Commission. The power to make individual instruments is scattered around the Treaty of Rome but Article 189 provides a general description of the particular secondary law sources. This provides:

" In order to carry out their task the Council and the Commission shall, in accordance with the provisions of this Treaty, make regulations, issue directives, take decisions, make recommendations or deliver opinions.

A regulation shall have general application. It shall be binding in its entirety and directly applicable in all Member States.

A directive shall be binding, as to the result to be achieved, upon each Member State to which it is addressed, but shall leave to the national authorities the choice of form and methods.

A decision shall be binding in its entirety upon those to whom it is addressed.

Recommendations and opinions shall have no binding force."

As can be seen from that wording regulations are directly applicable whereas directives are not. This clear picture has been slightly obfuscated by recent decisions [2] of the European Court which have established that in certain circumstances a directive can take direct effect whereas a regulation may not. This is where the directive's terms are sufficiently explicit for it to take immediate effect without the intervention of a national legislative or administrative act. This sophistry seems to blur the clear distinction drawn by Article 189 and is perhaps for that reason to be regretted.

Interpretation by the European Court

The jurisdiction of the European Court is threefold.[3] First it is an administrative tribunal concerned with the acts of the EEC institutions and officials. Secondly it is an international court deciding disputes between Member States under the treaties. Thirdly it has exclusive jurisdiction in the interpretation of the primary and secondary law in cases between Member States and their nationals and between their nationals. There are detailed provisions which govern the relationship between the Court and the courts of Member States, in the exercise of the latter jurisdiction. On this a distinction is drawn between interpretation and application of the treaties. On the former the European Court is the supreme tribunal; on the latter the courts of the Member States have the last word.[4] The judges of the Court are elected by the governments of the Member States, in practice from the judiciary, professors of law, private practitioners and government lawyers. In addition they are assisted by two advocates-general from similar backgrounds who perform a role based on French practice but unprecedented in English law. The task of the advocates-general is threefold: to propose a solution to the case; to relate that solution to the existing law and thirdly to outline probable future developments in the law. Their submissions are an invaluable supplement to the rather terse judgments which the Court itself delivers.

The basic method of interpretation is the literal approach but there is something which approximates to the so-called golden rule, in that it has been stated that the clear language of an act of an EEC institution must not be allowed to prevail if, *in the light of the treaties*, it leads to an absurdity.[5] It has also been suggested that one cannot expect the treaties to demonstrate the same standard of draftsmanship as national legislation.[6]

The Court often seems to adopt a purposive approach. Sometimes, using the terminology of French law, this has been called a logical approach, sometimes a teleological approach.[7] There is a growing body of authority supporting this kind of approach. In the case of *Costa* v. *ENEL*,[8] Advocate General Lagrange stated that excessive formalism should give way to the community spirit.

In ascertaining the "spirit" or the intention underlying the treaties or a particular instrument the Court appears to allow resort to extrinsic materials where these are available and they are often referred to in the submissions of the advocate general. The Court itself on the other hand appears to resort to them not to arrive at its decision but to confirm its decision.[9] At least this is what the Court says it does.

Precedent in the European Court

The Court being a supranational court borrows general principles from the laws of the Member States. Sometimes these consist of particular rules of Member States; sometimes they consist of "general principles of law" in the more technical sense used in continental and international law embracing such things as natural justice and equity in the ethical sense.

Like other continental courts the Court is not strictly bound by its previous decisions. This was stated in *Da Costa N.V.* v. *Nederlandse Belastingadministrie* [10] in 1963. It has no doctrine of *stare decisis*. In the words of Lord Denning M.R. in the recent case of *H. P. Bulmer Ltd.* v. *J. Bollinger S.A.*[11]: " Its decisions are much influenced by considerations of policy and economics; and, as these change, so may their rulings change."

The structure of the reports of its decisions which are divided into two parts—the *motifs* (reasons) and the *dispositif* (ruling)—differs from that of English reports [12] (see Appendix 1). The terms *ratio decidendi* and *obiter dicta* do not appear to be used. In a case in 1967 [13] Advocate-General Roemer referred to the large number of cases cited and said " It is, therefore, appropriate ... to resort to these decisions with discretion, even where the general terms of the propositions suggest their application to problems not arising in the case before the court when they were formulated."

Although the European Court refuses to be bound by its own decisions the fact remains that under section 3 of the European Communities Act 1972 the English courts are now bound not only by its decisions but also by the principles laid down by it. This seems to blur the distinction between *ratio decidendi* and *obiter dicta* even within the English legal system. The European Court nevertheless seems *in practice* to follow its own precedents.

Last, the European Court pays much more attention to " doctrine " in the sense of the writings of jurists. This is in line with continental law and marks a further difference from English law although even here the practice has been changing in recent years, as we saw in Chapter 10, and the old rule that one could only cite the writings of authors after they had died seems to have disappeared.

Some General Problems for English Legal Method

England, Wales and Ireland have grown up as common law systems. Scotland, as we saw in Chapter 3, has had a separate legal tradition with its own customary law which has been successively influenced by the civilian and English traditions. The common law is a case law system governed by a doctrine of binding precedent. These points, however, can be over-emphasised since as we saw more and more of modern law emanates from legislation and there are considerable leeways within the doctrine of precedent. Scotland seems to pursue a doctrine of precedent but to place the emphasis more on principle than a rather myopic concentration on facts which often seems to characterise the English system.

The other Member States (with the exception of Denmark) have grown up with customary systems influenced by the Roman law tradition which eventually gave way to codification in the Napoleonic period. The reasons for this were usually political— either conquest or a desire for national unity. Nevertheless the fact remains that continental lawyers seem to English lawyers to pursue a more deductive approach and to pay little attention to precedent. However, both of these are exaggerations and the two traditions seemed even before 1973 to be moving closer together. The theory suggests a difference which is often not reflected in practice. The main reasons are that law can never be an act of mechanical deduction—facts refuse to fit neatly into the legislator's categories. Also natural conservatism and pure convenience suggest the wisdom of treating like cases as like, while common sense suggests the folly of making a fetish of precedent.

It is dangerous to speculate on future developments but it seems reasonable to assume that the influence of the European Court and the continental tradition may well result in a slackening of the doctrine of precedent and that the emphasis in future will be more on purpose and principle than on fact. The rather misleading concepts of *ratio decidendi* and *obiter dicta* may well lose their influence. Indeed the distinction between them already seems to be blurred in Scots law.[14]

In the immediate future a major source of controversy is likely to arise over the differing style of legal draftsmanship. The Statute Law Society in their memorandum *Statute Law: A Radical Simplification* describe the English style of detailed draftsmanship as " legalistic, often obscure and circumlocutious. Sentences are long and involved, the grammar is obscure, and archaisms, tortuous language and a penchant for the double negative over the single positive abound." This is not, however, a necessary consequence of legislation in detail.

The continental style on the other hand often prefers general principles giving a more creative role to the courts in fact if not in theory. The Statute Law Society in paragraph 160 of their memorandum sum up the position thus:

> " It is impossible to say at this stage where the balance between the two approaches will come to rest. But in fields in which United Kingdom legislation will be subject to Community legislation, directives or rules [*sic*] it would be at least prudent for Parliament to have regard to the Continental approach when framing its own legislation when in the last resort such legislation will be governed by the courts and tribunals of the Community. In other words, unless and to the extent that the Community adopts the United Kingdom approach, it is prudent for Parliament to consider and follow as far as possible the Continental approach in fields in which the final decision lies on the Continent."

One can only hope that we shall shed some of the ghastly aspects of our drafting while not necessarily abandoning the detailed approach where this is appropriate. As we saw in Chapter 8 a single approach may not be desirable. There are areas of law which require the emphasis to be placed on certainty and other areas which require the emphasis to be placed on flexibility.

Notes

[1] See generally J. W. Bridge, " Community Law and English Courts and Tribunals: General Principles and Preliminary Rulings " [1975] *European Law Review* 13. For a detailed study of the scrutiny of EEC

secondary legislation see T. St. John N. Bates, " The Scrutiny of European Secondary Legislation at Westminster," *loc. cit.* p. 22.

[2] *e.g. Grad* v. *Finanzamt Traunstein* [1971] C.M.L.R. 1 and *Van Duyn* v. *Home Office* [1974] E.C.R. 1337; [1975] 1 C.M.L.R. 1. A distinction is drawn between direct applicability and direct effect.

[3] See Dr. Bernard Dickens, " The Community Constitution and Legal Effects " in *Introduction to the Common Market*, p. 24.

[4] See Lord Denning M.R. in *H. P. Bulmer Ltd.* v. *J. Bollinger S.A.* [1974] Ch. 401, 419c–E, but see the criticisms of that case in *Encyclopedia of European Community Law*, Vol. BII, paras. B10–394–6.

[5] See Professors D. Lasok and J. W. Bridge, *Introduction to the Law and Institutions of the European Communities* (2nd ed.), p. 92 and the authorities cited there.

[6] *Ibid.* p. 92.

[7] *Vide supra*, Chap. 8.

[8] [1964] C.M.L.R. 425, 448.

[9] Lasok and Bridge, *op. cit.* pp. 94–95. See also *Stauder* v. *City of Ulm* [1970] C.M.L.R. 112; [1963] C.M.L.R. 224.

[10] [1963] C.M.L.R. 224.

[11] [1974] Ch. 401, 420c–D.

[12] Lasok and Bridge, p. 97.

[13] *Brasserie de Haecht* v. *Wilkin* [1968] C.M.L.R. 26.

[14] See T. B. Smith, *Judicial Precedent in Scots Law*, p. 107.

BOOK III

Problems of the Law and Legal Method

CHAPTER 12

LAW AND SOCIO-ECONOMIC CHANGE

A Complex Set of Problems

THE relationship of law to society in a western democratic country is interesting but complex. Law is a cause and effect of both stability and change in social behaviour although modern commentators tend to emphasise the process of social change.[1] By social change is meant an alteration in the ways in which people in a society relate to each other with regard to such matters as family life, morality, government and other basic social activities.[2] Social change covers both incidental change within a particular social structure in society such as the changing role of women, or an alteration of the fundamental structure of society itself such as a change from an agricultural, feudal society to an industrialised democracy.

Social and legal change are important in themselves but cannot be divorced from the materialist or economic base of society.[3] Marxist social theory emphasises this dependence and regards law as part of the general cultural superstructure which is built upon the economic base or mode of production of society. As such it operates as a form of coercive and ideological domination by the ruling economic class.[4] However, as Marx himself recognised, the relationship is even more complex than that. Thus transformations in the economic system ultimately produce changes in the law but sometimes changes in economic relations are the result of legal developments. Karl Renner[5] has pointed out that in any event transformations in the economic system do not automatically produce changes in the law. The changes in the law are usually brought about by political development and invariably there is a time-lag, often of centuries. During this time-lag, as Professor Kahn Freund puts it, " norms which, at an earlier period of history may have been a true mirror of social relations, may cease to be an accurate expression of factual conditions."[6] Some laws will fall into disuse but others will be transformed in their social function. A classic illustration of the latter is the changing function of land ownership from the basis of feudal power to the attainment of home ownership through building society finance. Renner's analysis is useful but ultimately fails to give adequate recognition to the malleability of law itself and the possibilities of legal change. At the forefront of his thinking were Roman law and the continental codes. All legal systems have *internal* dynamics which activate legal change but constant legal change is inevitable with an open and pluralistic system such as the common law. Its list of categories is never closed, their form never finally settled and there is no fixed and immutable order of principles. Let us examine this question in more detail.

Dynamics of the Legal System

The common law system has an internal dynamism which produces legal change in an empirical way. The classical theory was that the judiciary merely declared and applied the pre-existent law. This was a childish, but, in its time, no doubt a convenient fiction. The truth is that from the beginning the judges fashioned and developed the law from case to case in accordance with their perceptions of the needs of a changing society. Thus the development of contract, tort and the trust for example were each a response to what was felt to be a social need. The growth of commerce demonstrated the formal covenant to be too cumbrous a formality and rendered the development of a more flexible approach to contract necessary. The growth of a more sophisticated and mobile society, and the Industrial Revolution made a system of compensation for civil injury based primarily on property rights inadequate, and the need or wish to keep land in the family and to provide less formal and expensive means of association led to the development of the trust.

We have seen in Chapter 7 the role conflict inherent in the judicial function and how judges have been categorised into " bold spirits " and " timorous souls." The latter is a convenient description of the *extremes* of judicial attitudes and it belies the fact that many modern judges fall somewhere in the middle. It is difficult to identify a common ideology of this centre group but perhaps it can be found in the speech of Lord Reid in *Pettitt* v. *Pettitt* [1970] A.C. 777, 794–795 when he recognised that the courts had an important function in developing or adapting the common law to meet new conditions in appropriate cases. He emphasised, however, his reference to " appropriate cases " because he thought the judges should recognise a difference between cases where they were dealing with " lawyer's law " and cases where they were dealing with

> " matters which directly affect the lives and interests of large sections of the community and which raise issues which are the subject of public controversy, and on which laymen are as well able to decide as are lawyers. On such matters it is not for the courts to proceed on their view of public policy for that would be to encroach on the province of Parliament."

As broad guidelines these seem adequate although the concept of " lawyer's law " is rather a vague one.[7] It appears to cover the case law and legislation which over the centuries have been developed almost exclusively by lawyers and which are regarded as too technical for laymen to handle. Trust law is the classic example but there are problems. Is the law of contract and tort within the concept? Is the concept a *desirable* one anyway? Should certain areas be regarded as lawyers' provinces? Alternatively it might be argued that the existence of such a concept inhibits interest by lawyers in developing areas such as public law and poverty law. Clearly in areas outside lawyers' law the laws will appear in the form of legislation which must be interpreted and applied by the courts. Thus the courts still have an important role to play but it is one which they themselves regard as more passive. They are the interpreters rather than the formulators of policy in these areas.

In a recent lecture [8] Lord Devlin gave a lucid analysis of the judicial function with regard to social and legal change. He distinguished between *activist lawmaking* by which he meant keeping pace with change in the consensus of a community (the area of which might be difficult to discern) and *dynamic or creative lawmaking*, by which he meant the use of law to generate change in the consensus. The first was a legitimate province for the judge at least as far as the common law was concerned, the second not. Even in relation to the first the judicial role could be exaggerated since 90 per cent. or more of English judges, he thought, were engaged for 90 per cent. of their time in the disinterested application of known law.

He contrasted the British courts with the American Supreme Court which has engaged in dynamic lawmaking and pointed to the distinctly political character of that court as an organ of government under the American Constitution. The Supreme Court like the vines of France was not for transportation.

Although British judges were concerned with justice in the sense of legal justice and equity they were not concerned with *social* justice which was more political and partisan in character.

He then considered arguments against judicial activism as opposed to dynamic lawmaking. The first was that it was undemocratic. This, he thought, was an argument against dynamic lawmaking since judicial activism as he had defined it operated within the consensus. He seems to be identifying democracy with substance rather than process here since *the judicial process* itself is arguably always undemocratic. In the United Kingdom judges are not democratically elected and the public only participate to a limited extent in the judicial process. Secondly, there was the objection of retroactivity which he felt was a strong one. This could be tempered by extended legal aid but not, he thought, by the American system of prospective overruling *i.e.* upholding the law in the instant case but announcing change in future. Last, the most telling argument was that the judges even in relation to lawyers' law were ill-equipped in litigation to play the role of lawmaker. They had limited knowledge and the assistance of counsel was insufficient for *this* purpose. New law ought only to be made after adequate consultation. Lord Devlin thus represents a view which is perhaps a little right of centre if one may use a term more appropriate to the political world.

The law is, then, an ever-changing mass of rules, principles and standards shaped by the legislators and the judiciary. Clearly, the whole mass does not change at any one time otherwise there would be chaos. A legal system, like all social institutions, represents an attempt to pursue the disparate goals of stability and change. In the end the law naturally tends towards compromise. Some people get impatient. They feel that the law does not adequately represent their interest or their particular set of values. They often form pressure groups. Pressure groups are an important channel of public opinion in a form convenient to government. They can be broadly classified into two categories—interest groups and cause groups. Interest groups represent a particular section of society, whereas cause groups usually represent particular values such as justice or the prevention of cruelty to children. I have attempted elsewhere to trace the role of pressure groups in public opinion and social change.[9]

Added to these are the permanent law reform agencies such as the Criminal Law Revision Committee and the Law Commissions. These act as a filter for reform ideas at least in the area of " lawyers' law." Again, I have attempted to describe these bodies and their activities in more detail elsewhere.[10]

We have considered the question of judicial law-making in relation to legislation. An important general question which faces English law at the moment is the proper role of the judiciary and the law reform bodies in the process of legal change. With the establishment of the Law Commission in 1965 and its plans to codify wide areas of English law it looked to some commentators as if the status of the judiciary was being reduced to that of mere interpreter of the largely codified law. Obviously, interpretation often involves a certain measure of imagination and creativity but clearly not as much as judicial development of case law. There are signs, however, that the early reforming zeal has diminished and that we are unlikely to have codified English law for some time, if at all. What remains, therefore, is a mixture of judge-made law and legislation with more major reforms being effected through the latter medium. If the United Kingdom adopts a modern Bill of Rights then this may increase the role of the judiciary. Although expressed in legislative form, a Bill of Rights in a sense represents a " higher law " and is likely to be expressed in terms which are more suggestive of common law principles than ordinary statutory rules. It might legitimate a limited amount of what Lord Devlin calls dynamic law-making.

The Impact of Social and Economic Change

Let us now look at key areas of the law and examine some of the major trends of social, economic and legal change. All that will be attempted will be a very brief and impressionistic sketch.[11]

Criminal Law

As we saw in Chapter 3, this is the area of law where the penal technique is applied.

The major controversies which have taken place in recent years have centred around the justification and efficacy of the use of the penal technique.

An important debate was that which took place between Lord Devlin [12] and Professor Hart [13] round about 1960. This highlighted two opposing views of modern society. Lord Devlin adopted what was fundamentally a consensus approach, maintaining that a society consists partly of shared moral ideas; this gave it a right to enforce that morality and to use the weapon of the law to do so. It should desist from this only where for various reasons it was inexpedient. The criterion of immorality for legal purposes should be the intolerance, indignation and disgust of the man (*sic*) in the jurybox. In the subsequent case of *Shaw* v. *Director of Public Prosecutions* [1962] A.C. 220, where the accused had published a directory of prostitutes after the legislature had prohibited soliciting in the streets, the House of Lords seemed to accept these views when it invented the criminal offence of conspiracy to corrupt public morals to supplement the legislation. The decision has been much criticised,[14] and the Law Commission has recently recommended a change in the law in favour of more specific offences. Arguably *Shaw* was an example of dynamic law-making where it would be difficult to establish a consensus in favour of the creation of such a wide and general offence.

Professor Hart basically adopted the standpoint of John Stuart Mill's essay *On Liberty* where he said that " the only purpose for which power can be rightfully exercised over any member of a civilised community, against his will, is to prevent harm to others." Hart maintained that recognition of individual liberty as a value involves " as a minimum, acceptance of the principle that the individual may do what he wants, even if others are distressed when they learn what it is that he does—unless, of course, there are other grounds for forbidding it." [15] Hart's " other grounds " cover a limited degree of paternalism protecting people from harming themselves.

The debate arose out of the Wolfenden Report on Homosexuality and Prostitution which led to the legalisation of homosexual behaviour between consenting adults in private in England and Wales and the prohibition of public prostitution. Much of the controversy in the debate has centred around sex, the public/private dichotomy and the question of obscenity. It has also featured the need to protect children from corruption and exploitation. Clearly what amounts to corruption and exploitation in our society are matters of controversy in themselves.[16] The debate is primarily a

social, political and moral one although the idea of economic
exploitation is introduced by some participants. It basically represents a continuation of the Victorian clash between the old traditional values of a predominantly Christian culture and a new secular approach based on utilitarianism—the greatest happiness of the
greatest number. Utilitarianism was the product of a middle-class
dominated capitalist society. " What is the use of you? " it asked and
answered its own question by an attempt to calculate the tendency
of each social practice to produce pleasure and avoid pain. Alvin
Gouldner, an American sociologist in *The Coming Crisis of
Western Society*, p. 67 describes the general influence of utilitarianism on society in this way:

> " . . . utilitarianism has a built-in tendency to restrict the sphere
> of morality; to enlarge the importance attributed to purely
> cognitive judgment; . . . to select courses of action on grounds
> independent of moral propriety or impropriety; and in its
> future-orienting dependence on consequences not yet realized,
> to defer moral judgment by making it auxiliary to cognitive
> judgment."

We shall return to utilitarianism as a set of values in Chapter 14.
It has exercised considerable influence on law reform in the United
Kingdom and Commonwealth in the past 150 years although there
are now signs that its influence is beginning to wane.

Another aspect of criminal law which has reflected economic and
social change is the growth of so-called " administrative penal
law." [17] This growth is largely the result of increased government
intervention and the application of the administrative regulatory
technique. Thus there are offences which relate to road safety,
safety at work, minimum quality of food and drugs and so on.
Many of these are what are known as offences of strict liability or
absolute prohibition. Normally there are two ingredients in a
crime—*mens rea*, a guilty mind and *actus reus*, a guilty act. With
this type of offence there is merely a need to prove the guilty act.
The reason is the sheer practical difficulty and cost involved in
having to prove *mens rea* in each case. Nevertheless, many lawyers
react strongly to the existence of such offences and the Law Commission has recommended that in the absence of clear wording
there shall be a presumption of *mens rea*. This is an instance of
lawyers, in the interests of what they conceive to be underlying

values of the legal system, resisting an undesirable legal consequence of social change.

Gradually we are learning more about deviant behaviour in general and also the futility of many of our penal practices.[18] Unfortunately, little of this knowledge seems to have had an impact on the basic concepts of substantive criminal law. As Professor Radzinowicz has written " A Victorian lawyer would still feel at home with our basic offences, but he would be puzzled and bewildered by our basic methods of punishment and treatment. . . ." [19] The penal system nevertheless has a momentum of its own and public opinion on crime tends to be conservative. The legislature and the judiciary appear to reflect this conservatism although the legislature is more open to direct pressure from well-organised pressure groups. In both the United States and Canada, the Supreme Court has a wider role than the British courts and operates under a Bill of Rights. This sets out basic values of the legal system and often results in causes being litigated and enables the court frequently to be in the vanguard of reform although it must be admitted that the American court has so far been much more adventurous than the Canadian. Clearly there are risks involved if the court is too active in dynamic law-making in what is construed to be the political arena.

Family Law [20]

We saw in Chapter 2 how the law provides a framework of rules for private arranging. One of the main areas of private arrangement is of course the family. The law prescribes the form for a valid marriage and procedures for nullity and divorce. These matters passed from ecclesiastical to secular administration in the mid-nineteenth century. The law also provides a framework of grievance remedial rules for determining the ownership of family property on the dissolution of a marriage and the custody and care of children.

The main movement over the last decade has been the rationalisation of the divorce laws. This has been a shift away from the old notions of matrimonial offences towards legal recognition of the sociological fact of the breakdown of a marriage. Even before these reforms took place, the pressures of social change were forcing the judges to enlarge the concepts of cruelty and desertion. Nevertheless the principal reforms were effected through legislation, and at the planning stage the Law Commission sought guidance on the question of values and social attitudes from public bodies rather than attempt to superimpose its own value system or its intuition of consensus values on society.

The social and economic position of a married woman has changed drastically in the last hundred years and this is being reflected in the law relating to matrimonial property. Continental countries, unlike English law, have long recognised some system of community of property. The matter is under active consideration by the Law Commission at present and has been the subject of a social survey.

With regard to children, the movement has been away from parental power over children to parental responsibility for them with an increasing trend towards local authority involvement to protect their welfare.

Contract

We tend to think of the nineteenth century as a period of *laissez-faire*. In fact, this was only true generally of the first half of the nineteenth century. The second half was marked by increasing paternalism and collectivism.[21]

Nevertheless, the law of contract which prescribes the private arranging and grievance-remedial rules for contract situations was built up on *laissez-faire* principles. This lends some support for the old adage that when political causes fail they go to Oxford and when economic theories decline they go to the law courts.[22] The Sale of Goods Act 1893, which was a legal code applying to contracts for the sale of goods, enshrines this particular philosophy, as does the doctrine prohibiting the restraint of trade which was developed by the courts.

With the rise of mass production and the growth of public utilities, more and more contracts have been reduced to standard forms which the French quite properly call contracts of adhesion *e.g.* H.P. agreements, insurance policies and contracts for the supply of electricity. Here the consumer has to take it or leave it on the terms offered and clearly this practice can be abused, particularly where sweeping clauses are inserted excluding liabilities.

Gradually through the doctrine of fundamental breach of contract, which in most cases negates the effect of an exemption clause in a contract where the breach goes to the root of the contract, the courts have been able to check some unfair practices. The problem has been that the law of contract at least in the last hundred years has developed as a monolithic whole applicable both to commercial and consumer transactions. There has been a need for greater specific protection for the consumer and this has been achieved through legislation. Thus we have had the Hire-Purchase Acts, the Misrepresentation Act 1967, the Trade Descriptions Act 1968, the Supply of Goods (Implied Terms) Act 1973, the Fair Trading Act 1973 and now the Consumer Credit Act 1974. Each of these measures has brought in statutory protection for consumers, sometimes backed up by the use of the administrative-regulatory and penal techniques as we saw from our examples in Chapter 3.[23]

Tort

The law of tort is concerned with the remedy of grievances in cases where there is civil injury but (usually) no contractual relationship.

In the nineteenth century and early this century the courts had adapted a tort system, which had developed in an agrarian society, to meet the increasing demands of an industrialised society. The major development was the evolution of the tort of negligence which is traced in Appendix 3. There the movement was from a gradual extension of the list of situations where the court recognised a duty of care to a generalised formulation. In many of the cases which are discussed in Appendix 3, the facts demonstrate the changing social conditions. Thus a manufactured oil lamp, transport, gas mains and eventually mass-manufactured ginger pop all appear in the cases.

The fault concept which is based on the notion of a duty of care and enables legal change to reflect social change has begun to prove inadequate to service modern conditions. Proof of fact, proof of fault and the orthodox paraphernalia of law and legal litigation may be too cumbrous, costly and inefficient a method for handling the large number of cases of personal injury which occur, for example with traffic " accidents."

In the United Kingdom, a Royal Commission is currently looking into the law to ascertain whether a system of state insurance would be preferable. Already there are precedents in National Insurance, and elsewhere in the Commonwealth such schemes have been introduced. Clearly compensation for road traffic accidents is one crucial area where such a scheme would probably be an improvement on the present " forensic lottery." [24]

A further extension of liability has been achieved at common law by means of the concept of vicarious liability whereby an employer was held liable for the torts committed by his employees in the course of their employment. The rationale of this was that as the employer had control over the employee and was gaining financial benefit from the activity in question he should therefore bear the loss. From the employer's point of view this can be seen as a species of strict liability although in practice he covers himself with insurance and treats the premium as an expense of the business.

Property and Economic Power [25]

The protection of private property was one of the earliest functions of the law. However, gradually since the nineteenth century there have been more and more restrictions imposed on the enjoyment of property. Also the increase in the incidence of taxation has tended to break up the large concentrations of property in private hands although there has been an almost corresponding increase of property concentration in large corporations.

Use of property in the form of land is now controlled by town planning legislation which regulates " development " and seeks to preserve our national heritage. Also the Community Land Act 1975 imposes further controls. Most rented property is regulated by the Rent Acts which deal with rent limits and security of tenure.

In the case of personal property, in addition to the legislation we have mentioned in the discussion of the law of contract, there are the restrictive trade practice provisions of the Restrictive Trade Practices Act 1956 and the Fair Trading Act 1973. The latter also contains provisions which attempt to deal with monopoly situations which are against the public interest. Clearly the definition of " public interest " is difficult and inevitably changes with the times. Added to these are the provisions of Articles 85 and 86 of the Treaty of Rome, which deal with restrictive trade practices and monopolies with an EEC element and which are in some ways even more far-reaching. We have learned that size can produce some advantages but it can easily lend itself to abuse in a market economy.

Abuse of economic power can also be perpetrated by trade unions and we have seen various attempts by governments to cope with this problem, ranging from legislative control to a non-legal " social contract." The Conservative Government's Industrial Relations Act 1971 proved to be a disaster because it met with organised opposition from a sizeable section of society. We learned something about the ideological nature and practical limits of law from this experiment.

Social Stratification and Legal Services [26]

Before the last war access to legal services and representation was almost exclusively a middle-class privilege. Working people generally could not afford to pay, and solicitors by and large were not particularly interested in the problems of the poor. Since the post-war period we have had a legal aid system in criminal and civil cases which has been administered by the magistrates' courts and Law Society respectively. To these has been added legal advice and assistance under the so-called £25 or " Green Form Scheme." The availability of legal aid in all its forms depends on eligibility in terms of low income and capital and the type of case, and clearly the choice of criteria is likely to be controversial. In addition to this particular controversy there is at present a general debate as to the continuing " unmet need " for legal services. That there is such a need despite the legal aid system is recognised by the Law Society, the Society of Labour Lawyers, the Society of Conservative Lawyers, the Lord Chancellor's Legal Aid Advisory Committee and by many authors of books, articles and pamphlets. Various reasons have been put forward for this " unmet need "—the lack of lawyers in poor areas for financial reasons, the distrust of the legal profession by the poor, the tendency by lay people to classify a problem as a non-legal one, and so on. What had been lacking hitherto is quantitative data about the range of unmet legal needs. In areas where full-time or part-time neighbourhood law centres have been established (usually by private initiative) this has been done on the basis of personal knowledge of the area and an intuitive assessment of needs rather than a systematic survey. Usually it has been found that housing, family law and personal injuries constitute the majority of problems on which advice is sought. A pioneering study was carried out by Brian Abel Smith, Michael Zander and Rosalind Brooke [27] in the London Boroughs of Islington, Tower Hamlets and Southwark which indicated that not much more than a quarter of the cases which in their view needed a lawyer's attention had received it. On the basis of this, despite a disappointingly low response to their questionnaire, the authors conclude " Our survey has shown substantial unmet need particularly among those with low incomes and of low social class in three London Boroughs which were relatively well provided with services." [28] A major factor in the need being unmet was the ineffectiveness and inefficiency of the advisory services but there was also the problem of the attitudes of people to lawyers and the legal system. As many as 11 per cent. of the people questioned said they would never go to a lawyer.

The question of " unmet need " for legal services is being actively considered by the Lord Chancellor's Department and is the subject of a special report prepared by Richard White. It is known that the present Lord Chancellor is keen to extend legal services in poor areas. The introduction of the " Green Form Scheme " means that some of this work is being handled by solicitors in private practice since the legal advice system pays a reasonable rate of remuneration but many feel that what is needed is the establishment of more full-time neighbourhood law centres in the poorer areas. In some areas the establishment of such centres out of public funds has been attacked by the legal profession who see this as unfair competition, but the pendulum seems to be swinging in favour of the establishment of more of such centres with local people represented on the boards of management.

Socio-Economic Change and Obedience to Law

The common law evolved out of custom but has owed something to the charisma of particular judges. It has developed as a system based on tradition which has responded to the forces of change in the ways we have considered. Nevertheless we live in times of rapid economic and social change which necessitate ever-increasing legislative intervention and have resulted in a growth of the power of the state. The result is that we have a mixed economy and a mixed legal system: a mixed economy in the sense of a combination of public and private enterprise and a mixed legal system in the two senses of legislation and case law, and " legal " and " administrative " approaches to social problems. We are in the slightly paradoxical position that the common law and the legal profession have manfully resisted comprehensive rationalisation in terms of codification but have retreated before the advance of rationalisation in terms of administration.

Continuing public respect for law in all its forms depends on its adequate recognition of human needs. With the breakdown of the family and larger kinship units and the increasing urbanisation of society we have moved from what a German writer [29] called " gemeinschaft "—an organic society—to " gesellschaft "—a fragmented society. More pressure and demands are now being placed on law and the legal system to maintain social order. At the same time, and partly for the same reasons, law cannot command the uncritical obedience it used to. Charisma and tradition perhaps count less than they did. The area of obvious consensus is difficult to discern and the law must now satisfy the test of rationality in terms of intellectual coherence and efficiency, egalitarianism and the other prevailing values of society if it is to sustain its legitimacy in a changing world.[30] This is a daunting challenge. Can law meet it? We shall pursue this topic further in Chapter 13 when we examine some of law's limitations.

Notes

[1] See Wolfgang Friedmann, *Law in a Changing Sosiety*, Chap. 1; Y. Dror, " Law and Social Change," 33 Tulane L.R. 749 (1959); Stuart S. Nagel, " Overview of Law and Social Change," in *Law and Socia. Change*, ed. by Stuart S. Nagel, p. 7; Lawrence M. Friedman, " General Theory of Law and Social Change," in *Law and Social Change*, ed. by Jacob S. Ziegel, p. 17; and for social change generally, see *Social Change*, ed. by Robert Nisbet.

[2] Nagel, *op. cit.* p. 8.

[3] Nagel, *op. cit.* p. 10.

[4] For a useful discussion of this, see Alan Hunt, " Law, State and Class Struggle," in *Marxism Today*, June 1976, p. 178.

[5] *The Institutions of Private Law and their Social Functions.*

[6] Renner, *op. cit.* Introduction by O. Kahn-Freund, pp. 4–5.

[7] See my *Law Reform and the Law Commission*, Chap. 1.

[8] "Judges and Lawmakers" (1976) 39 M.L.R. 1.

[9] Farrar, *op. cit.* Chap. 6.

[10] *Ibid. passim.*

[11] See further Friedmann, *op. cit.* and *The State and Rule of Law in a Mixed Economy.*

[12] *The Enforcement of Morals.*

[13] *Law, Liberty and Morality.*

[14] See Hart, *op. cit.* p. 6.

[15] *Op. cit.* p. 47.

[16] See further Friedmann, *op. cit.* Chap. 6. This was highlighted in the *Oz* obscenity trial which demonstrated a conflict of values on the question of corruption.

[17] Friedmann, *op. cit.* p. 202.

[18] See Friedmann, *op. cit.* pp. 212 *et seq.*

[19] *In Search of Criminology*, p. 181.

[20] For a more detailed treatment, see Friedmann, *op. cit.* Chap. 7.

[21] See A. V. Dicey, *Law and Opinion in England in the Nineteenth Century.*

[22] I have been unable to trace this adage but remember reading it in an old company law textbook.

[23] See further Friedmann, *op. cit.* Chap. 4.

[24] See further Friedmann, Chap. 5. See also *The Forensic Lottery* by T. Ison.

[25] See further Friedmann, Chap. 3 and Part 3.

[26] See *In Search of Justice* by Brian Abel-Smith and Robert Stevens, Chap. 8. This book was written before the Legal Advice and Assistance Act 1972 which set up the new legal advice and assistance scheme. See also *Social Needs and Legal Action* by P. Morris, R. White and P. Lewis.

[27] *Legal Problems and the Citizen.*

[28] *Ibid.* p. 226.

[29] Tönnies, *Community and Society.*

[30] See Sir Leslie Scarman, *English Law—The New Dimension*, and J. H. Farrar, "Law Reform Now; a Comparative View" (1976) 25 I.C.L.Q. 214, 223 *et seq.*

CHAPTER 13

THE LIMITATIONS OF LAW

LAW has natural and conventional limits as you will have discerned in our journey so far. In order to understand the role of law in society one needs to know something about those limitations. Let us take a closer look at them. One can roughly divide them into three groups: first, the limited social functions of law and viewpoint of lawyers, secondly, the limitations on the methods of social control through law, and, thirdly, the specific limitations of legal method. The first group might be described as sociological and political limitations, the second as administrative limitations, and the third as philosophical limitations—although these are obviously not completely exclusive categories.

The Limited Social Functions of Law and Viewpoint of Lawyers

The prime object of law is not the understanding but the regulation of social life. Law is an instrument or set of techniques of social control with the purpose of achieving social order. This it does by maintaining public order, fostering co-operation, regulating power and reinforcing social standards.

There are, of course, whole areas of life which are unregulated by law. Thus the most personal parts of one's life are really outside the law's domain. Law cannot give you health or comfort or love. It does not directly promote the aesthetic side of life. Even for the more obviously public activities such as economic production and politics, all that law can do is to provide a framework. Again, although law can be used to enforce morality the moral standards emanate from elsewhere. Law provides a means rather than the end.

Nevertheless, law does pervade our kind of society and act as a possible scheme of interpretation of social reality. It is easy to assume that the prescriptions of the law are descriptions of social reality.

Marxist writers maintain that law is an instrument of ideological domination and consequently in a capitalist country it tends to distort real social relations between people into relations between things. In the words of a recent writer, Alan Hunt,[1]

> "... legal rules appear abstracted from social relations, and are therefore a 'fetishistic' expression of social relations. Legal rules are further divorced from the social relations to which they refer because they (like the state itself) appear separated, independent of society; they seem to have an independent origin and life of their own. Thus as ideological forms of social relations legal rules are doubly removed from the real world."

There is, however, a certain naïveté in this analysis since it neglects the inescapable problems involved in applying general categories to specific situations in times of change. Also the independence of *the legal system from the government* can be interpreted as a strength rather than a weakness of capitalist countries. It may be misleading to equate law and the legal system in this context. Law undoubtedly needs to reflect contemporary society, but the legal system arguably needs to be independent of government.

An American writer, Judith Shklar echoes some of the Marxist ideas when she maintains that law fosters a social outlook which she calls "legalism" and which, she argues, is an important political ideology in the western world. The characteristics of legalism are, according to her, "the dislike of vague generalities, the preference for case-by-case treatment of all social issues, the structuring of all possible human relations into the form of claims and counterclaims under established rules, and the belief that the rules are there."[2] One might also add a desire artificially to limit the scope of the issue under discussion at any given time. This traditional outlook is "an openly, intrinsically, and quite specifically conservative view, because law is itself a conservatizing ideal and institution. In its epitome, the judicial ethos, it becomes clear that this is the conservatism of consensus."[3]

"Legalism" put in these somewhat vague terms is really a set of social attitudes manifested by some but not all lawyers and by certain laymen which finds its intellectual rationale in the concept of the rule of law. Whilst it may be unrealistic to expect coherence in social attitudes one can reasonably expect consistency in their intellectual rationalisation and justification. The rule of law nonetheless has proved a vague and unsystematic umbrella concept for a number of possibly conflicting values going beyond legality.

Equality, liberty and justice have all been brought under the umbrella at different times. The principal defect seems to spring from the fact that like all sweeping generalities it purports to apply to a large number of things of differing nature and quality. The concept of the rule of law comprehends the totality of laws and institutional practices, some of which may be regarded as good, others as bad. Obviously the criteria of goodness and badness are inherently controversial.

It is arguable that legalism, the rule of law and consensus ideas of society are less commonly held viewpoints today. There is perhaps a greater tendency to look at the merits or demerits of a particular law or practice rather than uncritically accept the legitimacy of the law as a whole. Society seems to have less unity and cohesion and people seem to have become more sceptical and pluralistic. It may be that there is still in fact a consensus of opinion on matters such as the continuing need to prohibit murder and to give recognition to certain truisms about human nature but there are large areas of social life where the existence of such a consensus would now be difficult to establish. It is, however, difficult to prove the presence or absence of a consensus except by a ballot or the most well-planned and scrupulous polling of opinions and this is not often done. It is costly and it would be irksome to do it for a number of issues.

The judiciary, as Judith Shklar has indicated, nevertheless seem attached to a consensus view of society. One can appreciate their dilemma. On what can the legitimacy of the modern law, particularly the common law, be based if not on consensus? Critics of the legal system point to the dependence of the legal system on coercion and the way in which that coercion protects property and privilege. Others stress the subtle forms of ideological domination which it represents. There is some truth in these criticisms although they fail to do adequate justice to the complexity of a legal system in a country such as ours. It is possible nevertheless as we mentioned at the end of Chapters 1 and 12 to base the legitimacy of law on its rationality. It is suggested that this need not depend on a consensus view of society as a whole, still less on force or ideological domination. It does, however, depend not only on intellectual coherence but also on some degree of evaluation—and the selection of the value element in rationality is a difficult question in a rapidly changing, and increasingly pluralistic society. We shall return to the question of values in Chapter 14.

The Limitations on the Methods of Social Control Through Law

In order to measure the limits of law as a set of methods of social control one has to have a conception of something like a social goal or cluster of goals for particular laws. What is the particular law aimed at? Sometimes this will be difficult to discern and it will then be a matter of attribution.

Assuming one can identify a goal then one can attempt to measure the efficacy or efficiency of the law in fulfilling that goal. Efficacy means taking effect at all, efficiency means working well. Clearly the latter involves some scheme of evaluation. This is quite apart from the general moral question of the justification of the use of law in a particular context.

General Factors [4]

What general factors tend to limit law's efficiency? First, as we have seen in Chapter 4 there are problems involved in the ascertainment of fact. We shall return to this in a moment when we consider the limits of legal method. Secondly, there are some social obligations which cannot sensibly or practically be enforced through law, for example, sexual relations between husband and wife. All that the law can do here is to deal with the consequences of refusal. Some legal rights can be subtly encroached upon. Thus someone can trespass through my garden and I may not know of it and even if I do know, the law for common-sense reasons denies me a remedy if he does no damage. The law in any event traditionally has at its command only a limited range of remedies. The common law tried to deal with everything in terms of money compensation. Equity acted *in personam* but would not interfere in matters which required constant supervision. The use of the administrative regulatory technique enables intervention to take place in the latter area but this is often regarded as administration rather than law. This is, however, merely a matter of convention and in many countries this particular approach is regarded as law.

Another factor is that many laws depend for their efficacy and efficiency on the co-operation of the citizen which is not always forthcoming, often these days for reasons of finance or desire for non-involvement.

At the planning stage the legislator may not have enough knowledge of social facts to formulate adequate legislation. In the past many law reforms have taken place on the basis of assumptions rather than proof of social fact. The existence of the Law Commissions and Royal Commissions mitigates against this to some extent today. Again, in spite of careful planning a law may encompass conflicting goals. Values and policies can conflict. Cheapness and efficiency in dealing with small claims for example might result in short cuts which could produce injustice to a particular defendant.

There are also the perennial problems of language and failure of communication. Language we have already considered. Often these days there is inadequate promulgation and sometimes for example it is impossible to obtain a Queen's Printer's copy of a statute or statutory instrument.

Once a law is in operation there may be failures by officials to enforce it for various reasons such as under-staffing, lack of motivation, corruption or errors of judgment. Non-intervention is not always a bad thing. The police for example do not always prosecute offenders particularly when a law is regarded as obsolete. The major criticism of this practice arises out of the lack of public knowledge of the criteria they are applying.

When a matter is before the courts the constraints which quite properly result from basic values of the legal system such as the rules of natural justice sometimes limit the effectiveness of penal laws. We shall examine such values in the next chapter.

Last, there are the all-pervasive factors of cost and lack of resources with which we are all too familiar today.

Particular Factors [5]

In Chapter 3 we basically applied Professor Summers's classification of law into separate methods or techniques of social control. Let us examine particular factors which jeopardise the use of each of the techniques.

The penal technique

Here there are strong policy reasons why the law should be detailed and explicit. Case law concepts, such as conspiracy, are

dangerous weapons and have been much criticised. Ironically perhaps, the vaguer the offence the more effective it can be in the
hands of the police as an instrument of control. On the other hand,
the existence of such vague concepts in the law jeopardises public
respect for law.

Allied to vagueness and uncertainty is the lack of adequate
promulgation of some laws particularly some offences of absolute
prohibition in the field of motoring. If one of the purposes of penal
law is exhortation to compliance, then it will fail if there is
inadequate publicity.

Some penal laws are really trivial and prosecution of such offences
and also of some technical infringements of laws, which are themselves intrinsically not trivial, damage public respect for law and
render enforcement difficult or purposeless. An over-zealous police
can engender social hostility to law enforcement.

Some breaches of the criminal law are difficult to detect, particularly the so-called crimes without a victim, such as sexual deviations.
The sanctions of the criminal law are often unable to effect deterrence or the subsequent rehabilitation of the criminal. Last, there
is a constant tension between the penal laws and the changing values
of society as we have seen throughout this book.

The grievance-remedial technique

As with criminal law, the civil law prescribing remedies for
grievances is sometimes vague, obscure or archaic. Some grievances, such as intrusions on privacy, are not clearly definable in law.
Often the loss suffered is not really measurable in financial terms
so that legal redress is a gesture rather than adequate restitution.
Frequently grievances are difficult to establish because of problems
of proof of fact or to remedy because the plaintiff is not legally
aided and lacks funds.

The private arranging technique

Since the purpose of the law here is to provide facilities for
effecting socially desirable activities much depends on adequate information about the law but ultimately the matter rests on the
particular aims of the parties. Is there an intention to create legal
relations? Is it sufficiently clear? Do the aims of the parties conflict? Usually legal redress is a matter of last resort for the parties.

The constitutive technique

Here the first question is how accessible to the general public is a particular method of incorporation. Obviously, in the early period few groups were allowed the privilege of incorporation by royal charter or could afford the luxury of a private Act of Parliament. The formalities are still reasonably strict but the cost of incorporating a limited liability company is cheap and it is possible to buy one " off the peg " from company formation specialists. From the public's point of view the corollary of limited liability is disclosure and much depends on the efficiency of the Department of Trade in enforcing the law against those in default.

The administrative-regulatory technique

This technique, which involves the creation of an administrative agency to regulate a particular area of social activity, depends heavily on adequate state resources and adequate knowledge of social practices in the particular areas sought to be regulated. It is sometimes affected by the conflict of social goals implicit in the law and the inability to formulate appropriate standards of commercial behaviour. At times this is exacerbated by political machinations. Added to these factors is the constant risk of the development of subtle methods of evasion. For its optimum efficiency it depends on the acceptance of the standards as good morals by the majority of people in the relevant sections of the community.

The fiscal technique

As life gets more complicated fiscal legislation acquires nightmarish qualities. In this country we have a tradition of using very detailed legislation and the problems of complexity and consequent unintelligibility are made worse by tax avoidance and the subsequent grafting of anti-avoidance provisions onto the original text. Unless the system is to be overburdened with administrators the law here must rely on voluntary co-operation by the majority of taxpayers in disclosing their income and wealth. In the past this has been forthcoming although one perhaps detects signs of a changing attitude arising from radical disagreement as to the social justice of particular taxes.

Conferral of social benefits

Some benefits such as education are pretty intangible! Sometimes, for perfectly natural reasons, it is impossible to achieve equality of treatment; some people are more gifted or resourceful or articulate. Lack of resources and lack of social knowledge clearly limit the application of the law in this area.

Proof of Fact

We have already mentioned the difficulties involved in ascertainment in each case of the facts to which legal rules are to be applied. In the striking words of Oliver Wendell Holmes, Sr., in his book *The Professor at the Breakfast Table*: "Every event that a man must master must be mounted on the run, and no man has ever caught the reins of a thought except as it galloped by him." According to another American writer, Roscoe Pound, proof of fact "is one of the oldest and most stubborn problems of the administration of justice." [6]

At first, at an early period the law seems to have coped with this problem on the basis of some mechanical test such as the casting of lots. This involved no personal judgment on the part of the judge and could not therefore be challenged. In the past reliance has been placed on the oath; it is still used but the religious and social beliefs which made this effective have lost a lot of their force. To guard against the unreliability of oral evidence, the law often requires important transactions to be evidenced in writing and sometimes to be witnessed. Unfortunately these requirements of form can, if strictly enforced, easily lead to injustice.

The problem of proof of fact is not simply one of perjury. Since nearly every event which comes before a court is a past event, the court's object is to reconstruct that event. Clearly, in strict terms this is impossible. Every event is unique and no reconstruction will exactly reproduce it. The law has to fall back on the evidence of witnesses of what they said, saw, heard or did and also upon the production of objects. There can easily be mistaken observation, misunderstanding, misinterpretation and straightforward forgetfulness even in the case of the most honest and intelligent witness. [7]

Use of Fact

In its approach to fact, law is rigorous and systematic. In this it resembles the physical sciences but at the end of the day law is non-scientific because its purposes and functions differ from those of the sciences. The dominant characteristic of scientific thinking is description and analysis of cause and effect or processes over a period of time. Lawyers are admittedly interested in cause and effect but "their delimitation and sometimes their interpretation are narrowly defined by normative considerations." [8]

Lawyers use fact to enable a decision to be reached. Making the decision involves categorisation but for a normative purpose *i.e.* the ascription of responsibility or liability. Thus, unlike the scientist, the courts are not concerned with falsification of their theories or assertions. Although a defence counsel will seek to disprove the prosecution's case, the court itself will take the jury's finding as a datum and act on it. Also the court will not afterwards in the ordinary course be concerned with the falsification of its assumptions as regards a particular prisoner unless he comes up before it again and reference has to be made to the earlier punishment. Further, law is not concerned with probability as such. Thus, although the burden of proof in civil matters rests upon a balance of probability, the *finding* is not that event X probably occurred but that it *did* occur.

The essential nature of most litigation before the courts is conflict. This is obvious in proceedings at common law where there are either prosecutors and the accused or plaintiffs and defendants. It is obscured in Chancery proceedings which are usually more concerned with the consideration of a particular *matter*, and which have more in common with the continental practice of inquisitorial proceedings. In the words of Vilhelm Aubert:

> "There is no room [in law] for pure fact-finding in the sense in which this is possible in the laboratory, in the privacy of the doctor's office, or in the anonymity of the sociological survey. The question of establishing a fact becomes almost inevitably a question of making a fact public, and always of laying it open to the partisan normative interpretation of legal counsel, unrestricted by demands for strict objectivity." [9]

The Unfathomable Policy Element in Legal Method

We have referred rather generally to policy in Chapter 7 when we considered case law as a source of law and method of reasoning. Let us examine it in more detail in the context of judicial decision-making. The diagram on p. 157 attempts to depict the main factors operating in this aspect of case law.

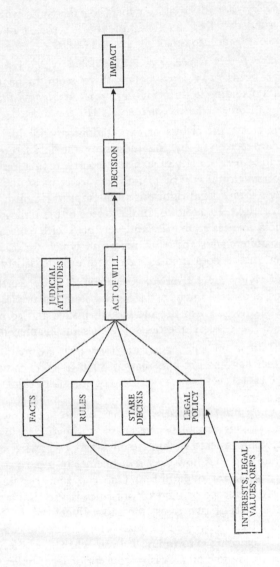

The Structure of Judicial Decision Making

The inputs—*facts, rules* (which we use in a wide sense to cover principles and standards), the particular *stare decisis principles*, and *legal policy*—are all variables which, together with what one American writer described as " within-puts " [10] (*i.e. judicial attitudes*) influence the decision-making by the court.

Legal policy is a species of public policy which is hard to define in clear terms.[11] In legal policy there seem to be three sets of variables operating and interacting: *interests, legal values*, and what I shall call *other relevant factors*—ORFs for short.[12]

Interests are the claims or expectations of individuals or groups which are perceived by the judges or the legislature to exist in society in respect of matters such as property, reputation and freedom from personal injury.[13] By claims we do not mean the enforcement of an *established* legal right but an attempt to establish the existence of such a right. In addition, in the words of the philosopher, Henry Sidgwick, there is a " borderland, tenanted with expectations which are not quite claims and with regard to which we do not feel sure whether Justice does or does not require us to satisfy them." [14]

Legal values are the broad measures of social worth which are accepted and acted upon in the legal system. Examples are the rule of law, the freedom of the individual, justice and so on. We shall return to the general question of values in Chapter 14.

ORFs are a miscellaneous category which are mainly concerned with efficiency and include matters such as cost, convenience and political expediency which we do not normally think of as social values.

The main limitations here are that we do not know what influence the various variables have on the ultimate decision of a court. All that you can learn in our present state of knowledge is that they do operate and that how they *will* operate in a particular case is to a degree a matter of intuition. One can state certain tendencies. Obviously the scope of the existing rules is very important and the closer the facts of two cases, the more likely one is to follow the other, all other things being equal. The higher the court, the more likely a later court is to follow it even where the rule is contained in *obiter dicta*. The all-pervasive concept of legal policy, although I have tried to simplify it in the above analysis is, however, a fluid one which is difficult to tie down. It seems to be relevant to ascertaining the scope of the *ratio decidendi* of a case and in determining whether the facts of an earlier case are sufficiently analogous to justify following it in a later case. It seems to have some bearing on *stare decisis* in that a later court will be influenced by it in ascertaining the *ratio* of an earlier case for the purposes of considering whether it is bound by the earlier case or whether it can distinguish it. Legal policy is crucial to the process of distinguishing cases. We can describe it as a factor or variable in each of these situations. We cannot say more. The nature of judicial attitudes and their possible relationship to legal policy are also relatively uncharted seas, certainly as far as this country is concerned.

Notes

[1] Allan Hunt, " Law, State and Class Struggle," *Marxism Today*, June 1976, 178, 183.

[2] J. Shklar, *Legalism*, p. 10. Legalism is to be contrasted with legality which in this book refers to internal consistency in the use of legal authorities. Legality is sometimes used in American literature to refer to the rule of law. See *e.g.* Philip Selznick, *Law, Society and Industrial Justice*, pp. 11–18.

[3] *Ibid.*

[4] See generally R. Pound, " The Limits of Effective Legal Action " (1917) 27 *Ethics* 150; Harry W. Jones, *The Efficacy of Law* and R. S. Summers, *Law; its Nature, Functions and Limits* (2nd ed.).

[5] See Summers, *op. cit. passim.*

[6] *Jurisprudence*, Vol. III, p. 355.

[7] See Pound, *op. cit.* p. 357 and Max Radin, " The Permanent Problems of the Law " in *Jurisprudence in Action*, pp. 411 *et seq.*

[8] V. Aubert, " The Structure of Legal Thinking " in *Legal Essays: A Tribute to Frede Castberg*, p. 49.

[9] *Ibid.* p. 52.

[10] Glendon Schubert, *Judicial Policy Making* (rev. ed.), p. 139. Compare his *Systematic Model of Judicial Policy Making* at p. 140. Schubert categorises the three major attitudes as (1) *political* liberalism and conservatism (2) *social* liberalism and conservatism and (3) *economic* liberalism and conservatism.

[11] *Cf.* D. Lloyd, *Public Policy*, Lord Radcliffe, *Law in its Compass*, Chap. II and Clive Symmons (1971) 34 M.L.R. 394, 528.

[12] *Cf.* Benjamin N. Cardozo, *The Paradoxes of Legal Science*, p. 75.
[13] See Roscoe Pound, *An Introduction to the Philosophy of Law*, pp. 89 *et seq.* For a recent critique, see M. D. A. Freeman, *The Legal Structure*, pp. 71 *et seq.*
[14] *The Methods of Ethics* (7th ed.), p. 270.

Chapter 14

VALUES IN LAW AND LAW REFORM

WE ended the first chapter with a quotation from Roscoe Pound to the effect that law must be stable yet it cannot stand still. The appropriateness of that epigram should by now have become clear. We have seen how the relationship of legal to social change is a complex one. Law must provide a stable basis for society yet it must accommodate change.

We have seen how questions of policy permeate law-making by Parliament and the case law function of the judges. We have seen that legal policy can be represented as an interraction of three sets of variables and that one important set of variables is values.

Value questions in fact arise in law in a number of quite different ways. Values arise in the *structure of law* particularly as we saw in Chapter 4 where " open textured " concepts are used in the formulation of legal rules, principles and standards. Then there are some values which represent the *hallmarks of good legal craftsmanship* in making laws and devising legal procedures. Professor Fuller of Harvard has described these latter values as " the inner morality of law." [1] It is, however, probably preferable not to think of them either as inner or as morality since this can lead to confusion.[2] These values can be classified into *legislative process values*, *judicial process values* and *legal administration values*. The first are the standards of good legal craftsmanship involved in producing legislation. The second are the standards involved in the adjudication of cases and the third are the standards of legal administration outside the legislature and the courts. The third is obviously a wide category. Some of these values are sometimes subsumed under the concept of " the rule of law." The law also to differing degrees pursues as goals certain *substantive values* such as freedom of the individual and justice. Lastly there is the large and difficult problem of which values and value systems are appropriate as the general *criteria of rational criticism of law*. This latter question is a practical matter as far as law reform bodies are concerned. The most difficult problems for such bodies are to assess whether there is a consensus on a particular topic, what it is and whether they should follow it. They are also concerned with priorities. Let us, therefore, consider in turn each of these major aspects of values.

Values in the Structure of Law

Law frequently uses words which involve questions of degree, open texture and evaluation.[3] The first require comparisons to be made and some kind of yardstick to be applied whereas the second are words where " we can never fill up the possible gaps through which a doubt may seep in." [4] Both of these factors often overlap with evaluation. Concepts such as fairness and reasonableness are examples of both open texture and evaluation. The virtue of a precedent system is that it records a number of situations which have been assessed to be on one side of the line or the other (*i.e.* inside or outside a legal category) and which can be used analogically in future cases.

The Hallmarks of Good Legal Craftsmanship

In some ways law is a craft. Karl Llewellyn described a craft as a body of skills and men for getting something done [5] which (*inter alia*) included a known goal or set of goals.[6] In the Western world lawyers include in their set of goals certain criteria of good legal craftsmanship. Certain qualities tend to produce good law and their negation or absence, bad law. Profession Lon Fuller in *The Morality of Law* listed eight of these [7]: generality, adequate promulgation, avoidance of retroactive laws, clarity, avoidance of contradiction, avoidance of laws requiring the impossible, constancy through time and consistency between the declared rule and official action. Ultimately these helped to ensure " the success of the enterprise of subjecting human conduct to the governance of rules." [8]

In a recent article Professor Robert Summers [9] has used the term " process values " to refer to " standards of value by which we may judge a legal process to be good as a process, apart from any good result efficacy it may have." [10] This concept clearly overlaps with Professor Fuller's so-called " inner morality " to some extent. Professor Summers uses the term " process value " in a general way but we shall follow our plan to subdivide such values into three categories—legislative process values, judicial process values and legal administration values. Thus in this analysis most of Fuller's examples are legislative process values but his last one would be a legal administration value since it refers to the behaviour of officials under the law. The utility of adopting our threefold classification is that particular process values might be applicable to one process and not to the others.

Professor Summers lists as his catalogue of process values—

(1) participatory governance,
(2) process legitimacy,
(3) process peacefulness,
(4) humaneness and respect for individual dignity,
(5) personal privacy,
(6) consensualism,
(7) procedural fairness,
(8) the procedural rule of law,
(9) procedural rationality and
(10) timeliness and finality.

Participatory governance, which means government involving public participation, is rather general and is perhaps best thought of in terms of a legislative process value. Process legitimacy potentially covers legality, public assent or acquiescence, or moral respect. Professor Summers uses it to cover the second. This would apply to all three categories of process. Process peacefulness—the avoidance of violence and disorder—would mainly apply to legal administration and the judicial process. Humaneness and respect for personal privacy are self-explanatory. Consensualism shows a bias against coercion and in favour of voluntary behaviour. Humaneness, respect for privacy and consensualism could apply to all three aspects of process. Procedural fairness probably involves what the late J. L. Austin [11] would call a " trouser word " situation in that we often only know what is fair by identifying what is unfair and thus unfairness wears " the trousers," *i.e.* controls the definition. The " procedural rule of law " may mean that law officials are subject to rules or that there are mechanisms to ensure that they obey the rules. Procedural rationality, according to Professor Summers, covers the following maxims:

(1) carefully ascertain relevant evidence and canvass relevant argument,
(2) carefully weigh that evidence and argument,
(3) deliberate calmly and carefully,
(4) resolve issues impartially and solely on their merits

This is pre-eminently a value of the judicial process.

A number of the values identified by Professor Fuller and Professor Summers have in the past been subsumed under the concept of the rule of law. This is a vague concept as we have seen but was interpreted by Dicey [12] to cover amongst other things the supremacy of the law and equality before the law. During the past 40 years it has been fashionable to criticise Dicey's analysis but nevertheless the rule of law seems to survive as a supra-national concept in the western world, although there is an increasing tendency to define it in terms of recognition of certain basic human rights.[13] There is, as we shall see later, a growing desire to crystallise these into operative legal principles.

Substantive Legal Values

In addition to a general compliance with what we have described as the hallmarks of good legal craftsmanship the law gives differing degrees of recognition to certain substantive values.[14] Sometimes it does this by the crystallisation of an explicit legal principle such as "No man shall profit from his own wrong." Often these are then eroded by exceptions contained in particular legal rules, *e.g.* the recognition by the law of title to land arising from a period of adverse possession by squatters. More generally, however, a particular value is not crystallised as a defeasible universal in this way, but is given a measure of recognition in the sense that a number of legal rules and principles are laid down which are aimed towards it as a goal and the goal is on occasion used to explain or justify the particular rules or principles. (In these respects a system like the common law is an open system.) Law as a practical system is, however, concerned with social harmony in everyday life rather than the realisation of a utopia.

Bearing all this in mind let us try to discover what are examples of substantive legal values.

The Roman jurist, Ulpian, summed up the basic precepts of the law as being "*honeste vivere, alterum non laedere, suum cuique tribuere*" which being roughly translated means that the law should cause one to live honestly, not to harm another and to give to each man his due. Clearly, these values are rather general and vague. Nevertheless, they were adopted by Justinian's *Institutes* [15] which were produced as a manual for Roman law students and to a certain extent they are reflected in the content of modern writings.

As regards the basic values recognised within a modern legal system, Roscoe Pound[16] identified in 1910 what he called the "jural postulates" of American society. These comprised security of the person from intentional aggression; security of possession of property under the existing social order; good faith in transactions; due care not to cause unreasonable risk of injury upon others; and control of dangerous things. Pound intended these as the basic underlying assumptions of the law. In 1942, he updated the list to include job security and the absorption by society of risk of misfortune to individuals. The actual list has been attacked for being out-dated and for omitting important matters such as the sanctity of family life and the rule of law. Also, there is no attempt at ranking the postulates into any kind of hierarchy.

More recently, R. W. M. Dias has attempted to extract contemporary legal values from English case law. Like Pound, he has listed the sanctity of the person and property but he has also included the safety of the state, social welfare and equality (under which he subsumes justice). Last, he has included a miscellaneous quartet of fidelity to tradition, morality, convenience and international comity. It is obvious that there is a measure of overlap between some of them, for example between morality and justice. His overall conclusion based on a study of the English cases seems a reasonable one applicable to the whole of the United Kingdom, namely, that "national and social safety override all other considerations and sanctity of the person is superior to sanctity of property, but beyond this the pattern is kaleidoscopic, not hierarchical."[17]

Even more recently, Professor Peter Stein and John Shand in their book *Legal Values in Western Society*, have identified what appear to them to be the three master values of a western democratic legal system—law and order, justice and freedom of the individual. It is not altogether clear on what basis the choice has been made and indeed whether "law and order" is a value at all rather than a state of affairs. It appears, however, to be a reference to the rule of law. The other values which they identify are the values of life, privacy, property and certain other more particular values which they perceive in commercial transactions. They also mention briefly utility but do not rate it highly.

The United Kingdom is a party to the European Convention on Human Rights and the United Nations Declaration of Human

Rights, although these do not *per se* take internal effect.[18] The Convention and Declaration both set out basic statements of human rights to which the law should give effect. In some countries these rights take internal effect as law by virtue of a Bill of Rights or by automatic adoption of the Convention or Declaration. Currently there is active controversy [19] as to whether the United Kingdom should adopt an up-dated Bill of Rights to set out expressly these or similar basic values. It is argued that the remnants of Magna Carta, the Bill of Rights 1688 and the general law give inadequate recognition to these rights. Conversely it is argued that the adoption of a new Bill of Rights would give the British judiciary a more overtly political role, in that they could veto legislation, and this would be undesirable.

Further values against which legal development in the European Economic Community as a whole must now be measured are the socio-economic goals set out in Article 2 of the Treaty of Rome. The establishment of a Common Market and the approximation of economic policies in the Member States are simply the means to defined ends. The ends are the promotion of a harmonious development of economic activities; continuous and balanced expansion; an increase in stability; a raising of the standard of living and closer relations between Member States. These are goals and arguably values.

It can be seen from this summary that apart from the provisions of the Treaty of Rome which we have just considered there is no closed set of values operating in the United Kingdom and at present no firmly established hierarchy amongst them.[20]

Values and the Criteria of Rational Criticism

Lastly we have values which are used to criticise and evaluate the law. There is a certain amount of confusion in some legal literature in that it is not always clear whether a particular value is being used as an internal operative value of the law or as a criterion of external criticism. Some substantive values as we have seen are constantly referred to as values enshrined *in* the law. The problem arises because the common law is a pluralistic system which includes principles, and also because the analogical reasoning aspect of case law involves a process of justification. It is thus sometimes difficult to see clearly whether the particular discussion is concerned with law internally or the rational external evaluation of law.

Accepting the possible overlap in practice between particular values recognised (to differing degrees) internally and those used in the process of rational criticism, let us now concentrate on sets or systems of values used for the latter purpose. Values used for rational criticism need not belong to a set but in the past coherent criticism has tended to have been made on the basis of those which did. It is common to identify general values by their place in a particular religion or school of morality. Thus, for centuries in western countries the dominant values within this set were traditionally Christian values. Existing institutions such as law were evaluated by reference to Christian values. It must be admitted, however, that the exact values recognised by Christianity and their relationship to each other has sometimes been a matter of controversy and there is a general tendency amongst Christians to follow Christ's teaching to render unto Caesar the things which are Caesar's and unto God the things which are God's. In other words, Christianity for a variety of reasons has often been a fairly conservative influence.

In the nineteenth century, with the rise of the middle class and the growth of parliamentary democracy, the doctrine of utilarianism was developed by Bentham and others, as a secular system of values. This recognised the master value of utility: the promotion of the greatest happiness of the greatest number. The aim was to promote pleasure and to prevent pain. The interest of the community was, according to Bentham, " the sum of the interests of the several members who compose it." [21]

This principle provided a valuable criterion for the criticism of law and legal institutions in the nineteenth century. It was simple (indeed, it was oversimple in a number of respects) but at the time it appeared eminently reasonable to politicians of both parties. Consequently, it resulted in a great deal of constitutional and legal reform.

Nevertheless, it suffered from a number of defects which an apologist such as John Stuart Mill attempted to explain away in his famous essay on utilitarianism. The main criticisms were focused on its rationality as the basis of a system of private ethics. Later, some telling criticisms were made, drawing attention to certain possible totalitarian consequences which might follow if utility were to be the *sole* criterion of *public* morality. The interests of minorities and the underprivileged would suffer since utility is concerned with the interests of the majority. It has, however, never been effectively discredited as a basic criterion of law and legal institutions. Indeed, in its latter-day form of consumerism it has played an important part in the reasoning of the Law Commissions.[22]

Recently, at the level of ethics and political philosophy, utility has been challenged by Professor John Rawls [23] who has produced an alternative model of social values which attempts to combine the notion of social justice with that of individual freedom. In this model, the underprivileged are given a measure of preference. His theory rests on the hypothesis of a social contract entered into by men from whom are concealed by a veil of ignorance certain facts of life which motivate men away from equality.

The theory which is built on the foundations laid by the classical social contract philosophers and Kant uses the contract hypothesis as a justification of the rationality of the principles which are eventually chosen. In some ways, it is a simplified abstract reconstruction of the type of situation which led to the adoption of the American Constitution. The theory starting from this hypothesis arrives at two basic principles which are (in order of priority), first, each person is to have an equal right to the most extensive system of basic liberties compatible with a similar system of liberty for all and, secondly, social and economic inequalities are to be arranged so that they are attached to positions open to all, under conditions of equality of opportunity and are to the greatest benefit of the least privileged. It then proceeds to design the basic structure of institutions and practices in accordance with these principles.

The theory is complex and has many aspects. Numerous criticisms have been made of it which range from the basic intellectual techniques adopted to the minutiae of particular propositions. The most important criticisms for our purposes at this stage are centred on Rawls' notion of the veil of ignorance, which is a vast and crucial assumption to make, even in the postulation of a theory of this kind. A detailed analysis of the theory and the criticisms of it, however, must be postponed until later in your course of academic studies. It is sufficient to note at this stage that it represents the most elaborate analysis of the concept of justice that has been attempted in recent times and is the most coherent expression of a set of values for rational evaluation of law in a Western democratic society.

Values in Law Reform

The problem of identifying values is one which faces anybody charged with the task of law reform. Normally the role of such bodies is that of adviser to Government or Parliament. Other bodies which are influential in promoting particular reforms are specialised pressure groups whose task is to persuade rather than advise.

In its Second Annual Report published in 1973, the Law Reform Commission of Canada gave its views on the correct approach for a Law Reform Commission advising Government. In its opinion, the Commission, which was a small, unelected body consisting mainly of lawyers, had no mandate to impose its own values on the rest of society. At the same time, it did not seem right simply to view the matter as one for market research and public opinion polls. The correct approach seemed to be: first, discover legal values by looking at the law and its operation; secondly, consider whether these are the values which the public wants to see in their law; and, thirdly, consider whether the prevailing legal values in the particular law are the values which ought to be there and whose presence can be supported by rational argument. This seems a sensible and fair approach although the notion of rational argument is inevitably a little vague.

Priorities

A further problem faced by law reform bodies and indeed by everyone is: how does one determine priorities in values for the purposes of rational evaluation? As we saw earlier, sometimes where a particular value is recognised as a legal value, the law itself may postulate a value hierarchy, e.g. by a Bill of Rights or the general provisions of the Treaty of Rome. Generally, however, it does not do so and the matter has to be resolved in a pragmatic way. How then can the matter be dealt with outside the legal system in the rational criticism of law?

Bentham, as we saw, operated on the basis of a master value of utility. This was an all-embracing value rendered so because of his simplistic but elastic conceptions of happiness, pleasure and pain. Nonetheless, he found it necessary to devise what was called a *felicific calculus* in which he tried to reduce the qualities of intensity, duration, certainty, remoteness, fecundity and purity of pleasure to mathematical proportions.[24] This was rather absurd and one cannot subject values to such a precise analysis. Some argue in consequence that ordering of values is impossible or must always be based on an *ad hoc* intuitive choice.

Professor Rawls [25] has used a new method which he has described as lexical ordering of principles whereby one tries to give effect to one value before moving on to another. This seems to be an interesting approach with a useful practical application although opinions will always tend to differ on the original choice of order and also on questions of degree.

Questions of identifying particular values and weighing and ordering them are very much live issues today. The whole area represents an area of intellectual anarchy since the decline of the authority of the Church and of classical utilitarianism. Your teachers in the universities and polytechnics are stumbling around (some of them) groping for the answers. Pluralism and some ordering of values are not necessarily inconsistent as Professor Rawls has shown.[26] The legal system resists an immutable order and copes with the problems of evaluation from day to day and from case to case. It may be, rather paradoxically, that while frequently seeking the *criteria* of rational criticism outside the legal system we shall return at the end of the day to the operation of the legal system to understand more about the ultimate question of *weighing and ordering* those values we have discerned and accepted. A distinguished Belgian philosopher put it in this way—

" . . . in studying with attention and analysing with care the techniques of legal procedure and interpretation which permit men to live under the Rule of Law, the philosopher, instead of dreaming of the Utopia of an ideal society, can derive inspiration . . . from what secular experience has taught men, charged with the task of organising a reasonable society on earth." [27]

Notes

[1] *The Morality of Law*, Chap. II.

[2] See H. L. A. Hart's book review in 78 Harv.L.R. 1281 (1965) and R. S. Summers, " Professor Fuller on Morality and Law " (1965) 18 *Journal of Legal Education* 1, 24–27.

[3] *Supra*, Chap. 4.

[4] Friedrich Waismann, " Verifiability " in *The Theory of Meaning*, ed. by G. H. R. Parkinson, p. 38.

⁵ See W. Twining, *Karl Llewellyn and the American Realist Movement*, p. 505.

⁶ *Ibid.* p. 507.

⁷ Fuller, *op. cit.*, Chap. II.

⁸ *Ibid.* p. 91.

⁹ " Evaluating and Improving Legal Processes—A Plea for Process Values," 60 Cornell L.R. 1 (1974).

¹⁰ *Ibid.* p. 3.

¹¹ *Sense and Sensibilia*, p. 70.

¹² A. V. Dicey, *Law of the Constitution*, Chap. IV.

¹³ See *The Rule of Law and Human Rights, Principles and Definitions* (International Commission of Jurists) and Norman Marsh, " The Rule of Law as a Supra-National Concept " in *Oxford Essays in Jurisprudence* (1st series) ed. by A. G. Guest, Chap. IX.

¹⁴ *Cf.* R. Dworkin, " Is Law a System of Rules? " in *Essays in Legal Philosophy*, ed. by R. S. Summers, p. 25.

¹⁵ *The Institutes of Justinian*, Book I, tit. I 3–4 (translated by J. B. Moyle), p. 3.

¹⁶ See *Social Control Through Law*, pp. 112–116.

¹⁷ See R. W. M. Dias, *Jurisprudence* (4th ed.), p. 260.

¹⁸ It may, however, be legitimate to refer to the Convention in construing a statute—see *Waddington* v. *Miah* [1974] 1 W.L.R. 683 and *Birdi* v. *Secretary of State for Home Affairs* (1975) 119 S.J. 322. See the comments of P. Wallington [1975] C.L.J. 9, A. Drzemczewski [1976] 92 L.Q.R. 33 and Sir Leslie Scarman, *English Law: The New Dimension*, pp. 12, 13. Sir Leslie in fact suggests that since the passing of the European Communities Act 1972 the Convention may have become part of English law presumably because the European Court will refer to it.

¹⁹ See *Legislation in Human Rights*—a Discussion Document issued by the Home Office; Sir Leslie Scarman, *English Law—The New Dimension*, Part II; Michael Zander, *A Bill of Rights?* and Lord Lloyd of Hampstead, " Do We Need a Bill of Rights " (1976) 39 M.L.R. 121.

²⁰ See further M. D. A. Freeman, *The Legal Structure*, Chap. 4.

²¹ *Principles of Morals and Legislation*, Books I, IV.

²² See my *Law Reform and the Law Commission*, Chap. 6. See also L. C. B. Gower, " Reflections on Law Reform," U. of Toronto L.J. 257, 268 (1973).

²³ In his *Theory of Justice*.

²⁴ See Chap. IV of *Principles of Morals and Legislation*.

²⁵ *A Theory of Justice*, p. 43.

²⁶ *Ibid.* pp. 263–265.

²⁷ C. Perelman, *Justice et Raison*, p. 255 (my translation).

APPENDICES

1. Specimen Sources.

2. The Law Library, Legal Materials and Their Use.

3. The Case Law Process in Operation—The Conceptual Development of Negligence.

SPECIMEN SOURCES

Education Act 1975

1975 CHAPTER 2

An Act to make further provision with respect to awards and grants by local education authorities; to enable the Secretary of State to bestow awards on students in respect of their attendance at adult education colleges; and to increase the proportion of the expenditure incurred in the maintenance or provision of aided and special agreement schools that can be met by contributions or grants from the Secretary of State.

[25th February 1975]

BE IT ENACTED by the Queen's most Excellent Majesty, by and with the advice and consent of the Lords Spiritual and Temporal, and Commons, in this present Parliament assembled, and by the authority of the same, as follows:—

1.—(1) Section 1 of the Education Act 1962 (local education authority awards for designated first degree courses or comparable courses) shall apply also to such courses at universities, colleges or other institutions in Great Britain and Northern Ireland as may for the time being be designated by or under regulations made for the purposes of that section as being—

Awards and grants by local education authorities.
1962 c. 12.

> (a) full-time courses for the diploma of higher education or the higher national diploma; or
>
> (b) courses for the initial training of teachers.

(2) Paragraph (b) of subsection (1) of the said section 1 (eligibility for award dependent on possession of requisite educational qualifications) shall apply only in relation to courses for the time

---

1. Short Title.   **2.** Number.   **3.** Long Title.
4. Note absence of Preamble.   **5.** Date of the Act.   **6.** Enacting words.
7. Section.   **8.** Marginal note.   **9.** Subsection.

being designated for the purposes of that section as being comparable to first degree courses.

(3) Section 2(1) of the said Act of 1962 (local education authority awards for courses of further education not falling within section 1 of that Act) shall apply also to any course for the training of teachers (whether held in Great Britain or elsewhere) to which section 1 of that Act does not apply including, in relation to a person undergoing training as a teacher, any course which he attends as such training and which is for the time being designated under section 4 of the Education Act 1973 (postgraduate courses).

1973 c. 16.

(4) Subsections (2) and (3) of section 4 of the said Act of 1962 (regulations under sections 1 to 3 of that Act) shall apply also in relation to subsection (1) above; and subsection (6) of that section (meaning of " training " and " person undergoing training " in section 2 of that Act) shall apply also in relation to subsection (3) above.

10

Awards by Secretary of State for students at adult education colleges.
1962 c. 12.

1944 c. 31.
1962 c. 47.

2. In section 3 of the Education Act 1962 (awards by Secretary of State for certain courses) after paragraph (c) there shall be inserted—

" (d) to bestow awards on persons who, at such time as may be prescribed by the regulations, have attained such age as may be so prescribed, being awards in respect of their attendance at courses at any institution which—

(i) is in receipt of payments under section 100 of the Education Act 1944 or section 75 of the Education (Scotland) Act 1962; and

(ii) is designated by or under the regulations as a college providing long-term residential courses of full-time education for adults ";

and for the words " in the case of awards bestowed in accordance with paragraph (b) or paragraph (c) of this section " there shall be substituted the words " in the case of awards bestowed in accordance with paragraph (b), (c) or (d) of this section ".

Contributions and grants for aided and special agreement schools.
1967 c. 3.

3. In sections 102 and 103 of the Education Act 1944 and section 1(2) of the Education Act 1967 (contributions and grants by Secretary of State equal to or not exceeding four-fifths of certain expenses incurred in the maintenance or provision of aided and special agreement schools) for the words " four-fifths " there shall be substituted the words " 85 per cent.".

Repeals.

11

4. The enactments mentioned in the Schedule to this Act are hereby repealed to the extent specified in the third column of that Schedule.

---

10. Amendment Provision.   **11.** Repeal.

5.—(1) This Act may be cited as the Education Act 1975.

(2) The Education Acts 1944 to 1973 and this Act may be cited together as the Education Acts 1944 to 1975.

(3) Any reference in this Act to any enactment is a reference to that enactment as amended by any subsequent enactment.

(4) Subsection (2) of section 1 above shall not come into force until 1st September 1975; and subsection (3) of that section and Part I of the Schedule to this Act shall not come into force until the first regulations made by virtue of subsection (1)(*b*) of that section come into operation.

(5) Nothing in section 3 above or in Part II of the Schedule to this Act affects contributions or grants in respect of expenditure on work which was begun before 6th November 1974 or on the provision of the site on which, or buildings to which, any such work was done.

(6) This Act does not extend to Scotland or Northern Ireland.

Citation, interpretation, commencement and extent.

12

12. Area of operation.

SCHEDULE

Repeals

Part I

Chapter	Short Title	Extent of repeal
10 & 11 Eliz. 2. c. 12.	The Education Act 1962.	In section 2, in subsection (1) the words " (other than persons undergoing training as teachers) " and subsection (3).
1974 c. 7.	The Local Government Act 1974.	In section 1(5)(*b*) the words " or section 2(3) (grants to persons undergoing training as teachers) ". In section 8(2), paragraph (*b*) together with the word " and " immediately preceding that paragraph.

Part II

Chapter	Short Title	Extent of repeal
1967 c. 3.	The Education Act 1967.	Section 1(1).

PRINTED IN ENGLAND BY HAROLD GLOVER
Controller of Her Majesty's Stationery Office and Queen's Printer of Acts of Parliament

LONDON: PUBLISHED BY HER MAJESTY'S STATIONERY OFFICE

13. Schedule.

1

1974 No. 654

WAGES COUNCILS

2

The Boot and Floor Polish Wages Council (Great Britain) (Abolition) Order 1974

Made - - - -	1*st April* 1974
Laid before Parliament	10*th April* 1974
Coming into Operation	13*th May* 1974

3

Whereas the Secretary of State in accordance with section 4 of and Schedule 1 to the Wages Councils Act 1959(**a**) published notice of his intention to make an order abolishing the Boot and Floor Polish Wages Council (Great Britain):

And whereas no objection has been made with respect to the draft order referred to in the said notice:

Now, therefore, the Secretary of State in exercise of powers conferred by section 4(1)(*b*) of, and paragraph 4 of Schedule 1 to, the said Act and now vested in him (**b**), and of all other powers enabling him in that behalf, hereby makes the following Order:—

4

1. The Boot and Floor Polish Wages Council (Great Britain) is hereby abolished.

2.—(1) This Order may be cited as the Boot and Floor Polish Wages Council (Great Britain) (Abolition) Order 1974 and shall come into operation on 13th May 1974.

(2) The Interpretation Act 1889(**c**) shall apply to the interpretation of this Order as it applies to the interpretation of an Act of Parliament.

Signed by order of the Secretary of State.

5

1st April 1974.

6

Harold Walker,
Joint Parliamentary Under Secretary of State,
Department of Employment.

(**a**) 1959 c. 69.
(**b**) S.I. 1959/1769, 1968/729 (1959 I, p. 1795; 1968 II, p. 2108).
(**c**) 1889 c. 63.

---

1. Number.   **2.** Title.   **3.** Preamble.   **4.** Paragraph.
5. Date.   **6.** Signature.

EXPLANATORY NOTE
(This Note is not part of the Order.)

This Order abolishes the Boot and Floor Polish Wages Council (Great Britain), which was established as a Trade Board under the Trade Boards Acts 1909 and 1918 (c. 22 and c. 32), and became a Wages Council by virtue of the Wages Councils Act 1945 (c. 17).

The abolition of the Council was recommended by the Commission on Industrial Relations on the grounds that the Council is no longer necessary in order to maintain adequate pay and conditions for the workers in the boot and floor polish industry.

Printed in England by McCorquodale Printers Ltd., and published by Her Majesty's Stationery Office

A

[COURT OF APPEAL]

REGINA *v.* VENNA

1975 July 8, 17; 31   James and Ormrod L.JJ. and Cusack J.

B *Crime—Assault—Mens rea—Defendant's reckless behaviour causing
    injury to police officer—Whether recklessness sufficient mens
    rea for assault occasioning actual bodily harm*
   *Crime—Public order—Charge under Act—Disturbance at night
    by youths shouting and singing—Intervention by police—
    Threatening behaviour—Whether appropriate charge—Public
    Order Act 1936 (1 Edw. 8 & 1 Geo. 6, c. 6), s. 5*

C   The defendant and other youths created a disturbance in
    a street in the early hours of the morning and continued to
    do so after a police officer had tried to persuade them to go
    home. The officer placed his hand on one youth and said
    " You are all under arrest." Other police officers arrived and
    assisted in the arrest of the youths. While resisting arrest, the
    defendant fought violently, was knocked or fell to the ground
    and two officers held him by the arms. He continued to kick
    and, in doing so, fractured the hand of an officer who was
D   trying to pick him up. He was charged with threatening
    behaviour contrary to section 5 of the Public Order Act 1936
    and with assault occasioning actual bodily harm. He was
    convicted.
        On appeal against conviction on the ground, inter alia,
    that the judge erred in law in directing the jury that the mental
    element of recklessness was enough, when coupled with the
    actus reus of physical contact, to constitute the offence of
E   assault occasioning actual bodily harm:—
        Held, dismissing the appeal, that recklessness in the use
    of force was sufficient to satisfy the mental element necessary
    to form the intent to commit a criminal assault and, accord-
    ingly, the judge had correctly directed the jury that a physical
    injury inflicted deliberately or recklessly constituted the offence
    of assault occasioning actual bodily harm (post, pp. 428H—
    429B).
F   *Ackroyd* v. *Barett* (1894) 11 T.L.R. 115, D.C. and *Fagan*
    v. *Metropolitan Police Commissioner* [1969] 1 Q.B. 439, D.C.
    considered.
        Per curiam. The behaviour of the defendant and his
    friends was not the sort of incident that Parliament had in
    mind when enacting the Public Order Act 1936. The court
    is not prepared to say that it was wrong in this case to prefer
    a charge under the Act but those who have the responsibility
G   of deciding what charges to prefer should consider very care-
    fully, before having recourse to section 5 of the Act, whether
    the facts reveal a state of affairs which justifies proceedings
    under that statute (post, p. 425B–E).

The following cases are referred to in the judgment:

Ackroyd v. *Barett* (1894) 11 T.L.R. 115, D.C.
H *Fagan* v. *Metropolitan Police Commissioner* [1969] 1 Q.B. 439; [1968]
        3 W.L.R. 1120; [1968] 3 All E.R. 442, D.C.

[Reported by MISS EIRA CARYL-THOMAS, Barrister-at-Law]

---

1. The Court.   **2.** Date.   **3.** Headnote.   **4.** Cases cited.

422

Kenlin v. *Gardiner* [1967] 2 Q.B. 510; [1967] 2 W.L.R. 129; [1966]
   3 All E.R. 931, D.C.   A

Reg. v. *Ambrose* (1973) 57 Cr.App.R. 538, C.A.

Reg. v. *Bradshaw* (1878) 14 Cox C.C. 83.

Reg. v. *Cunningham* [1957] 2 Q.B. 396; [1957] 3 W.L.R. 76; [1957]
   2 All E.R. 412, C.C.A.

Reg. v. *Duffy* [1967] 1 Q.B. 63; [1966] 2 W.L.R. 229; [1966] 1 All
   E.R. 62, C.C.A.

Reg. v. *Fennell* [1971] 1 Q.B. 428; [1970] 3 W.L.R. 513; [1970] 3 All   B
   E.R. 215, C.A.

Reg. v. *Lamb* [1967] 2 Q.B. 981; [1967] 3 W.L.R. 888; [1967] 2 All
   E.R. 1282, C.A.

Rex v. *Osmer* (1804) 5 East 304.

The following additional cases were cited in argument:

Christie v. *Leachinsky* [1947] A.C. 573; [1947] 1 All E.R. 567, H.L.(E.).   C

Reg. v. *Chisam* (1963) 47 Cr.App.R. 130, C.C.A.

Reg. v. *Martin* (1881) 8 Q.B.D. 54.

Reg. v. *Wilson* [1955] 1 W.L.R. 493; [1955] 1 All E.R. 744, C.C.A.

Reg. v. *Wood* (1859) 1 F. & F. 470.

APPEAL against conviction.

On December 6, 1974, at Gloucester Crown Court (Judge Bulger), the   D
defendant, Henson George Venna, was convicted of using threatening
behaviour in a public place whereby a breach of the peace was likely to be
occasioned, contrary to section 5 of the Public Order Act 1936, and of
an assault occasioning actual bodily harm to a police officer. A co-
defendant, Edwards, was also convicted of threatening behaviour and
assault on a police constable, contrary to section 5 (1) of the Police Act
1964. The co-defendant, Allison, was acquitted of criminal damage to a   E
police officer's uniform and threatening behaviour. At the close of the
prosecution case, by direction of Judge Bulger, a third co-defendant,
Robinson, was acquitted of the charge of threatening behaviour. The
defendant appealed against conviction on the grounds, inter alia, that his
conviction was inconsistent with the acquittals of the co-defendants Allison
and Robinson; that the judge had wrongly left to the jury the question   F
whether the defendant, Edwards and Allison had been guilty of threatening behaviour, and that the judge had erred in law in directing the jury
that the mental element of recklessness was enough, when coupled with
the actus reus of physical contact, to constitute the battery involved in
assault occasioning actual bodily harm. On July 17, 1975, the Court of
Appeal dismissed the appeal, but reserved their reasons.

The facts are stated in the judgment.   G

Jonathan Woods for the defendant. The jury were directed that, to
constitute the mens rea of assault, recklessness is sufficient. The direction
was wrong in law because the intention to do the physical act, the subject
matter of the charge, is necessary to constitute the offence and that element
was not left to the jury.   H

[CUSACK J. If someone lashes out and lands a blow, are you saying
that no offence was committed? The defendant's mind was going with
his feet; he kicked out and intended to do so.]

---

5. Nature of Appeal.   **6.** Summary of earlier proceeding.
7. Summary of Counsel's arguments.

A   Intent to make contact is necessary. The defence of accident is of course not available if A is struck when B was aimed at.

An assault is not established by proof of a deliberate act which had consequences which were not intended: *Reg.* v. *Lamb* [1967] 2 Q.B. 981. Recklessness is not sufficient to constitute the mens rea in battery: *Ackroyd* v. *Barett* (1894) 11 T.L.R. 115. Since there is no authority to the contrary any extension to the law must be made by the legislature. There

B   is a distinction where offences are assaults which by statute include the element of " malice," e.g., unlawfully and maliciously wounding, contrary to section 20 of the Offences against the Person Act 1861: there recklessness is sufficient to support the charge (*Reg.* v. *Cunningham* [1957] 2 Q.B. 396). [Reference was made to *Glanville Williams' Criminal Law*, 2nd ed. (1961), para. 27, p. 65; *Smith and Hogan, Criminal Law*, 3rd ed. (1973),

C   pp. 284, 286; *Kenny's Outlines of Criminal Law*, 19th ed. (1966), paras. 157 and 158, p. 210 and para. 164, p. 218; and *Russell on Crime*, 12th ed. (1964), pp. 652, 656.] Reliance is also placed on what was said in *Fagan* v. *Metropolitan Police Commissioner* [1969] 1 Q.B. 439.

On the question of the right to resist unlawful arrest and how much force may be used, see *Christie* v. *Leachinsky* [1947] A.C. 573; *Reg.* v. *Wood* (1859) 1 F & F. 470; *Reg.* v. *Wilson* [1955] 1 W.L.R. 493 and

D   *Kenlin* v. *Gardiner* [1967] 2 Q.B. 510. On the question of the right to assist others who are being arrested unlawfully, see *Reg.* v. *Duffy* [1967] 1 Q.B. 63; *Rex* v. *Osmer* (1804) 5 East 304; *Reg.* v. *Fennell* [1971] 1 Q.B 428 and *Reg.* v. *Chisam* (1963) 47 Cr.App.R. 130.

Francis Barnes for the Crown (on the question of recklessness). The jury were told that either intention or recklessness would do. " Recklessness" is sufficient: *Reg.* v. *Martin* (1881) 8 Q.B.D. 54, 58. If a man

E   foresees that injury is likely to follow a deliberate act, but nevertheless he commits the act and injury results therefrom, that will suffice to constitute the offence: *Reg.* v. *Cunningham* [1957] 2 Q.B. 396. It would not be appropriate that different criteria, so far as mens rea is concerned, should apply to assaults occasioning actual bodily harm (section 47 of the Offences against the Person Act 1861) and malicious wounding (section 20 of the

F   Act of 1861), merely because the adverb " maliciously " does not appear in section 47. If, as on the authorities it does, recklessness suffices for wounding, it should also suffice for assaults. It would not be right that liability should depend upon what might be a matter of mere chance, whether the skin of the victim was broken or not; e.g., whether a bone fracture were simple or compound.

G   The conviction on count 2 supports the finding of lawful arrest. The appellant, therefore, went to Allison's rescue at his own peril.

Cur. adv. vult.

8

9

H   July 31. JAMES L.J. read the judgment of the court. This is an appeal against conviction by the defendant who, on December 6, 1974, in the Crown Court at Gloucester, was convicted of threatening behaviour contrary to section 5 of the Public Order Act 1936 and of an assault occasioning actual bodily harm. A co-defendant, Edwards, was also convicted of threatening behaviour and of an assault on a police constable

---

8. Reserved judgment.   **9.** Judgment.

Reg. v. Venna (C.A.) [1976]

contrary to section 51 (1) of the Police Act 1964, of which he was
separately charged. Another co-defendant, Allison, separately charged with A
criminal damage to a police officer's uniform, was acquitted of that offence
and also of the charge of threatening behaviour. The third co-defendant,
Robinson, charged only with the offence of threatening behaviour was
acquitted by direction of the trial judge at the close of the prosecution
case.

Mr. Woods for the defendant relied substantially upon the acquittals B
of Allison and Robinson and argued that the convictions of the defendant
are inconsistent with those acquittals.

The various charges against the four defendants arose out of an
incident which occurred in the early hours of August 30, 1974, in Station
Road, Gloucester. The four defendants and another youth called
Patterson, who was not arrested, were creating a disturbance in the public
street by shouting and singing and dancing. At one stage there was a C
banging of dustbin lids. The local residents were disturbed and at least
one complaint of the noise was made to the police. A police officer named
Leach went to investigate. What took place between him and the youths
was described in evidence by three taxi drivers. Leach patiently and
tactfully tried to persuade the four youths to be quiet and to go home.
The response was a remark by Robinson, " Fuck off," and the continua- D
tion of the noise and dancing. Leach told them there had already been a
complaint about their unruly behaviour and ordered them on their way.
Robinson thereafter stood apart from the others and did nothing. That
was the foundation of his subsequent acquittal. The others continued a
sort of war dance and went on singing. Leach told them that if they
continued to create a disturbance and obstruct the pavement they would
be arrested. Allison in defiance sat down on the pavement. Leach moved E
towards him to arrest him and the defendant, Edwards and Patterson
crowded around. As he placed his hand on Allison, Leach said, " You
are all under arrest.""

The defendant's evidence at the trial was that he did not hear these
words and did not appreciate that he was being arrested until a later
stage of the incident. As Leach picked Allison up, Allison struggled to F
free himself and the defendant, Edwards and Patterson tried to pull
Allison out of the officer's grip. Leach held on to Allison and called for
help on his pocket radio. The scene was such that the taxi drivers were
about to intervene. A passer-by, referred to as " the fat man," did intervene on the officer's behalf. The defendant in evidence surmised that he
did so because " he thought the copper's head might be bashed in." Other
police officers arrived and assisted Leach in the arrest of the defendant G
and the co-defendants. Before those who were resisting arrest were
finally overpowered, Allison had torn Leach's uniform, Edwards had
seized Leach's left thumb and bent it forcibly backwards causing physical
injury, and the defendant had fought so violently that four officers were
required to restrain him. In the course of the defendant's struggles he
was knocked or fell to the ground. Two police officers held him by the H
arms. On the defendant's own admission he then knew he was being
arrested and he continued to " lash out " wildly with his legs. In doing
so he kicked the hand of a police officer who was trying to pick him

---

10. Judgment summarizes facts.

A up. The kick caused a fracture of a bone and was the subject of the charge of assault occasioning actual bodily harm.

The defendant's evidence was to the effect that he and his friends were not told that they were creating a disturbance and that all he had done was to tell Leach that he could not arrest Allison. He said that he had been struck on the chin and knocked to the ground and that he had lashed out with his feet in an effort to get up. He did not know or

B suspect that there was a police officer in the way or that his foot might strike a police officer's hand.

The whole incident leading to the charges was, unfortunately, a very ordinary and all too common one. On any view the defendant and his friends were behaving in an unruly and disgraceful anti-social manner, but it was not a very grave or serious incident. It was certainly not the sort of incident that Parliament had in mind when enacting the Public

C Order Act 1936. We are not prepared to say that in this case it was wrong to prefer a charge under the provisions of that Act. The jury did find that there was threatening behaviour and, although the police officer, Leach, agreed in evidence that he did not think the initial behaviour was threatening he made the arrest on the basis of belief that a breach of the peace was imminent.

D There was ample evidence on which the jury could find that there was behaviour within the terms of section 5. But those who have the responsibility of deciding what charges to prefer should consider very carefully, before having recourse to section 5 of ·the Public Order Act 1936, whether the facts reveal a state of affairs which justifies proceedings under that statute. In *Reg.* v. *Ambrose* (1973) 57 Cr.App.R. 538, 540, Lawton L.J. issued a clear warning against the misuse of section 5 of the

E Act, which warning we repeat. In the end this comparatively minor matter occupied the time of the Crown Court for four days and the argument in this court extended into a second day.

The argument for the defendant was first that the judge erred in law in his directions to the jury in a number of respects, and was wrong, having regard to the state of the evidence and the way the case was put

F for the prosecution, to leave to the jury the question whether the defendant, Edwards and Allison had been guilty of threatening behaviour and to invite the jury to consider whether the conduct of the defendant, after the point of time when the officer said, "You are all under arrest," was threatening behaviour. This argument drew together a number of the heads enumerated in the grounds of appeal. It was essentially dependent upon the premise that the arrest of Allison was unlawful.

G The pattern of summing up suggested to the jury that they could regard the incident as comprising two stages separated by the arrest of the defendants; that they might reach the conclusion, as the judge expressly stated he had done, that up to the time of arrest there was little if any threatening behaviour; that on that view of the facts the jury might think that Leach, who had said that the arrest was made under his powers derived

H from section 7 (3) of the Public Order Act 1936, had made the arrest technically for the wrong reason; and that the jury, if they so found, should approach the case on the basis that the arrest was unlawful. The judge then gave directions to the jury upon the duty of a person purport-

11

---

11. Judgment then summarizes Counsel's arguments.

ing to effect an arrest to make known to the person arrested the reason A
for the arrest, upon the right of a person to resist an unlawful arrest, and
upon the right of a person to assist another who is the subject of an
unlawful arrest to free himself from the unlawful restraint.

We find it unnecessary to recite the argument of Mr. Woods on this
aspect of the appeal in any detail. The judge had rightly told the jury
that they were not bound to accept the police officer's opinion as to
whether there was threatening behaviour prior to the arrest. He B
correctly directed the jury as to what constitutes threatening behaviour,
that noise is not enough and that the behaviour has to be menacing or
alarming in relation to a breach of the peace. He reminded them of the
evidence of the taxi drivers.

In our view the judge rightly left the evidence to the jury on the
charge of threatening behaviour in relation to the time before the arrest,
although he said he was not impressed by the evidence and although he C
had in the exercise of his discretion directed a verdict of not guilty in
respect of Robinson. The jury reached the conclusion that the evidence
established threatening behaviour before the arrest. This is clear not
only from the verdicts of guilty on count 1 but also, and conclusively
from the verdict of guilty, of the charge of assaulting a police officer in
the execution of his duty in relation to Edwards. That verdict could be D
returned only if the jury had decided that the arrest was a lawful arrest.

The argument pressed in this court that the jury were or may have
been returning a verdict of guilty of common assault because of the form
in which the court clerk asked for the verdict is simply not tenable.
The jury had a copy of the indictment. They had agreed on the verdict
before the clerk put the question. There was no room for confusion.
At the trial it was accepted that the jury's verdict on count 2 must be E
construed as a finding that the arrest was lawful.

What Mr. Woods was able to do was to point to the acquittal of
Allison on count 1 and to the evidence which, on the face of it, implicated
Allison as much as, if not more, than the other defendants in their
behaviour before arrest. We think there is force in the argument that
the verdict in respect of Allison is inconsistent with the verdicts in F
respect of the defendant. It does not follow that the verdicts in
respect of the defendant are unsafe or unsatisfactory. Due to the pattern
of the summing up Allison may well have been regarded by the jury
as the one defendant remaining in their charge who did not strike a blow
or aim kicks from first to last and as one who, although he sat down on
the pavement, did not himself directly threaten a breach of the peace.

The terms in which the case against Allison was summed up were G
such as the jury may have construed to be an invitation to acquit. This
may have been unduly favourable to Allison. It does not afford a basis
for thinking the verdicts in respect of the defendant are unsafe or unsatisfactory. Mr. Woods invited our attention to authorities both old
and recent in order to demonstrate that the judge misdirected the jury
by telling them as a matter of law that, whereas a person who is unlaw- H
fully arrested may reasonably resist the arrest, a person is not entitled to
go to the aid of another who is unlawfully arrested unless he genuinely
believes that other person to be in imminent danger of physical injury,

A and by directing the jury in terms which by use of the word "resist" put too low a standard on the right to match force with force. The authorities cited such as *Rex* v. *Osmer* (1804) 5 East 304; *Kenlin* v. *Gardiner* [1967] 2 Q.B. 510 and *Reg.* v. *Duffy* [1967] 1 Q.B. 63 have no relevance to a situation in which the arrest is a lawful arrest.

Mr. Barnes for the Crown argued that in any event the directions of the judge were correct in law and cited *Reg.* v. *Fennell* [1971] 1 Q.B.
B 428 in support. We do not find it necessary to decide in this case whether the directions of the judge in relation to these matters were right or wrong. The finding of fact by the jury that the arrest was lawful is conclusive.

The jury having found the arrest to be a lawful arrest were not concerned with the directions given by the judge as to the right to resist
C arrest or the right to assist a person resisting an unlawful arrest. The finding that the arrest was lawful presupposes a finding of threatening behaviour before the arrest and there was no reason why the jury should not regard the evidence of behaviour of the defendant after the moment Allison was seized by the officer as part and parcel of the same incident. It was not suggested in this court nor was it suggested at the trial that the defendant could be acting lawfully if, contrary to his own evidence,
D he tried to release Allison from the lawful custody of Leach.

The second substantial ground of appeal relates to the conviction of assault occasioning actual bodily harm. Having summed up to the jury the issue of self defence in relation to the alleged assault the judge directed them in these terms:

E "However, you would still have to consider, on this question of assault by Venna, whether it was an accident. If he is lashing out . . . Let me put it this way. Mr. Woods on behalf of Venna says 'Well, he is not guilty of an assault because it was neither intentional nor reckless. It was a pure accident that he happened to hit the officer,' and that is quite right. If you hit somebody accidentally, it cannot be a criminal offence so you have got to ask
F yourselves, 'Was this deliberate, or was it reckless?' If it was, then he is guilty. To do an act deliberately hardly needs explanation. If you see somebody in front of you and you deliberately kick him on the knee, that is a deliberate act and, no two ways about it, that is an assault but it can equally well be an assault if you are lashing out, knowing that there are people in the neighbourhood or that
G there are likely to be people in the neighbourhood and, in this case, it is suggested that he had two people by his arms and he knew that he was being restrained so as to lead to arrest. If he lashes out with his feet, knowing that there are officers about him and knowing that by lashing out he will probably or is likely to kick somebody or hurt his hand by banging his heel down on it, then
H he is equally guilty of the offence. Venna can therefore be guilty of the offence in count 3 in the indictment if he deliberately brought his foot down on Police Constable Spencer's hand or if he lashed out simply reckless as to who was there, not caring an iota as to

Reg. v. Venna (C.A.)   [1976]

whether he kicked somebody or brought his heel down on his   A
hands."

Mr. Woods argued that the direction is wrong in law because it
states that the mental element of recklessness is enough, when coupled
with the actus reus of physical contact, to constitute the battery involved
in assault occasioning actual bodily harm. Recklessness, it is argued, is
not enough; there must be intention to do the physical act the subject   B
matter of the charge. Counsel relied on *Reg.* v. *Lamb* [1967] 2 Q.B.
981 and argued that an assault is not established by proof of a deliberate
act which gives rise to consequences which are not intended.

In *Fagan* v. *Metropolitan Police Commissioner* [1969] 1 Q.B. 439,
444, it was said:

" An assault is any act which intentionally—or possibly recklessly—
causes another person to apprehend immediate and unlawful personal   C
violence."

In *Fagan* it was not necessary to decide the question whether proof of
recklessness is sufficient to establish the mens rea ingredient of assault.
That question falls for decision in the present case. Why it was considered necessary for the Crown to put the case forward on the alternative bases of " intention " and " recklessness " is not clear to us. This   D
resulted in the direction given in the summing up.

On the evidence of the defendant himself one would have thought
that the inescapable inference was that the defendant intended to make
physical contact with whoever might try to restrain him. Be that as it
may, in the light of the direction given, the verdict may have been
arrived at on the basis of " recklessness." Mr. Woods cited *Ackroyd* v.   E
Barett (1894) 11 T.L.R. 115 in support of his argument that recklessness,
which falls short of intention, is not enough to support a charge of
battery, and argued that, there being no authority to the contrary, it is
now too late to extend the law by a decision of the courts and that any
extension must be by the decision of Parliament.

Mr. Woods sought support from the distinction between the offences   F
which are assaults and offences which by statute include the element
contained in the word " maliciously," e.g. unlawful and malicious wounding contrary to section 20 of the Offences against the Person Act 1861,
in which recklessness will suffice to support the charge: see *Reg.* v.
Cunningham [1957] 2 Q.B. 396. In so far as the editors of textbooks
commit themselves to an opinion on this branch of the law they are
favourable to the view that recklessness is or should logically be sufficient   G
to support the charge of assault or battery: see *Glanville Williams
Criminal Law,* 2nd ed. (1961), para. 27, p. 65; *Kenny's Outlines of the
Criminal Law,* 19th ed. (1966), para. 164, p. 218; *Russell on Crime,* 12th
ed. (1964), p. 656 and *Smith and Hogan, Criminal Law,* 3rd ed. (1973),
p. 286.

12

We think that the decision in *Ackroyd* v. *Barett* is explicable on the   H
basis that the facts of the case did not support a finding of recklessness.
The case was not argued for both sides. *Reg.* v. *Bradshaw* (1878) 14
Cox C.C. 83 can be read as supporting the view that unlawful physical

---

12. *Ackroyd* v. *Barett* distinguished.

A force applied recklessly constitutes a criminal assault. In our view the element of mens rea in the offence of battery is satisfied by proof that the defendant intentionally or recklessly applied force to the person of another. If it were otherwise the strange consequence would be that an offence of unlawful wounding contrary to section 20 of the Offences against the Person Act 1861 could be established by proof that the defendant wounded the victim either intentionally or recklessly but, if the

B victim's skin was not broken and the offence was therefore laid as an assault occasioning actual bodily harm contrary to section 47 of the Act, it would be necessary to prove that the physical force was intentionally applied.

We see no reason in logic or in law why a person who recklessly applies physical force to the person of another should be outside the

C criminal law of assault. In many cases the dividing line between intention and recklessness is barely distinguishable. This is such a case. In our judgment the direction was right in law and this ground of appeal fails.

There are other grounds of appeal which we do not propose to consider in detail. In particular it was contended that the judge did not put

D the defence that the defendant had the right to use force which matched the unlawful use of force, and that the issue of failure to inform the defendant of the reason for his arrest, which bore on the lawfulness of his arrest, was in effect withdrawn from the jury. There is no substance in the argument advanced in support of these grounds. The finding that Leach was acting in the execution of his duty and lawfully is an insuperable obstacle in the defendant's path.

E For these reasons we dismissed the appeal.

13

Appeal dismissed.

Solicitors: *Registrar of Criminal Appeals; G. R. Archer, Gloucester.*

F

G

———

H

———

13. Order.

1975
—
Auditeur
du Travail
(Mons) v.
Cagnon
—
European
Court
of Justice

1 AUDITEUR DU TRAVAIL AT THE TRIBUNAL DE
MONS *v.* CAGNON AND TAQUET (Case 69/74)

BEFORE THE COURT OF JUSTICE OF THE EUROPEAN COMMUNITIES

2

(*The President*, Judge R. Lecourt; Judges J. Mertens de Wilmars,
Lord Mackenzie Stuart, A. M. Donner, R. Monaco, P. Pescatore,
H. Kutscher, M. Sørensen and A. O'Keeffe.) Herr Gerhard Reischl,
Advocate General.   18 February 1975

Reference by the Tribunal de Police de Mons under **Article 177** EEC.

3

Road transport. Driving conditions. Daily rest periods. In
Article 11 (2) of the Road Transport (Driving Conditions)
Regulation (543/69), the phrase ' every crew member... shall
have had ... a ... rest period ' of at least 10 consecutive hours
means that the provisions on daily rest must be observed both
by the crew members (*e.g.*, drivers) themselves, who are required
to stop all activities referred to in Article 14 of the Regulation
for the minimum period laid down, and also by the employer
running a road transport undertaking, who is required to take
the necessary measures to permit the crew members to have the
daily rest laid down. [10]

The Court interpreted Article 11 (2) of Regulation 543/69 (the Road
Transport (Driving Conditions) Regulation 1969) to the effect that its
provisions relating to a daily rest period are binding not only on the
employer but also on the drivers of road transport vehicles.

> *Marc Sohier*, legal adviser to the E.C. Commission, for the
> Commission as *amicus curiae*.
> *Maître Detaeye* for the defendants.

No cases were referred to.

Facts

4   Article 11 (2), first paragraph, of Council Regulation 543/69 of
25 March 1969 on the harmonisation of certain social legislation
relating to road transport provides:

---

1. Case name.   **2.** Court.   **3.** Headnote.   **4.** Summary of facts.

'Every crew member engaged in the carriage of passengers shall have had, during the twenty-four-hour period preceding any time when he is performing any activity covered by Article 14 (2) (c) or (d):
—a daily rest period of not less than ten consecutive hours, which shall not be reduced during the week, or
...'

1975
—
*Auditeur
du Travail
(Mons)* v.
Cagnon

European
Court
of Justice

Article 14 (2) (c) of the same regulation refers to ' driving periods '.

The present proceedings result from an action pending before the Tribunal de Police de Mons in which the Auditeur du Travail (at the Tribunal du Travail de Mons) is prosecuting Jean-Pierre Cagnon, coach driver, as the defendant and Jean-Paul Taquet, his employer who is civilly and jointly liable. In the summons the defendant is charged with not having complied with the provisions of the first paragraph of Article 11 (2) of the aforementioned Council Regulation 543/69 of 25 March 1969 and of section 2 of the Belgian Royal Decree of 23 March 1970 implementing the said regulation by reason of the fact that during a trip to Germany,

' being a member of a crew engaged in the carriage of passengers, not having had, during the twenty-four-hour period preceding any time when he is performing an activity covered by Article 14 (2) (c) of Regulation 543/69, a daily rest period of not less than ten consecutive hours.'

During the main proceedings the defendant did not dispute the facts with which he was charged, but objected that the Community provision in question did not involve any obligation on his part in that it was only employers who were bound to respect the daily rest period and not crew members of road vehicles.

The Tribunal de Police de Mons found first of all that since the defence raised by the employer, according to which Mr. Cagnon had been instructed to spend the night at Dortmund, the destination of the vehicle driven by the defendant, had not been challenged, there was no misconduct on the part of Mr. Taquet. It then stated that the defence related to the interpretation of the first paragraph of Article 11 (2) of Regulation 543/69 since it was a question of whether ' the driver must have had the possibility of taking the rest laid down by the legislation or whether, on the other hand, he is required to respect the regulation, that is to say, to have in fact rested '.

Following a suggestion by the prosecutor to request the Court of Justice to give a ruling on the question of interpretation thus raised, the Tribunal de Police de Mons by judgment of 6 September 1974 stayed the proceedings and referred to the Court of Justice under Article 177 of the EEC Treaty the question:

' What is the meaning of the words " shall have had . . . a . . . rest period " in the first paragraph of Article 11 (2) of Regulation 543/69.'

1975

*Auditeur
du Travail
(Mons)* v.
Cagnon

European
Court
of Justice
—
Submissions
(Reischl
A.G.)

Submissions of the Advocate General (Herr Gerhard Reischl)

In connection with a case pending before it, the Tribunal de Police de Mons has requested the Court's interpretation of a provision of Council Regulation 543/69 on the harmonisation of certain legislation relating to road transport.

That regulation, which *inter alia* was made to implement a common transport policy on the basis of **Article 75** of the EEC Treaty, provides—in so far as we are concerned here—in Article 11 (2) that every crew member engaged in the carriage of passengers shall have had, during the 24-hour period preceding any time when he is performing any activity covered by Article 14 (2) (c) or (d) (that is driving or attending at work) a daily rest period of not less than 10 consecutive hours, which shall not be reduced during the week. Article 14 (2) of the regulation further provides that members of the crew shall enter in the daily sheets of the individual control book details *inter alia* of breaks from work of not less than 15 minutes. It is the task of the member-States under Article 18 of the regulation to adopt such laws, regulations or administrative provisions as may be necessary for the implementation of the regulation and such measures have to cover, *inter alia*, penalties to be imposed in case of breach.

A Royal Decree was accordingly issued on 23 March 1970 in Belgium. Section 3 thereof refers to section 2 of the Transport Treaties Implementation Act of 18 February 1969 (*Loi relative aux mesures d'exécution des traités et actes internationaux en matière de transport par route, par chemin de fer ou par voie navigable*) and declares that infringements of the said Council regulation are punishable in a certain manner.

Criminal proceedings were brought against Jean-Pierre Cagnon, coach driver, and his employer, Jean-Paul Taquet, transport contractor, under those provisions. Apart from failure to enter breaks from work of not less than 15 minutes under Article 14 (2) of the Council regulation, an infringement which does not concern us further here, the former is charged with being engaged in the carriage of passengers in Germany and not having had, during the 24-hour period preceding the time when he was performing his activity, a daily rest period of not less than 10 consecutive hours. The employer, who stated that the driver had been directed to spend the night in question at the destination in Germany, was, in view of his evidence, not criminally liable. Should the driver indeed have committed an infringement in performing the work entrusted to him by the employer, the latter would, however, be jointly liable under section 2 (4) of the Act of 18 February 1969 for all the fines imposed on the driver, and the costs of the proceedings. This is the reason that he was not dismissed from the case.

The accused driver's main defence to the proceedings was the argument that Article 11 (2) of the regulation gave rise to obligations

5. Submissions of Advocate General.

1975
—
*Auditeur
du Travail
(Mons)* v.
Cagnon
—
European
Court
of Justice
—
Submissions
(Reischl
A.G.)

only on the part of the employer and not the crew members. He alleged that it was sufficient under this provision for the employer to see that the possibility existed of taking the daily rest period and that it was not necessary for crew members in fact to rest. If this interpretation were correct, it would obviously not be possible after the statements made in the main proceedings to impose penalties on the accused driver.

In view of these facts, which require an interpretation of Regulation 543/69, the Tribunal de Police de Mons considered it proper to stay the proceedings by the order of 6 September 1974 and to refer for a preliminary ruling under **Article 177** of the EEC Treaty the question of how the words ' shall have had . . . a . . . rest period ' in Article 11 (2) of Regulation 543/69 are to be understood.

Only the Commission of the European Communities has made observations on this question. It has recommended an interpretation according to which Article 11 of the regulation also imposes an obligation on crew members actually to observe the daily rest periods, that is breaks from the activities referred to in Article 14 (2) (c) or (d).

I find this view and reasons convincing and propose that the Court should adopt them.

First it is important to maintain that the provision requiring interpretation is part of a regulation, that is a document which under **Article 189** of the EEC Treaty has general application, is binding in its entirety and directly applicable in all member-States.

The Commission is also right in stating that the wording of Article 11 (2) makes it clear that there is an obligation not only on the transport contractor to provide the possibility of having daily rest periods but also on the crew members actually to observe the provisions on daily rest periods. In fact it is stated in Article 11 (2) —so far as it concerns us here: ' every crew member engaged in the carriage of passengers shall have had, during the twenty-four hours preceding any time when he is performing any activity covered by Article 14 (2) (c) or (d): a daily rest period of not less than ten consecutive hours, which shall not be reduced during the week. . . . ' This provision would certainly have been differently worded if it had been the intention of the draftsman of the regulation simply to require the transport contractors to give their drivers the possibility of daily rest periods. Daily rest periods within the meaning of Article 11 of the regulation—as the Commission likewise rightly stresses—must be contrasted with the driving periods and other periods of attendance at work mentioned in Article 11 by reference to Article 14. This means that crew members doubtless have a certain freedom in how they use their rest periods; what however is ruled out, in any event, is driving activity and attendance at work.

The correctness of this interpretation does not appear from Article 11 (2) alone. Support is obtained from a glance at Articles 7 and 8

1975
—
*Auditeur
du Travail
(Mons)* v.
Cagnon
—
European
Court
of Justice
—
Judgment
(Monaco J.)

of the regulation, in which the limitation on driving periods is related to the daily rest periods. This accords with the interpretation that there is a direct and clear obligation on crew members to respect not only the driving periods but also the rest periods.

Finally, the objectives of the regulation as expressed in its pre-amble must not be forgotten. The objective is the harmonisation of certain provisions affecting competition in transport by rail, road and inland waterway, as is shown by the reference to the Council Decision of 13 May 1965.[1] Reference is made to the promotion of ' social progress ' and, not least, to the improvement of road safety. It appears to me quite obvious that these objectives could not be achieved if Article 11, as the accused in the main proceedings thinks, were limited to providing the possibility of observing the rest periods. In such circumstances nothing would be done for the harmonisation of the provisions affecting competition and certainly no improve-ment in road safety would be achieved, nor could there be any promotion of social progress but rather regression in comparison with the previous legal situation obtaining in the member-States.

For all these reasons the question from the Tribunal de Police de Mons should be answered as follows:

Article 11 (2) of Regulation 543/69 is to be interpreted as meaning that it also gives rise to an obligation on the part of crew members to observe the provisions on rest periods, so that during the periods provided for, the activities mentioned in Article 14 (2) (c) or (d) are not pursued.

JUDGMENT (drafting judge, Monaco J.)

6

[1] By judgment dated 6 September 1974, filed at the Registry of the Court on 18 September 1974, the Tribunal de Police de Mons requested a preliminary ruling under **Article 177** of the EEC Treaty on the interpretation of the first paragraph of Article 11 (2) of Council Regulation 543/69 of 25 March 1969 on the harmonisation of certain social legislation relating to road transport.

[2] The question arose in police proceedings in which a coach driver was charged with not having taken, as a crew member engaged in the carriage of passengers, the daily rest referred to in the aforementioned first paragraph of Article 11 (2).

[3] The defendant challenged the validity of the proceedings on the ground that only employers had to observe the requirement for daily rest and not crew members of road vehicles.

[4] The Court is requested for this purpose to rule as to the meaning which must be given to the words ' shall have had . . . a . . . rest period '.

[5] The first paragraph of Article 11 (2) of Regulation 543/69

[1] J.O. 1500/65.

---

6. Judgment. Note formality and brevity.

1975

*Auditeur
du Travail
(Mons)* v.
Cagnon

European
Court
of Justice

Judgment
(Monaco J.)

provides ' every crew member engaged in the carriage of passengers shall have had, during the twenty-four-hour period preceding any time he is performing any activity covered by Article 14 (2) (c) or (d): a daily rest period of not less than ten consecutive hours, which shall not be reduced during the week . . .'.

[6] Article 14 (2) (c) and (d) refers to ' driving periods ' and ' other periods of attendance at work '.

[7] The third and tenth recitals of Regulation 543/69 show that the regulation has among other objectives ' to improve road safety ' for which purpose it is desirable ' to lay down the minimum duration of and other conditions governing the daily and weekly rest periods of crew members '.

[8] Such an objective would not be achieved if the provisions enacted in relation to daily and weekly rest applied only to the employer running the road transport service, and did not likewise apply to crew members by requiring them to have in fact rested for the prescribed minimum period.

[9] For the precise purpose of ensuring that this requirement is observed, Article 14 of the said regulation provides that crew members shall carry an individual control book.

[10] As a result the phrase ' shall have had . . . a . . . rest period ' in the first paragraph of Article 11 (2) of Regulation 543/69 of 25 March 1969 must be interpreted as meaning that the provisions on daily rest must be observed both by crew members themselves, who are required to stop all activities referred to in Article 14 of the regulation for the minimum period laid down, and by the employer running a road transport undertaking, who is required to take the necessary measures to permit the crew members to have the daily rest period laid down.

7

Costs

[11] The costs incurred by the Commission of the European Communities, which has submitted observations to the Court, are not recoverable.

[12] Since the proceedings are, in so far as the parties to the main action are concerned, a step in the action before the national court, costs are a matter for that court.

On those grounds, THE COURT, in answer to the question referred to it by the Tribunal de Police de Mons by judgment of 6 September 1974,

HEREBY RULES:

The phrase ' shall have had . . . a . . . rest period ' in the first paragraph of Article 11 (2) of Regulation 543/69 of 25 March 1969 must be interpreted as meaning that the provisions on daily rest must be observed both by crew

8

---

7. Reasons.   **8.** Ruling.

1975
—
*Auditeur
du Travail
(Mons)* v.
Cagnon
—
European
Court
of Justice
—
Arrêt
(Monaco J.)

members themselves, who are required to stop all activities referred to in Article 14 of the regulation for the minimum period laid down, and by the employer running a road transport undertaking, who is required to take the necessary measures to permit the crew members to have the daily rest period laid down.

ARRET

[1] Attendu que, par jugement du 6 septembre 1974, parvenu au greffe de la Cour le 18 septembre 1974, le Tribunal de Police de Mons a posé, en vertu de l'**article 177** du traité C.E.E., une question concernant l'interprétation de l'article 11, § 2, al. 1er du règlement n° 543/69 du Conseil du 25 mars 1969, relatif à l'harmonisation de certaines dispositions en matière sociale dans le domaine des transports par route;

[2] que la question a été soulevée à l'occasion d'une procédure de police, au cours de laquelle il est notamment reproché au conducteur d'un car de ne pas avoir pris, en qualité de membre d'un équipage affecté au transport de voyageurs, le repos journalier visé à l'article 11, § 2, al. 1er précité;

[3] que le prévenu a contesté le bien-fondé de cette procédure, en soutenant que le respect de l'obligation du repos journalier ne s'imposerait qu'aux employeurs et non aux membres des équipages des véhicules routiers;

[4] qu'à ces fins il est demandé à la Cour de dire dans quel sens doit être comprise l'expression ' avoir bénéficié d'un repos ';

[5] Attendu qu'aux termes de l'article 11, § 2, al. 1er du règlement n° 543/69, ' tout membre d'un équipage affecté aux transports de voyageurs doit avoir bénéficié, au cours de la période de 24 heures précédant tout moment où il exerce une des activités indiquées à l'article 14, § 2 sous (c) et (d), d'un repos journalier de 10 heures consécutives au moins, sans possibilité de réduction au cours de la semaine . . .';

[6] que l'article 14, § 2 se réfère, sous (c) et (d), à des ' periodes de conduite ' et aux ' autres périodes de présence au travail ';

[7] qu'il ressort des troisième et dixième considérants que le règlement n° 543/69 a, parmi d'autres objets, notamment celui d' ' améliorer la sécurité routière ' aux fins de laquelle il est apparu nécessaire de ' fixer les durées minimales et les autres conditions auxquelles les repos journalier et hebdomadaire des membres d'équipages sont soumis ';

[8] qu'un tel objectif ne serait pas atteint si les dispositions arrêtées en matière de repos journalier et hebdomadaire ne devaient s'imposer qu'au seul employeur, exploitant d'un service de transport routier, et ne devaient également s'appliquer aux membres d'équipages, en les obligeant à prendre effectivement le repos minimal prescrit;

75

1975
—
*Auditeur
du Travail
(Mons)* v.
Cagnon
—
European
Court
of Justice
—
Arrêt
(Monaco J.)

[9] qu'en vue précisément d'assurer le respect de cette obligation, ledit règlement prévoit, à son article 14, l'institution d'un livret individuel de contrôle obligatoire pour les membres d'équipages;

[10] qu'en conséquence, l'expression ' avoir bénéficié d'un repos,' figurant à l'article 11, § 2, al. 1er du règlement (CEE) n° 543/69 du 25 mars 1969, doit être interprétée comme imposant le respect des dispositions relatives au repos journalier tant aux membres d'équipages eux-mêmes, auxquels il est fait obligation de suspendre effectivement, pendant la durée minimale prescrite, tout exercise des activités indiquées à l'article 14, § 2, sous (c) et (d) du même règlement, qu'à l'employeur exploitant d'un service de transport routier, tenu de prendre les mesures nécessaires afin de permettre aux membres d'équipages de bénéficier du repos journalier prescrit;

Sur les dépens

[11] Attendu que les frais exposés par la Commission des C.E., qui a soumis des observations à la Cour, ne peuvent faire l'objet de remboursement;

[12] que la procédure revêtant, à l'égard des parties au principal, le caractère d'un incident soulevé devant la juridiction nationale, il appartient à celle-ci de statuer sur les dépens;

par ces motifs, LA COUR, statuant sur la question à elle soumise par le Tribunal de Police de Mons par jugement du 6 septembre 1974,

DIT POUR DROIT:

L'expression ' avoir bénéficié d'un repos,' figurant à l'article 11, § 2, al. 1er du règlement (CEE) n° 543/69 du 25 mars 1969, doit être interprétée comme imposant le respect des dispositions relatives au repos journalier tant aux membres d'équipages eux-mêmes, auxquels il est fait obligation de suspendre effectivement, pendant la durée minimale prescrite, tout exercise des activités indiquées à l'article 14, § 2, sous (c) et (d) du même règlement, qu'à l'employeur exploitant d'un service de transport routier, tenu de prendre les mesures nécessaires afin de permettre aux membres d'équipages de bénéficier du repos journalier prescrit.

APPENDIX 2

THE LAW LIBRARY, LEGAL MATERIALS AND THEIR USE

You will spend a lot of your time working in the law library if you are at all conscientious as a law student. It is often said that a good lawyer is one who knows where to look for the law. At first it all seems a bit bewildering. You may have a library tour organised by a member of staff or librarian. If so what follows may duplicate what they say to some extent. It will also go over the same ground as Chapter 3 of Professor Glanville Williams' *Learning the Law*. I shall, however, go into a little more detail and also refer you to some Scottish, Irish, Commonwealth and American materials together with some sources of EEC and French and German law. Obviously you are not going to use all these at once but the references may be useful to you as your studies progress.

UNITED KINGDOM AND IRELAND

I will deal first with United Kingdom and Irish materials. These can be usefully classified into primary and secondary sources. Primary sources are those which actually make law—statutes, delegated legislation and reports of cases. Secondary sources are texts of various sorts which summarise and sometimes discuss the law—things like textbooks, legal encyclopedias, digests and legal periodicals.

Primary Sources

1. *Statutes*

Although we often talk of the " Statute Book " there is no such thing. Early statutes as we saw in Chapter 8 were decrees issued by the King or more usually the King in Council in a variety of forms. Later they became a tripartite enactment by the King, the Lords and the Commons in Parliament assembled.

Hawkins and Ruffhead made a useful unofficial collection in the eighteenth century of statutes then in force. There were other unofficial collections but in the period 1810 to 1822 Commissioners appointed by the House of Commons produced nine volumes known as *Statutes of the Realm* which covered the period 1235 to

1713 but excluding the interregnum. The interregnum is covered by Firth and Rait, *Acts and Ordinances of the Interregnum*.

In 1868 the Statute Law Committee was set up and produced *Statutes Revised* covering the period 1235 to 1948. From 1947 to 1965 there was a specialist branch of the Office of Parliamentary Counsel dealing with consolidation. In 1965 the Law Commissions took over responsibility for comprehensive consolidation and statute law revision. As a result of this work a new series is being produced entitled *Statutes in Force*. In the foreword to this Lord Hailsham, who was then Lord Chancellor, explained the nature and purpose of the new series in the following way:

" The Third Edition of *Statutes Revised* was published in 1950 under the supervision of the Statute Law Committee as part of the programme of statute law reform inaugurated soon after the end of the last war. At that time, it was recognised that a further edition would be needed when the projected work on consolidation and statute law revision had borne some fruit. The time has now been reached when a large amount of consolidation and revision has been done. The combined effect of this work and of the ordinary legislation passed since 1950 has been to repeal or amend a large part of the Acts contained in the Third Edition. The Committee has therefore decided to undertake the publication of a new official revised edition of the statutes.

The three editions of *Statutes Revised* published between 1885 and 1950 were bound collections of the Public General Acts as amended. The Third Edition and the succeeding annual volumes were supplemented by an annual noter-up service which provided details of subsequent amendments and repeals. This was a useful service, but noting up is a laborious process and can easily be a source of error.

The new edition is renamed *Statutes in Force*. It is designed as a self-renewing, self-expanding and thus permanent edition. The Acts will be printed as separate booklets and assembled in loose-leaf binders. In this way it will be possible to keep the new edition up to date without disfiguring the text.

It is to be an official edition of the statutes currently in force and is published by authority. An Editorial Board is responsible for developing the work until it includes all Public General Acts in force, and for keeping it continuously up to date.

The new edition offers an arrangement by subject-matter. Those who require all the statutes currently in force will be served by the complete edition so arranged. But those whose interest is limited and who require part only of the statute law do not have to buy the whole work. They will be able to make their own selection.

Statutes in Force is designed to meet the obligation of the State to provide an accurate and up-to-date text of all statutes currently in force, edited in a helpful and comprehensive way, but without commentary."

Copies of individual Acts can usually be obtained from the Government Bookshops which are branches of Her Majesty's Stationery Office. A copy of the Education Act 1975 with annotations is set out in Appendix 1 to this book.

Each year H.M.S.O. publishes volumes containing Public General Acts (with which you will usually be concerned) and Local and Private Acts. It also publishes a Chronological Table of Statutes. This covers *Statutes of the Realm* and all Public General Acts from 1714. Together with this is the *Index to Statutes in Force* which is arranged alphabetically. These are quite useful tools for historical research together with the annotated Halsbury's *Statutes* to which I shall refer below.

The Incorporated Council of Law Reporting publish statutes under the rather silly title *Law Reports—Statutes*. These cover the period 1866 onwards.

The old practice was to cite statutes by regnal year and chapter. The regnal year is the year of the reign of the particular monarch and the chapter refers to the place in the records of a particular session of Parliament. Thus the Sale of Goods Act 1893 is 56 & 57 Vict. c. 71. It is still sometimes used but statutes nowadays are generally cited by their short title which is usually set out for some odd reason at the end of an English statute. It gives a brief description of the subject-matter of the Act and the calendar year in which it was passed.

There is a series of Northern Ireland statutes, the name of which has differed from time to time. This goes up to 1973.

Statutes of the Republic of Ireland are contained in the series known as *The Acts of the Oireachtas* which is in English and Gaelic. There is an index volume covering 1922 to 1968.

2. Delegated legislation

The most important pieces of delegated legislation are usually referred to as statutory instruments because this term is used as a generic term in the Statutory Instruments Act 1946. It covers such things as Orders in Council and ministerial orders, rules and regulations. Like statutes they are sold separately by H.M.S.O. They are also collected annually and there is a collection called *Statutory Instruments* which is published by H.M.S.O. and kept up to date with annual volumes and an index. A *Table of Government Orders* records the effect of instruments made after 1949 on earlier instruments.

3. Law reports

As you can see from the report of *Regina* v. *Venna* [1976] 1 Q.B. 421 set out in Appendix 1, a modern law report gives the name of the case, its date, the court and the judges who sat in it, a headnote, an outline of the facts and pleadings, the name of counsel, sometimes a summary of their argument and always a detailed report of the judgment. This particular format became reasonably settled after 1765. It is useful to know a little of the history of law reporting since there have been significant changes in the system over the years. A chronological list of English law reports is set out on p. 205 and a list of authorised abbreviations for modern reports on p. 220.

The Year Books 1282–1537. As a beginner it is unlikely that you will be referred to the Year Books which are the oldest species of report. They are not complete reports but are thought to have been notes taken by students and practitioners, for educational or professional purposes. Originally the proceedings reported were in Norman French and the reports continued to be in what became known as "Law French" long after English had begun to be used in the courts.

Named reporters 1537–1865. Eventually the form of reports began to change to include summaries of counsel's arguments and the judgments. These eventually appear under the reporter's name. Some of them were made for the reporter's own use; gradually however, they became mainly commercial ventures. They differ greatly in style and quality.

In the early period the most famous reports are those of *Coke* and *Plowden* in the common law courts. Both were distinguished lawyers who added notes to their reports. Coke's reports were often very discursive and sometimes positively long-winded. They include much by way of commentary as well as actual reports. They are nevertheless an invaluable source of early law. *Burrow's Reports* in the eighteenth century are probably the first of the modern reports although even he often reported the sense rather than the words verbatim.

In Chancery the early reports known as *Cases in Chancery* are often very terse. The first good reports were those of *Piere Williams* from 1695 to 1736. *Vesey Senior* and *Junior*, *Hare* and *Beavan* were the other major reporters.

The English Reports Full Reprint. Most libraries do not hold the nominate reports but most of the reports can be found in convenient form in the English Reports which reprint about 100,000 earlier reports verbatim, with citations and editorial notes. The reports are arranged by courts and there are useful index volumes and a conversion wall chart which enables you to convert from a citation in the nominate report to the appropriate citation in the *English Reports*. See the list on pp. 205 *et seq.*

There is another series known as *Revised Reports*, which covers some of the same ground and has cases which do not appear in the *English Reports*, but many libraries do not stock it.

Law reports 1865 to date. The legal profession formed the Incorporated Council of Law Reporting in 1865 which superseded the nominate reporters and publishes a " semi-official " series of reports which are now known as the *Law Reports*. The judges revise them and it is the custom of the courts to require citation of them if a case is reported in them.

The first series covers the period from 1865 to the Judicature Acts' reorganisation of the courts. A proper citation is to refer to the court thus *e.g.* L.R. 8 Ex. 132 although it is now common to add the year as well.

The second series covers 1875 to 1890 and refers to the particular division. Thus *Heaven* v. *Pender* decided in 1883 is 11 Q.B.D. 503. Again it is now common to add the date.

The third series which is still current dates from 1891. Here the date appears in square brackets and the " D " disappears. Thus *Le Lievre* v. *Gould* is reported in [1893] 1 Q.B. 491.

The present reports are:

Appeal Cases covering the House of Lords and Judicial Committee of the Privy Council cited as A.C.; reports of the divisions: *Queen's Bench Division*—Q.B.; *Chancery Division*—Ch. and formerly the *Probate, Divorce and Admiralty Division*—P. but now the *Family Division*—Fam. Court of Appeal cases go not in Appeal Cases but in the reports of the Division from which the case came.

In addition there are specialist reports such as the *Reports of Restrictive Practices Cases* (R.P.) and the *Industrial Court Reports* (I.C.R.).

From 1866 to 1952 the Council published *Weekly Notes* (W.N.) which contained summary reports of recent cases before they appeared in the main reports. From January 1, 1953, these were replaced by the *Weekly Law Reports* (W.L.R.).

Other Series. The best known commercial series is the *All England Law Reports* still using the tedious abbreviation " All E.R." despite the attempt of some learned writers to convert it to " A.E.R." These reports began in 1936 and aim to be quicker than other series although there is now little to choose between them and the *Weekly Law Reports.* They incorporate the *Law Times Reports* (L.T.) from 1948 and the *Law Journal Reports* (*e.g.* L.J. 9 Q.B. 126) from 1950. There is a useful reprint of selected old cases which now covers the period 1558–1935.

The *Times Law Reports* (T.L.R.) cover the period 1884 to 1952 and *The Times* newspaper has reports which are cited by reference to the date of the particular issue.

Other reports are contained in *The Solicitors' Journal* (S.J.), the *Justice of the Peace* (J.P.) both of which date back to the nineteenth century.

Commercial firms also produce specialist reports such as *Lloyd's List Law Reports*—cited now as Lloyd's Rep.; *Criminal Appeal Reports*—Cr.App.R. and *Knight's Industrial Reports*—K.I.R.

Scotland. Scotland had nominate reports until the end of the nineteenth century. Now the principal cases are reported in *Session Cases*—S.C. and *Scots Law Times*—S.L.T.

Ireland. A number of Irish cases appear in nominate reports but the main series is now *Irish Reports*—I.R. since 1894. Northern Irish cases are reported in *Northern Ireland Law Reports*—cited N.I.

A CHRONOLOGICAL LIST OF THE ENGLISH LAW REPORTS ARRANGED UNDER
COURTS AND SHOWING THE CORRESPONDING VOLUMES IN THE REVISED
REPORTS AND IN THE ENGLISH REPORTS

This list, which shows the position up to 1962, is taken from Sweet
& Maxwell's *Guide to Law Reports and Statutes* (4th ed.).

	No. of vols.	Period covered	Corresponding vols. of Revised Reports	Corresponding vols. of English Reports
Reports in all the Courts				
English Reports	176	1378—1866		
The Revised Reports	152	1785—1865		
Law Journal	9	1823—1831		
Law Journal Reports, New Series	118	1832—1949		
Jurist	55	1837—1866		
Law Times (Old Series)	34	1843—1859		
Law Times Reports	177	1859—1947		
Weekly Reporter	54	1853—1906		
Common Law and Equity Reports	6 vols. in 9	1853—1855		
New Reports	6	1862—1865		
The Law Reports	601	1865—1962		
Times Law Reports	71	1885—1952		
Weekly Notes	87	1866—1952		
The Reports	15	1893—1895		
All England Law Reports	74	1936—1962		
Weekly Law Reports	30	1953—1962		
House of Lords				
Shower, 1876	1	1694—1699		1
Colles	1	1697—1714		1
Brown, by Tomlins, 1803	8	1702—1800		(1–3) 1; (4–6) 2; (7, 8) 3
Dow	6	1812—1818	14–16, 19	3
Bligh	4	1819—1821	20–22	4
Bligh. New Series	11	1827—1837	30–33, 35, 36, 38, 39, 42, 51	(1–3) 4; (4–9) 5; (10, 11) 6
Dow and Clark	2	1827—1832	35	6
Clark and Finnelly	12	1831—1846	36, 37, 39, 42, 47, 49, 51, 54, 57, 59, 65, 69	(1–3) 6; (4–9) 7; (8–12) 8
Maclean and Robinson	1	1839		9
West	1	1839—1841	51	9

	No. of vols.	Period covered	Corresponding vols. of Revised Reports	Corresponding vols. of English Reports
House of Lords—contd.				
House of Lords Cases (Clark) (with Index)	12	1847—1866	73, 81, 88, 94, 101, 108, 115, 125, 131, 138, 145	(1, 2) ⁚ (3–6) 1((7–11) 1
Birkenhead's Judgments, 1923	1	1919—1922		
Privy Council				
Acton. (And Vol. II. Part I.)	1	1809—1811		12
Knapp	3	1829—1836	38, 40	12
Moore	15	1836—1862	43, 46, 50, 59, 70, 79, 83, 97, 105, 110, 117, 124, 132, 134, 137	(1, 2) 12 (3–7) 13 (8–12) 14 (13–15) ℣
Moore (New Series)	9	1862—1873		(1, 2) 15 (3–6) 16 (7–9) 1
Moore. East India Appeals	14	1836—1871		(1–5) 18 (6–10) 19 (11–14) 2
Law Reports, Indian Appeals	78	1872—1950		
Chancery				
Cary, 1872	1	1557—1604		21
Choyce Cases in Chancery, 1870	1	1557—1606		21
Tothill, 1872	1	1559—1606		21
Dickens	2	1559—1798		21
Reports in Chancery, 1736	1	1615—1712		21
Bacon, ed. Ritchie, 1932	1	1617—1621		
Nelson, 1872	1	1625—1693		21
Equity Cases Abridged	2	1667—1744		(1) 21; (2 2
Cases in Chancery	1	1660—1688		22
Freeman	1	1660—1706		22
Finch (Sir H.)	1	1673—1681		23
Vernon	2	1681—1720		23
Precedents in Chancery	1	1689—1723		24
Peere Williams	3	1695—1736		24
Gilbert	1	1705—1727		25
Select Cases, temp. King	1	1724—1733		25
Moseley	1	1726—1731		25
Kelynge, W., 1873	1	1730—1732		25

	No. of vols.	Period covered	Corresponding vols. of Revised Reports	Corresponding vols. of English Reports
Chancery—contd.				
Cases, temp. Talbot	1	1730—1737		25
West, temp. Hardwicke	1	1736—1739		25
Atkyns	3	1736—1755		26
Ambler	2	1737—1783		27
Barnardiston	1	1740—1741		27
Ridgeway, temp. Hardwicke (*See also* K.B.)	1	1744—1746		27
Vesey, sen., and Belt's Supplement	3	1747—1756		(1) 27; (2–3) 28
Eden	2	1757—1767		28
Brown, by Eden	4	1778—1794		28
Brown, by Belt	4	1778—1794		(1) 28; (2–4) 29
Cox	2	1783—1796		(1) 29; (2) 30
Vesey, jun., with Index, and Hovenden's Supplement	22	1789—1816	1–13	(1–3) 30; (4–6) 31; (7–11) 32; (12–16) 33; (17–22) 34
Vesey and Beames	3	1812—1814	12, 13	35
Cooper, G., temp. Eldon	1	1815	14	35
Merivale	3	1815—1817	15–17	(1–2) 35; (3) 36
Swanston	3	1818—1819	18, 19	36
Jacob and Walker	2	1819—1821	20–22	37
Jacob	1	1821—1822	23	37
Turner and Russell	1	1822—1824	23, 24	37
Russell	5	1823—1829	25–29	38
Russell and Mylne	2	1829—1831	32, 34	39
Mylne and Keen	3	1832—1835	36, 39, 41	(1–2) 39; (3) 40
Mylne and Craig	5	1836—1840	43, 45, 48	(1–3) 40; (4, 5) 41
Craig and Phillips	1	1841	54	41
Phillips	2	1841—1849	65, 78	41
Macnaghten and Gordon	3	1848—1852	84, 86, 87	(1) 41; (2, 3) 42
De Gex, Macnaghten and Gordon	8	1851—1857	91, 95, 98, 102, 104, 106, 109, 114	(1, 2) 42; (3–6) 43; (7, 8) 44
De Gex and Jones	4	1857—1860	118, 119, 121, 124	(1–3) 44; (4) 45

	No. of vols.	Period covered	Corresponding vols. of Revised Reports	Corresponding vols. of English Reports
Chancery—contd.				
De Gex, Fisher and Jones	4	1860—1862	125, 129, 130, 135	45
De Gex, Jones and Smith	4	1862—1866	137, 139, 142, 146	46
COLLATERAL REPORTS				
Romilly's Notes of Cases	1	1767—1787		
Wyatt's Practical Register Wilson, 4 parts	1	1818—1819	18	37
Cooper, temp. Brougham	1	1833—1834	38	47
Donnelly	2	1836—1837		47
Cooper, C. P.	1	1837—1839	46	47
Cooper, temp. Cottenham	2	1846—1848	76	47
Hall and Twells	2	1848—1850	84	47
Rolls Court				
Tamlyn	1	1829—1830	31	48
Keen	2	1836—1838	44	48
Beavan	36	1838—1866	49, 50, 52, 55, 59, 63, 64, 68, 73, 76, 83, 85, 88, 92, 96, 99, 104, 105, 109, 111, 113, 116, 119, 122, 126, 131, 132, 135, 138, 140, 145, 147, 148	(1, 2) 48 (3–7) 4 (8–12) 50 (13–17 51; (18 22) 52 (23–26 53; (27 31) 54 (32–36) 5
Vice-Chancellors' Courts				
Maddock	6	1815—1822	15–18, 20–23	56
Simons and Stuart	2	1822—1826	24, 25	57
Simons	17	1826—1849	27, 29. 30, 33, 35, 38, 40, 42, 47, 51, 54, 56, 60, 65, 74, 80, 83	(1–3) 57; (4 7) 58; (8 12) 59 (13–17 6
Simons (New Series) (temp. V.-C.s Shadwell and Kindersley)	2	1850—1852	89	61
Drewry	4	1852—1859	94, 100, 106, 113	(1–3) 61; (4 6
Drewry and Smale	2	1860—1865	127	62
Younge and Collyer	2	1841—1843	57, 60	(1) 62; (2 6

	No. of vols.	Period covered	Corresponding vols. of Revised Reports	Corresponding vols. of English Reports
ce-Chancellors' Courts —*contd.*				
ollyer	2	1844—1845	66, 70	63
e Gex and Smale	5	1846—1852	75, 79, 84, 87, 90	(1) 63; (2—5) 64
male and Giffard	3	1852—1857	96, 97, 107	65
iffard	5	1857—1865	114, 128, 133	(1) 65; (2—5) 66
(temp. V.-C.s Knight, Bruce, Parker, and Stuart)				
are	11	1841—1853	58, 62, 64, 67, 71, 77, 82, 85, 89, 90	(1) 66; (2—6) 67; (7—11) 69
ay	1	1853—1854	101	
ay and Johnson	4	1854—1858	103, 110	(1—3) 69; (4) 79
hnson	1	1859	123	70
(temp. V.-C.s Wigram, Turner, and Wood)				
hnson and Hemming	2	1860—1862	128, 134	70
emming and Miller	2	1862—1865	136, 144	71
OLLATERAL REPORTS				
olt	2	1845		71
ing's Bench & Queen's Bench				
tate Trials (Cobbett and Howell)	34	1163—1820		
tate Trials (New Series)	8	1820—1858		
racton's Note Book	3	1218—1240		
ear Books (Horwood)	5	1292—1307		
ear Book (Selden Society)	22	1307—1318		
ear Books (Maynard)	11	1307—1537		
ear Books (Horwood and Pike)	15	1337—1346		
ellewe	1	1378—1400		72
eilway	1	1496—1531		72
loore	1	1512—1621		72
yer	3	1513—1582		73
rooke's New Cases				
larch's Translation of Brooke 1873	1	1515—1558		73
enloe	1	1531—1628		73
eonard	1	1540—1615		74
lowden	2	1550—1580		75
wen	1	1556—1615		74
oy	1	1559—1649		74
oke	6	1572—1616		(1—4) 76; (5, 6) 77

	No. of vols.	Period covered	Corresponding vols. of Revised Reports	Corresponding vols. of English Reports
King's & Queen's Bench—contd.				
Godbolt	1	1575—1638		78
Croke	4	1582—1641		(Eliz.) 7 (Jac., Ca
Gouldesborough	1	1586—1602		75
Popham	1	1592—1627		79
Yelverton	1	1603—1613		80
Hobart	1	1603—1625		80
Davies (Ireland)	1	1604—1612		80
Ley	1	1608—1629		80
Calthrop	1	1609—1618		80
Bulstrode	3	1610—1625		(1, 2) 8 (3) 8
Rolle	2	1614—1625		81
Palmer	1	1619—1629		81
Jones, W.	1	1620—1641		82
Latch	1	1625—1628		82
March (New Cases)	1	1639—1642		82
Style	1	1646—1655		82
Aleyn	1	1646—1649		82
Siderfin	2	1657—1670		82
Raymond, Sir T.	1	1660—1684		83
Levinz	3	1660—1697		83
Keble	3	1661—1679		(1) 83; (2 3) 8
Kelyng, J.	1	1662—1669		84
Saunders	3	1666—1673		85
Jones, T.	1	1667—1685		84
Ventris	1	1668—1688		86
Pollexfen	1	1669—1685		86
Modern	12	1669—1732		(1–2 86; (3 7) 87; (8 12) 8
Freeman	1	1670—1704		89
Shower	2	1678—1695		89
Skinner	1	1681—1698		90
Comberbaoh	1	1685—1699		90
Carthew	1	1686—1701		90
Holt	1	1688—1711		90
Salkeld	3	1689—1712		91
Raymond (Lord)	3	1694—1732		(1) 91; (2 3) 9
Fortescue	1	1694—1738		92
Comyns	2	1695—1741		92
Sessions Cases	2	1710—1748		93
Gilbert's Cases in Law and Equity	1	1713—1715		93
Strange	2	1716—1749		93

	No. of vols.	Period covered	Corresponding vols. of Revised Reports	Corresponding vols. of English Reports
King's & Queen's Bench—contd.				
Barnardiston	2	1726—1735		94
Fitzgibbons	1	1728—1733		94
Barnes' Cases of Practice	1	1732—1760		94
Ridgeway, temp. Hard-wicke (*See also* Chancery)	1	1733—1737		94
Cunningham, 1871	1	1734—1736		94
Lee, temp. Hardwicke	1	1733—1738		95
Andrews	1	1738—1739		95
Wilson	3	1742—1774		95
Blackstone, W.	2	1746—1780		96
Sayer	1	1751—1756		96
Kenyon	2	1753—1759		96
Wilmot's Notes and Opinions	1	1757—1770		97
Burrow	5	1757—1771		(1–3) 97; (4–5) 98
Lofft	1	1772—1774		98
Cowper	2	1774—1778		98
Douglas	4	1778—1785		99
Durnford and East	8	1785—1800	1–5	(1) 99; (2–7) 100; (5–8) 101
East	16	1801—1812	5–14	(1–6) 102; (7–11) 103; (12–16) 104
Maule and Selwyn	6	1813—1817	14–18	105
Barnewall and Alderson	5	1817—1822	18–24	106
Barnewall and Cresswell	10	1822—1830	25–34	(1–4) 107; (5–8) 108; (9, 10), 109
Barnewall and Adolphus	5	1830—1834	35–39	(1, 2) 109; (3–5) 110
Adolphus and Ellis	12	1834—1840	40, 42–48, 50, 52, 54	(1) 110; (2–5) 111; (6–9) 112; (10–12) 113
Queen's Bench (Adolphus and Ellis, New Series)	18	1841—1852	55, 57, 61, 62, 64, 66, 68, 70, 72, 74, 75, 76, 78, 80, 81, 83, 85, 88	(1) 113; (2–5) 114; (5–9) 115; (10–13) 116; (14–17) 117; (18) 118

	No. of vols.	Period covered	Corresponding vols. of Revised Reports	Corresponding vols. of English Reports
King's & Queen's Bench—contd.				
Ellis and Blackburn	8	1851—1858	93, 95, 97, 99, 103, 106, 110, 112	(1–3) 118 (4–7) 119 (8) 120
Ellis, Blackburn and Ellis	1	1858	113	120
Ellis and Ellis	3	1858—1861	117, 119, 122	(1) 120; (2, 3) 121
Best and Smith	10	1861—1869	124, 127, 129, 136, 141, 147, 148	(1, 2) 121 (3–6) 122
Cababé and Ellis	1	1882—1885		
COLLATERAL REPORTS				
Dunning	1	1753—1754		
Smith, J. P.	3	1803—1806	7, 8	
Dowling and Ryland	9	1821—1827	24–30	
Manning and Ryland	5	1827—1830	31–34	
Nevile and Manning	6	1831—1836	38–43	
Nevile and Perry	3	1836—1838	44–45	
Perry and Davison	4	1838—1841	48, 50, 52, 54	
Gale and Davison	3	1841—1843	55, 57, 62	
Davison and Merivale	1	1843—1844	64	
Harrison and Wollaston	2	1835—1836	47	
Willmore, Wollaston and Davison	1	1837	52	
Willmore, Wollaston and Hodges	2	1838—1839	52	
Arnold and Hodges' Practice Cases		1840—1841		
Bail Court				
Chitty	2	1770—1822	22, 23	
Dowling	9	1830—1840	36, 39, 41, 46, 49, 54, 59, 61	
Dowling (New Series)	2	1841—1842	63, 65	
Dowling and Lowndes	7	1843—1849	67, 69, 71, 75, 79, 81, 82	
Saunders and Cole	2	1846—1848	82	
Lowndes, Maxwell and Pollock	2	1850—1851	86	
Lowndes and Maxwell	1	1852—1854		
Harrison and Wollaston	2	1835—1836	47	
Willmore, Wollaston and Davison	1	1837	52	

	No. of vols.	Period covered	Corresponding vols. of Revised Reports	Corresponding vols. of English Reports
ail Court—contd.				
*illmore, Wollaston and Hodges	2	1838—1839	52	
*ollaston	1	1840—1841		
*ew Practice Cases (Welford, Bittleston and Parnell)	3	1844—1848		
ommon Pleas				
*enloe and Dalison	1	1486—1580		123
*nderson	2	1534—1605		123
*rownlow and Gouldesborough	1	1569—1624		123
*aville	1	1580—1594		123
*utton	1	1612—1639		122
*ridgman, Sir J.	1	1613—1621		123
*inch	1	1621—1625		124
*ittleton	1	1626—1632		124
*etley	1	1627—1632		124
*ridgman, Sir O.	1	1660—1667		124
*arter	1	1664—1676		124
*aughan	1	1665—1674		124
*utwyche	2	1682—1704		125
*utwyche translated 8vo., 1718	2	1682—1704		125
*ooke, 1872	1	1706—1747		125
*arnes	1	1732—1760		
*illes	1	1737—1760		125
*lackstone, H., 1827	2	1788—1796	2, 3	126
*osanquet and Puller	5	1796—1807	4–	(1–2) 126; (3–5) 127
*aunton	8	1807—1819	9–91	(1–2) 127; (3–6) 128; (7–8) 129
*roderip and Bingham	3	1819—1822	212–2	129
*ingham	10	1822—1834	25, 27–31, 33–35, 38	(1–6) 130; (7–10) 131
*ingham (New Cases)	6	1834—1840	41–44, 50, 54	(1) 131; (2–6) 132
*anning and Granger	7	1840—1844	56, 58, 60, 61, 63, 64, 66	(1–3) 133; (4–6) 134; (7) 135
*ommon Bench (with Index)	19	1845—1856	68, 69, **71,** 73, 75, 77–79, 82, 84, 87, 92, 93, 98, 100, 104, 107	(1, 2) 135; (3–6) 136; (7–9) 137; (10–13) 138; (14–18) 139

	No. of vols.	Period covered	Corresponding vols. of Revised Reports	Corresponding vols. of English Reports
Common Pleas—contd.				
Common Bench New Series (with Index)	20	1856—1865	107, 109, 111, 114, 116, 120, 121, 125, 127, 128, 132, 134, 135, 137, 139, 142, 144, 147, 148	(1–4) 14 (5–8) 14 (9–1. 142; (13 16) 14 (17–2 1
COLLATERAL REPORTS				
Marshall	2	1814—1816	15, 17	
Moore	12	1817—1827	19–29	
Moore and Payne	5	1828—1831	29–31, 33	
Moore and Scott	4	1831—1834	34, 35, 38	
Scott	8	1834—1840	41–44, 50, 54	
Scott New Reports		1840—1845	56, 58, 60, 61, 63, 64, 66	
Hodges	3	1835—1837	42, 43	
Arnold	2	1838—1839	50	
Drinkwater	1	1840—1841	60	
Harrison and Rutherfurd	1	1865—1866		
Exchequer				
Jenkins, 1885	1	1220—1623		
Lane, 1884	1	1605—1612		145
Conroy's Custodiam Reports	1	1652—1788		145
Hardres	1	1655—1669		
Bunbury	1	1713—1742		145
Parker	1	1743—1767		145
Anstruther	3	1792—1797	3, 4	145
Forrest	1	1801	5	145
Wightwick	1	1810—1811	12	145
Price	13	1814—1824	15–27	145
McCleland	1	1824	28	(1) 145; (2 8) 146; (9 13) 14
McCleland and Younge	1	1825	29	148
Younge and Jervis	3	1826—1830	30–32	148
Crompton and Jervis	2	1830—1832	35, 37	148
Crompton and Meeson	2	1832—1834	38, 39	(1) 148; (14
Crompton and Meeson and Roscoe	2	1834—1836	40, 41	149

	No. of vols.	Period covered	Corresponding vols. of Revised Reports	Corresponding vols. of English Reports
Exchequer—cont.				
Meeson and Welsby (with Index)	17	1836—1847	46, 49, 51, 52, 55, 56, 58, 60, 62, 63, 67, 69, 71, 73, 74, 76, 77, 80, 82, 86	(1) 149; (2) 150 (1–4) 150; (5–8) 151; (9–12) 152; (13–17) 153
Exchequer Reports (Welsby, Hurlstone and Gordon)	11	1847—1856	91, 96, 102, 105	(1–4) 154; (5–8) 155; (9–11) 156
Hurlstone and Norman	7	1856—1861	108, 115, 117, 118, 120, 123, 126	(1) 156; (2–5) 157; (6–7) 159
Hurlstone and Coltman	4	1862—1865	130, 133, 140, 143	(1) 158; (2–4) 159
COLLATERAL REPORTS				
Price's Notes of Practice Cases (1 Part)		1830—1831		
Tyrwhitt	5	1830—1835	35, 37–40	
Tyrwhitt and Granger	1	1836	46	
Gale	2	1835—1836		
Murphy and Hurlstone	1	1836—1837	51	
Horn and Hurlstone	2	1838—1839	51	
Hurlstone and Walmsley	1	1840—1841	58	
Exchequer Equity				
Wilson (1 Part)		1805—1817	18	159
Daniell	1	1817—1820	18	159
Younge	1	1830—1832	34	159
Younge and Collyer	4	1833—1841	41, 47, 51–54	160
Nisi Prius				
Clayton	1	1631—1650		
Lilly, Assize	1	1688—1693		170
Peake	2	1790—1812	3, 4	170
Espinasse	6	1793—1807	5, 6, 8, 9	170
Campbell	4	1808—1816	10–16	(1–3) 170; (4) 171
Starkie	3	1815—1822	18–20, 23	171
Dowling and Ryland (1 Part)		1822—1823	25	171
Carrington and Payne	9	1823—1841	28, 31, 33, 34, 38, 40, 48, 50	(1) 171; (2–6) 172; (7–9) 173
Carrington and Marshman	1	1840—1842	66	174

	No. of vols.	Period covered	Corresponding vols. of Revised Reports	Corresponding vols. of English Reports
Nisi Prius—contd.				
Carrington and Kirwan	3	1843—1850	70, 80, 88	174, 175
Foster and Finlason	4	1858—1867	115, 121, 130, 142	175, 176
COLLATERAL REPORTS				
Bartholoman	1	1811		
Holt	1	1815—1817	17	171
Gow	1	1818—1820	21	171
Ryan and Moody	1	1823—1826	27	171
Moody and Malkin	1	1826—1830	31	173
Moody and Robinson	2	1830—1844	42, 62	174
Ecclesiastical				
Lee	2	1752—1758		161
Haggard (Consistory)	2	1788—1821		161
Phillimore	3	1809—1821		161
Addams	3	1822—1826		162
Haggard	4	1827—1833		162
Curteis	3	1834—1844		163
Robertson	2	1844—1853		163
Spinks (Ecclesiastical and Admiralty)	2	1853—1855		164
Deane and Swabey	1	1855—1857		164
Phillimore's Ecclesiastical Judgments	1	1867—1875		
COLLATERAL REPORTS				
Brodrick and Fremantle	1	1840—1864		
Joyce	1	1865—1881		
Brooke	1	1850—1872		
Dale	1	1868—1871		
Notes of Cases in the Ecclesiastical and Maritime Courts	7	1841—1850		
Cripp's Church and Clergy Cases (2 Parts)		1847—1850		
Tristram's Consistory Judgments	1	1872—1890		
Probate and Divorce				
Swabey and Tristram	4	1858—1865		164
Searle and Smith (2 Parts)		1859—1860		
Admiralty and Shipping				
Hay and Marriott	1	1776—1779		165
Robinson, C.	6	1799—1808		165
Edwards	1	1808—1810		165
Dodson	2	1811—1822		165

	No. of vols.	Period covered	Corresponding vols. of Revised Reports	Corresponding vols. of English Reports
Admiralty and Shipping —contd.				
Haggard	3	1822—1837	33, 35	166
Robinson, W.	3	1838—1852		166
Spinks (Ecclesiastical and Admiralty)	2	1853—1855		164
Spinks' Prize Cases	1	1854—1856		164
Swabey	1	1858—1859		166
Lushington	1	1860—1863		167
Browning and Lushington	1	1864—1865		167
COLLATERALS AND EXTRA VOLUMES				
Burrell and Marsden	1	1648—1840		167
Parker	1	1693—1774		
Roscoe's Prize Cases	2	1745—1859		
Lloyd's Prize Cases	10	1914—1922		
British and Colonial Prize Cases	3	1914—1922		
Notes of Cases in the Ecclesiastical and Maritime Courts	7	1841—1850		
Holt's Admiralty Cases	1	1863—1867		
Maritime Cases (Crockford)	3	1860—1871		
Maritime Cases (Aspinall)	19	1870—1940		
Lloyd's List Law Reports (2 vols. per year from 1951)	84	1919—1950		
Lloyd's Prize Cases	1	1940—1953		
Bankruptcy				
Rose	2	1810—1816		
Buck	1	1816—1820		
Glyn and Jameson	2	1821—1828		
Montagu and M'Arthur	1	1828—1829		
Montagu	1	1830—1832		
Montagu and Bligh	1	1832—1833		
Deacon and Chitty	4	1832—1835		
Montagu and Ayrton	3	1833—1838		
Deacon	4	1836—1839		
Montague and Chitty	1	1838—1840		
Montagu, Deacon and De Gex	3	1840—1844		
De Gex	2	1845—1850		
Fontblanque	1	1849—1852		
Bankruptcy and Insolvency Reports	2	1853—1855		
Morrell	10	1884—1893		
Manson (Bankruptcy and Companies Cases)	21	1894—1914		
Bankruptcy and Winding Up Cases	20	1915—1942		

	No. of vols.	Period covered	Corresponding vols. of Revised Reports	Corresponding vols. of English Reports
Company Cases				
Megone	2	1888—1891		
Manson (also under Bank-ruptcy)	21	1894—1914		
Bankruptcy and Winding Up Cases	20	1915—1942		
Railway and Canal Cases				
Nicholl, Hare, Carrow	7	1835—1855		
Beavan and Walford's Railway Cases (2 Parts)		1846		
Neville, Browne and Macnamara	29	1855—1949		
Traffic Cases (*continuation of above*) Vol. 30—		1949—1957		
Election Cases				
Glanville	1	1624		
Tomlins	1	1689—1795		
Douglas	4	1774—1776		
Phillips	1	1780—1781		
Luder	3	1785—1787		
Fraser	2	1790—1792		
Clifford	1	1796—1797		
Peckwell	2	1802—1806		
Corbett and Daniell	1	1819		
Cockburn and Rowe	1	1833		
Perry and Knapp	1	1833		
Knapp and Ombler	1	1834—1835		
Falconer and Fitzherbert	1	1835—1839		
Barron and Austin	1	1842		
Barron and Arnold	1	1843—1846		
Power, Rodwell and Dew	2	1847—1856		
Wolferstan and Dew	1	1856—1858		
Wolferstan and Bristowe	1	1859—1865		
O'Malley and Hardcastle (Election Petitions) *And Vol. 7, Parts 1–3*	6	1869—1929		
Registration Cases				
Cox and Atkinson's Registration Appeal Cases (2 Parts)		1843—1846		
Pigott and Rodwell	1	1843—1845		
Lutwyche	2	1843—1845		
Keane and Grant	1	1854—1862		
Hopwood and Philbrick	1	1863—1867		
Hopwood and Coltman	2	1868—1878		
Coltman	1	1879—1885		

	No. of vols.	Period covered	Corresponding vols. of Revised Reports	Corresponding vols. of English Reports
Registration Cases—contd.				
Fox and Smith	1	1886—1895		
Smith	2	1896—1915		
And Vol. 3, Part 1 only.				
Revision Courts				
Delane	1	1832—1835		
Manning	1	1832—1835		
Locus Standi Cases				
Clifford and Stephen	2	1867—1872		
Clifford and Rickards	3	1873—1884		
Rickards and Michael	1	1885—1889		
Rickards and Saunders	1	1890—1894		
Saunders and Austin	2	1895—1904		
Saunders and Bidder	2	1905—1919		
Bidder	7 pts.	1920—1936		
Newbon, Private Bills Reports	2	1895—1896		
Newbon, Private Bills Reports	3	1899		
Crown and Criminal Cases				
Kelyng, Sir J., 1873	1	1662—1669		84
Foster, 1792	1	1743—1761		168
Leach	2	1730—1815		168
Russell and Ryan	1	1799—1823		168
Lewin's Crown Cases on the Northern Circuit	2	1822—1838		168
Moody	2	1824—1844		(1) 168; (2) 169
Denison	2	1844—1852		169
Temple and Mew's Criminal Appeal Cases	1	1848—1851		
Dearsley	1	1852—1856		169
Dearsley and Bell	1	1856—1858		169
Bell	1	1858—1860		169
Leigh and Cave	1	1861—1865		169
Central Criminal Court Sessions Papers	158	1834—1913		
Cox's Criminal Law Cases	31	1843—1948		
Criminal Appeal Reports	46	1908—1962		
Local Government Cases				
Justice of the Peace	126	1837—1962		
Local Government Reports	60	1903—1962		
Cox's Magistrates Municipal and Parochial Cases	27	1859—1920		

	No. of vols.	Period covered	Corresponding vols. of Revised Reports	Corresponding vols. of English Reports
Patents and Trade Marks				
Davies	1	1785—1816		
Carpmael	2	1602—1842		
Webster	2	1601—1855		
Macrory	1	1847—1856		
Goodeve, 1884	1	1785—1883		
Griffin, 1887	2	1866—1887		
Reports of Patent, etc., Cases (1 vol. per year from 1958)	74	1884—1958		
Tax Cases				
Reports of Cases on Income Tax	39	1875—1962		
Taxation Reports	23	1939—1962		
Commercial Court				
Commercial Cases	46	1895—1941		
Town Planning and Compensation				
Planning and Compensation Reports	13	1949—1962		

AUTHORISED ABBREVIATIONS FOR MODERN LAW REPORTS

A.C.	Appeals Cases, 1891–
A.L.J.R.	Australian Law Journal Reports, 1958–
A.L.R.	American Law Reports, First series
A.L.R. 2d.	American Law Reports, Second series
A.L.R. 3d.	American Law Reports, Third series
A.L.R. Fed.	American Law Reports, Federal
A.T.C.	Accountant Tax Cases, 1922–26. Continued as Annotated Tax Cases, 1927–
All E.R.	All England Reports, 1936–
All E.R.Rep.	All England Reports, Reprint, 1558–1935
App.Cas.	Appeals Cases, 1875–90
B.I.L.C.	British International Law Cases
B.W.C.C.	Butterworths' Workmen's Compensation Cases, 1908–50
C.L.R.	Commonwealth Law Reports, 1903–
C.M.L.R.	Common Market Law Reports, 1962–

C.P.D.	Common Pleas Division, 1875–80
Ch.	Chancery, 1891–
Ch.D.	Chancery Division, 1875–90
Com.Cas.	Commercial Cases, 1895–1941
Cox C.C.	Cox's Criminal Law Cases, 1943–1941
Cr.App.R.	Criminal Appeal Reports, 1908–
D.L.R.	Dominion Law Reports, 1912–
E.R.	English Reports, 1220–1865
Ex.D.	Exchequer Division, 1875–80
Fam.	Family Division, 1972–
Gaz.L.R.	Gazette Law Reports, incorporated in New Zealand Law Reports
I.C.J. Reports	International Court of Justice Reports
I.C.R.	Industrial Court Reports, 1972–
I.L.R.	International Law Reports, 1950–
I.R. or Ir.R.	Irish Reports, 1838–
I.R.L.R.	Industrial Relations Law Reports, 1972
I.T.R.	Industrial Tribunals Reports, 1965–
J.P.	Justice of the Peace Reports, 1837–
K.I.R.	Knight's Industrial Reports, 1966–
L.Ed.	United States Supreme Court Reports, Lawyer's Edition, 1882–
L.J. or L.J.R.	Law Journal Reports, 1931–1949
L.J.C.C.A.	Law Journal Newspaper County Court Appeals, 1935
L.J.N.C.C.R.	Law Journal Newspaper County Court Reports, 1934–47
L.J.O.S.	Law Journal Reports, Old Series, 1822–31
L.R.A. & E.	Admiralty and Ecclesiastical, 1865–75
L.R.C.C.R.	Crown Cases Reserved, 1865–75
L.R.C.P.	Common Pleas, 1865–75
L.R.Ch.App.	Chancery Appeals, 1865–75
L.R.Eq.	Equity Cases, 1865–75
L.R.Ex.	Exchequer, 1865–75
L.R.H.L.	English and Irish Appeals to the House of Lords, 1865–75
L.R.P.C.	Privy Council Appeals, 1865–75
L.R.P. & D.	Probate and Divorce, 1865–75
L.R.Q.B.	Queen's Bench, 1865–75
L.R.Sc. & Div.	Scottish and Divorce Appeals, 1865 75

Lloyd's Rep.	Lloyd's List Law Reports, 1925–
N.I.	Northern Ireland Law Reports, 1925–
N.S.W.S.C.R.	New South Wales Supreme Court Reports, 1862–79
N.S.W.L.R.	New South Wales Law Reports, 1971–
N.S.W.R.	New South Wales Reports, 1880–1900
N.Z.L.R.	New Zealand Law Reports, 1883–
P.	Probate, 1891–1971
P. & C.R.	Planning and Compensation Reports, 1949–67 Continued as Property and Compensation Reports, 1968–
P.D.	Probate, Divorce and Admiralty Division, 1875–90
Q.B. or K.B.	Queen's (or King's) Bench, 1891–
Q.B.D. or K.B.D.	Queen's (or King's) Bench Division, 1875–90
R.P.	Restrictive Practices, 1958–1972
R.P.C.	Reports of Patent, Design and Trade Mark Cases, 1884–
S.A.L.R.	South African Law Reports, 1947–
S.C. or Sess.Cas.	Sessions Cases, 1906–
S.L.T.	Scottish Law Times (Reports), 1893–
S.R.(N.S.W.)	State Reports of New South Wales, 1901–1970
S.T.C.	Simon's Tax Cases, 1973–
T.C.	Tax Cases, 1875–
T.L.R.	Times Law Reports, 1884–1952
W.L.R.	Weekly Law Reports, 1953–
W.N.	Weekly Notes (Reports), 1866–1952

LAW REPORTS, 1ST, 2ND AND 3RD SERIES

1st 1865–1875   2nd 1875–1890   3rd 1891–

Appeals Cases and Predecessors, i.e.:

L.R.H.L.	1865–75	English & Irish Appeals to the House of Lords
L.R.P.C.	1865–75	Privy Council Appeals
L.R.Sc. & Div.	1865–75	Scottish and Divorce Appeals
App.Cas.	1875–90	Appeals Cases
A.C.	1891–	Appeals Cases

Chancery and Predecessors, i.e.:

L.R.Ch.App.	1865–75	Chancery Appeals
L.R.Eq.	1865–75	Equity Cases
Ch.D.	1875–90	Chancery Division
Ch.	1891–	Chancery

Queen's (or King's) Bench and Predecessors, i.e.:

L.R.C.P.	1865–75	Common Pleas
L.R.C.C.R.	1865–75	Crown Cases Reserved
L.R.Ex.	1865–75	Exchequer
L.R.Q.B.	1865–75	Queen's Bench
C.P.D.	1875–80	Common Pleas Division
Ex.D.	1875–80	Exchequer Division
Q.B.D.	1875–90	Queen's Bench Division
Q.B.	1891–	Queen's (or King's) Bench

Probate and Predecessors, i.e.:

L.R.A. & E.	1865–75	Admiralty and Ecclesiastical
L.R.P. & D.	1865–75	Probate and Divorce
P.D.	1875–90	Probate, Divorce and Admiralty Division
P.	1891–1971	Probate
Fam.	1972–	Family

Restrictive Practices

| R.P. | 1958–72 | Restrictive Practices |

Industrial Court Reports

| I.C.R. | 1972– | Industrial Court Reports |

Secondary Materials

Encyclopedias of English law

With the exception of Halsbury's *Laws of England*, " all general encyclopedias of English Law became casualties of the First or the Second World War." [1]

In 1866, a Commission was appointed to inquire into the exposition of a digest of the law. After publishing a first report, it died out but fortunately commercial publishers undertook the execution in its main outlines of the schemes recommended by the Commission. The basic aim was " to furnish a complete statement of English law in the convenient and accessible form of a series of connected treatises on every branch of the law, each written by experts in the particular subject." [2] The first edition was published under the General Editorship of Lord Halsbury who was then Lord Chancellor.

The work is entering its fourth edition. The contributors are judges, practising lawyers and academics whose names are disclosed. The structure is analytical. The law is divided into units which are sometimes smaller than the orthodox divisions of the law adopted by academic and professional writers. The work is set out in alphabetical order and contains cross-references to the companion work, Halsbury's *Statutes of England* and also to the *English and Empire Digest* which we will mention below.

Each volume is indexed with a table of cases and statutes and there is a useful general index for the whole series.

There are cumulative supplements published annually, a looseleaf current service and an annual abridgment. The latter is a survey of the legal developments in the particular year.

There are special editions for some Commonwealth countries for which supplementary volumes are added. Thus there is an *Australian Pilot* and a *Canadian Converter* which set out the Australian and Canadian authorities respectively.

Halsbury's *Statutes* are now in their third edition. The first edition was published in 1930. The primary purpose is to render easily available the correct and amended text of enactments together with explanatory notes. It contains almost all public Acts relating to England and Wales and London by-laws. For reasons which are not obvious, Acts or parts of Acts affecting Scotland only are not included but annotations are included concerning the application of Acts to Northern Ireland. The work is kept up to date by annual cumulative supplements and a loose-leaf current service.

Digests

Similar but less ambitious in scope to Halsbury are various digests and abridgments of the law. The best of the early abridgments and digests are those of *Rolle*, *Comyn* and *Bacon*. *Viner's* abridgment in the eighteenth century is more comprehensive but does not enjoy quite the same reputation as the others.

In modern times, Butterworths have produced the *English and Empire Digest* which is a digest of cases. It gives useful summaries of the cases and their subsequent history and is kept reasonably up to date by cumulative volumes. The writer has found its main use to be research in legal history. It is certainly not an easy source of the modern law.

Much more useful are *Current Law, Scottish Current Law* and the *Current Law Yearbooks* published by Sweet and Maxwell/Stevens and W. Green and Son. These began in 1947 and are the nearest approach to a complete and convenient index of recent law in one place. The separate Scots edition is even more useful, covering Scots material as well. The yearbooks provide a digest and index on an annual basis.

Textbooks

The question of doctrine has already been discussed in Chapter 10. Included under this head are the " classics " such as *Bracton, Coke, Hale,* and *Blackstone* and as we have seen greater weight is accorded them than more modern writings.

Later writers such as *Pollock, Anson* and *Dicey* are held in high repute.

For a detailed list of authors, see Sweet & Maxwell's *Legal Bibliography* and consult the catalogue of your law library.

The Scottish Institutional Writers

Reference has already been made to the Scottish approach to doctrine in Chapter 10.

The principal writers are Viscount Stair, *The Institutions of the Law of Scotland,* 1681; John Erskine, *An Institute of the Laws of Scotland,* 1773; and George Bell, *Commentaries on the Law of Scotland,* 1804, and *Principles of the Law of Scotland,* 1829.

Legal Dictionaries

The three best legal dictionaries are Stroud's *Judicial Dictionary,* Jowitt's *Dictionary of English Law* and *Words and Phrases Legally Defined.* Bouvier's *Law Dictionary* is a useful American legal dictionary.

Smaller and inexpensive dictionaries which you might find useful are Osborn's *Law Dictionary* (1976) and Mozley and Whiteley's *Law Dictionary* (8th ed., 1970).

On the whole, legal dictionaries are not of so much use except to check the meaning of a technical term when you begin your studies or to get research ideas later on. A word of caution even then must be uttered. Legal words and concepts are often chameleon-like. They change their meaning with their context. It is much better, therefore, to check their meaning if possible in the textbook in the particular area where the word crops up or in the particular part of Halsbury's *Laws*. It is easy to get misled by the meaning given in a different context by the dictionary.

Periodicals

These occupy roughly the same status as textbooks.

The main academic journals are the *Law Quarterly Review*, the *Cambridge Law Journal*, the *Modern Law Review*, the *Juridical Review*, the *Northern Irish Law Quarterly*, the *Irish Jurist*, *Current Legal Problems*, the *Cambrian Law Review* and the *Anglo-American Law Review*. These are general publications.

In addition, there are specialist journals such as the *Criminal Law Review*, the *Journal of Business Law*, *The Conveyancer*, the *International and Comparative Law Quarterly*, *Public Law*, *Family Law*, the *Industrial Law Journal*, the *British Journal of Law and Society*, the *British Journal of Criminology*, the *British Tax Review*, the *European Law Review*, and the *Journal of Planning and Environment Law*.

Useful practitioners' journals are the *New Law Journal*, the *Solicitors' Journal*, *Law Society's Gazette*, the *Scots Law Times* and the *Journal of the Law Society of Scotland*.

The American publication, *Index to Legal Periodicals*, is a valuable source of references to learned articles.

Law reform materials

You will often be referred to law reform proposals. Before 1965, the Law Revision Committee (later reconstituted as the Law Reform Committee), the Private International Law Committee, the Criminal Law Revision Committee and the Law Reform Committee for Scotland all produced reports. Since 1965, the English and Scottish Law Commissions have been set up and the practice is to issue programmes and working papers and only later to issue reports. Often draft legislation is appended. The Law Reform Committee and the Criminal Law Revision Committee still exist and produce reports.

Other sources of law reform proposals are the Reports of Royal Commissions and Departmental Committees.

All of these are obtainable from H.M.S.O., unless they are out of print.

The reports of *Justice*—the British branch of the International Commission of Jurists—are also useful materials and you will no doubt be referred to them.

AUSTRALIA

You will find a useful introduction to Australian law in the volume on Australia in the *British Commonwealth, Its Laws and Constitutions* series; *An Introduction to Law* by Derham, Maher and Waller; and *The Australian and the Law* by Geoffrey Sawer.

Primary Materials

Statutes

Australia is a federal jurisdiction. There are *Commonwealth Statutes* covering federal laws, and statutes for each state nearly all of which have been consolidated. For more detailed information, see *An Introduction to Law* by Derham, Maher and Waller (2nd ed.), pp. 211–214.

Law reports

Cases in the High Court and Privy Council are found in *Commonwealth Law Reports*, the *Australian Argus Law Reports* and the *Australian Law Journal Reports*. Privy Council cases also usually appear in the English Appeal Cases, *All England Reports* and the *Weekly Law Reports*.

There are various state reports. New South Wales had three sets—*State Reports (N.S.W.)*, *Weekly Notes (N.S.W.)* and *New South Wales Reports*, for a time.

Secondary Materials

Encyclopedias

Reference has been made to the *Australian Pilot* to Halsbury's *Laws*.

There is an *Australian Digest* which digests case law and Butterworths produce *Australian and New Zealand Annotations to the All England Reports*.

Textbooks

There are Australian editions of many English textbooks but there are many excellent textbooks of Australian law.

Periodicals

Most Australian universities produce their own law review although not all of these appear regularly.

The *Australian Law Journal* also has many useful articles.

Law reform materials

Each state has its own law reform committee which produces reports. There is also a federal law commission. Details of law reform activities in Australia and New Zealand are collated by the Federal Law Reform Commission which produces a regular bulletin called *Reform*.

CANADA

You will find a useful survey of Canadian law and the legal system in Bora Laskin, *The British Tradition in Canadian Law*.

Primary Materials

Statutes

Canada, like Australia, is a federal jurisdiction. Federal statutes are set out topic by topic in *Revised Statutes of Canada*. This is kept up to date by *Statutes of Canada*.

Each province produces its own set of statutes, *e.g. Revised Statutes of Ontario* which is kept up to date by *Statutes of Ontario*.

Law reports

Canada Law Reports report cases from the federal courts in Canada.

Dominion Law Reports is a very useful set of reports covering both federal and provincial cases.

There are various sets of reports for cases from particular provinces, *e.g.* the *Ontario Reports* and *Rapports Judiciaires Officiels* of Québec and regional reports, *e.g. Western Weekly Reports* which cover Alberta, British Columbia, Manitoba and Saskatchewan.

Secondary Materials

Encyclopedias

The *Canadian Abridgement* is a digest of cases from federal and provincial courts.

The Canadian Encyclopedia Digest is a law encyclopedia rather like the *Corpus Juris Secundum* in the U.S.A.

Textbooks

There are a number of specialist works by Canadian authors although the textbook writing tradition is not strong in Canadian law schools for a variety of reasons.

Periodicals

The most likely periodicals which you will consult are the *Canadian Bar Review* and the various university law journals. Unlike England, all the law schools tend to produce their own journals.

Law reform materials

Each province has its law reform body and there is a federal law reform commission. The latter has so far mainly operated in the areas of criminal and family law. Its reports show a fresh, popular style which is uncharacteristic of most commonwealth law reform reports.

NEW ZEALAND

There is a useful general survey of New Zealand law in the relevant volume in *The British Commonwealth Series* (edited by Dr. J. L. Robson, formerly Secretary for Justice) which is now in its second edition.

Primary Materials

Statutes

These are contained in a series known as *Statutes of New Zealand*. Prior to this series, which dates back to 1854, there are ordinances.

Law reports

The principal reports are the *New Zealand Law Reports*. Occasionally, you may get a case in a series known as the *Gazette Law Reports* which date from 1893–1953.

Secondary Materials

Encyclopedias

There is a *New Zealand Pilot* to Halsbury's *Laws*. In addition, there were numerous Digests of the case law in the nineteenth century.

Textbooks

Although English textbooks are often used, there is an increasing number of New Zealand specialist texts.

Periodicals

Nearly all the university law faculties produce journals. In addition, there is the *New Zealand Universities' Law Review*.

The *New Zealand Law Journal* is a practitioners' journal which sometimes contains articles useful to a student.

Law reform materials

There is a Law Reform Commission which has satellite committees.

THE UNITED STATES OF AMERICA

Primary Materials

Statutes

The United States is a federal jurisdiction with a written constitution. Federal legislation is contained in *Statutes at Large* but you are most likely to find it in your library in the form of the *United States Code Annotated* and the *Federal Code Annotated*.

There are separate sets of statutes of each state which are often called codes. These are broken down into subjects like the Canadian legislation.

Law reports

The American system of reports is complicated. Supreme Court cases are reported in *United States Supreme Court Reports*. Federal cases are covered in *United States Reports* and the *Federal Reporter*. Prior to these, there were nominate reports.

Each state has its own set of reports but you are most likely to find in your library some or all of the *National Reporter System* which divides the United States up into seven groups—Pacific, North-Western, South-Western, North-Eastern, Atlantic, South-Eastern and Southern. There is a very useful map showing the states covered by each group facing p. 70 of *How to Find the Law* (6th ed.) by William R. Roalfe.

Another set of reports which you may come across is *American Law Reports Annotated*.

Secondary Materials

Encyclopedias

There are two excellent encyclopedias of American law—the *American Jurisprudence* and the *Corpus Juris Secundum* which both resemble Halsbury's *Laws of England* in their coverage. There are some encyclopedias of state laws also but your library is unlikely to stock them.

The main digest is the *American Digest System* which follows the scheme of the *National Reporter System*.

Textbooks

The United States is rich in practitioners' text but the tendency in academic law nowadays is towards cases and materials books with brief interlocking texts.

Periodicals

The United States produces an abundance of university law journals. The articles to which you will be referred will tend to appear in magazines such as the *Harvard Law Review*, the *Yale Law Journal*, the *Columbia Law Review* and the *Chicago Law Review* although there are many other excellent journals.

It is unlikely that you will be referred to practitioners' journals but there are specialist journals such as the *Business Lawyer* to which occasional reference might be made.

Law reform materials

Each state has its own law reform body which produces reports. There are often *ad hoc* committees. In addition, you are likely to be referred to the *American Restatement* which emanates from the American Law Institute. It is drafted like law but has doctrinal influence rather than direct legal application.

FRANCE

Two very useful introductory books are Amos & Walton *Introduction to French Law* (3rd ed.), ed. by Lawson, Anton and Brown; and *A Source-book on French Law* by Kahn-Freund, Levy and Rudden. René David's *French Law—Its Structure, Sources and Methodology* is also useful.

Most of French law is codified. The Codes can be obtained in pocket editions in the series *Petits Codes Dalloz*. These have some annotations.

The major encyclopedia is the *Encyclopedie Dalloz*.

GERMANY

A really useful introduction is Dr. E. J. Cohn's two volume *Manual of German Law* (2nd ed.).

German law, like French law, is largely codified. Pocket editions of the codes are produced by C. H. Beck'sche Verlagsbuchhandlung of Munich.

There is no German equivalent of *Halsbury* or the *Encyclopedie Dalloz*. Reifferscheidt's *Erganzbares Lexikon des Rechts* is a large law dictionary.

EUROPEAN ECONOMIC COMMUNITY

The basic law, as we saw, is contained in the treaties. There is a useful edition of these produced by Sweet & Maxwell, now in its second edition. EEC legislation can be found in the legislation volumes of the *Official Journal of the European Communities*. There are official law reports of the European Court but the main English series is *Common Market Law Reports*.

Sweet & Maxwell produce an *Encyclopedia of European Community Law*.

There are a number of introductory texts, the simplest of which is Mathijsen's *Guide to European Community Law*.

Specialist journals include the *Common Market Law Review* and the *European Law Review*. Each Member State tends to produce its own literature to which the specialist must refer.

Notes

[1] Miles O. Price and Harry Bitner, *Effective Legal Research* (3rd ed.), p. 331.

[2] Viscount Hailsham in his Introduction to the second edition.

APPENDIX 3

THE CASE LAW PROCESS IN OPERATION—
THE CONCEPTUAL DEVELOPMENT OF NEGLIGENCE

In Chapter 7 we examined case law as a source of law and kind of reasoning. We saw how it was not exclusively deductive or inductive although sometimes such methods were used. At heart it involves a process of reasoning by analogy and rules with a superstructure of ground rules of *stare decisis*, and emanates from judicial decision-making. The word "process" here refers to the whole compendium of argumentation, methodology and historical development which produces legal rules, principles and standards. Concepts are necessary elements in the formulation of those rules, principles and standards. Edward Levi, who has been a Professor of Law and Attorney-General of the United States, has described the process as follows:

> "*In the long run a circular motion can be seen. The first stage is the creation of the legal concept which is built up as cases are compared. The period is one in which the court fumbles for a phrase. Several phrases may be tried out; the misuse or misunderstanding of words itself may have an effect. The concept sounds like another, and the jump to the second is made. The second stage is the period when the concept is more or less fixed, although reasoning by example continues to classify items inside and outside the concept. The third stage is the breakdown of the concept, as reasoning by example has moved so far ahead as to make it clear that the suggestive influence of the word is no longer desired.*" [1]

(Italics supplied.)

Levi illustrates this movement by reference to the development in Anglo-American law of the potential liability of a seller of an article which causes injury to a person who did not buy the article from the seller. We shall confine ourselves to the development in English law but then go on to consider the significance of the principles in the wider area of negligence at large.

The term negligence is used in lay speech to connote carelessness. As such it became a factor in establishing liability as the law became more sophisticated. In the modern law it is the name given to a specific tort (*i.e.* civil wrong) as well as a mode of committing certain other torts and crimes. In this appendix we shall be primarily concerned with its development as a specific tort. This development takes place in a period of great economic and social change which is marked by the gradual growth of mass manufacturing as a result of the industrial revolution.

THE DEVELOPMENT OF A CATEGORY OF DANGEROUS THINGS

The development begins with *Dixon* v. *Bell* (1816) 5 M. & S. 198; 105 E.R. 1023 which is not a case of sale at all. The defendant sent his servant girl to get a gun which he knew was loaded. She played with the gun and shot the plaintiff's son in the face. The court allowed recovery, Lord Ellenborough C.J. holding that the gun " by this want of care " had been " left in a state capable of doing mischief." In other words the gun was a thing which was dangerous through lack of care.

This simple picture is complicated by the case of *Langridge* v. *Levy* (1837) 2 M. & W. 519; 150 E.R. 863 where the plaintiff complained that the defendant had sold his (the plaintiff's) father a defective gun for the use of himself, and his sons. The gun exploded in the plaintiff's hand and mutilated it so badly that it had to be amputated. The court allowed recovery on the basis that there had been a false representation by the defendant that the gun was safe when he knew it was not and that the defendant had knowingly sold the gun to the father for the purpose of it being used by the son. The case thus appears to have been decided on the basis of fraud and direct dealing.

An argument had been raised for the defendant on the basis of *Dixon* v. *Bell* that there was a distinction between things " immediately dangerous ... by the act of the defendant " and " such as may become so by some further act to be done to it." The court rejected that distinction and indeed the whole category of dangerous things because it did not wish to create an authority for an action against vendors even of articles dangerous in themselves, " at the suit of any person whomsoever into whose hands they might happen to pass and who should be injured thereby."

The argument for a category of dangerous things was raised again in *Winterbottom* v. *Wright* (1842) 10 M. & W. 109; 152

E.R. 402. Here the plaintiff coachman had been injured when he was thrown from his seat on a coach. He sued the defendant who had supplied the coach under contract to the Postmaster-General. The court refused redress and to countenance the existence of a category of dangerous things. *Langridge* v. *Levy* was distinguished on the ground that it was a case of fraud and direct dealing. The court refused to extend either of those notions for the plaintiff's benefit.

However in *Longmeid* v. *Holliday* (1851) 6 Ex. 761; 155 E.R. 752 the court recognised the concept of things dangerous in themselves but disallowed recovery. This was a case of a lamp purchased by the plaintiff's husband which injured the plaintiff when she lit it. The court held that she had not shown that the defendant knew the lamp was unfit; he had not warranted it to be sound; and the lamp was not in its nature dangerous. The court recognised a distinction between " an instrument in its nature dangerous, or under particular circumstances dangerous," such as the gun in *Dixon* v. *Bell*, and a thing such as a coach not in itself dangerous but which might become so by a latent defect entirely unknown although discoverable by the exercise of ordinary care.

Thereafter the principle laid down in *Longmeid* v. *Holliday* was applied to other things. In *George* v. *Skivington* (1869) L.R. 5 Ex. 1 the concept of things dangerous or imminently dangerous was extended to include a defective hairwash. The case is odd in that the court did not refer to the concept, but equated the hairwash with the defective gun in *Langridge* v. *Levy*. *Longmeid* v. *Holliday* which had been cited in argument, was accounted for on the basis that no negligence had been proved. On the other hand the concept was extended to defective gas appliances in *Parry* v. *Smith* (1879) 4 C.P.D. 325 and *Dominion Natural Gas Co. Ltd.* v. *Colling & Perkins* [1909] A.C. 640 (P.C.).

In *Heaven* v. *Pender* (1883) 11 Q.B.D. 503 a defective scaffold was included in the concept. The plaintiff, a workman in the employment of a firm engaged to paint a ship in the defendant's dry dock, was injured when the scaffolding collapsed. The Court of Appeal allowed recovery. The majority rested their decision on a technical point about invitation. Brett M.R., however, was more adventurous and attempted to formulate a comprehensive general rule. He said at p. 509: (italics supplied)

" *The logic of inductive reasoning requires that where two major propositions lead to exactly similar minor premisses there must be a more remote and larger premiss which embraces both of the major propositions. That, in the present consideration, is, as it seems to me, the same proposition which will cover the similar legal liability inferred in the cases of collision and carriage. The proposition which these recognized cases suggest, and which is, therefore, to be deduced from them, is that whenever one person is by circumstances placed in such a position with regard to another that everyone of ordinary sense who did think would at once recognize that if he did not use ordinary care and skill in his own conduct with regard to those circumstances he would cause danger of injury to the person or property of the other, a duty arises to use ordinary care and skill to avoid such danger. Without displacing the other propositions to which allusion has been made as appli-cable to the particular circumstances in respect of which they have been enunciated, this proposition includes, I think, all the recognized cases of liability*. It is the only proposition which covers them all. It may, therefore safely be affirmed to be a true proposition, unless some obvious case can be stated in which the liability must be admitted to exist, and which yet is not within this proposition. There is no such case. Let us apply this proposition to the case of one person supplying goods or machinery, or instruments or utensils, or the like, for the purpose of their being used by another person under such circumstances that everyone of ordinary sense would, if he thought, recognize at once that unless he used ordinary care and skill with regard to the condition of the thing supplied or the mode of supplying it, there will be danger of injury to the person or property of him for whose use the thing is sup-plied, and who is to use it, a duty arises to use ordinary care and skill as to the condition or manner of supplying such thing. And for a neglect of such ordinary care or skill whereby injury happens a legal liability arises to be enforced by an action for negligence. This includes the case of goods, etc., supplied to be used immediately by a particular person or persons or one of a class of persons, where it would be obvious to the person supplying, if he thought, that the goods would in all proba-bility be used at once by such persons before a reasonable opportunity for discovering any defect which might exist, and where the thing supplied would be of such a nature that a neglect of ordinary care or skill as to its condition or the manner of supplying it would probably cause danger to the person or property of the person for whose use it was supplied, and who was about to use it. It would exclude a case in which the goods are supplied under circumstances in which it would be a chance by whom they would be used, or whether they would be used or not, or whether they would be used before there would probably be means of observing any defect, or where the goods would be of such a nature that a want of care or skill as to their condition or the manner of supplying them would not probably produce danger of injury to person or property. The cases of vendor and purchaser, and lender and hirer under contract need not be considered, as the liability arises under the contract, and not merely as a duty imposed by law, though it may not be useless to observe that it seems difficult to import the implied obligation into the contract except in cases in which if there were no contract between the parties the law would according to the rule above stated imply the duty."

Langridge v. *Levy* did not fit easily into his analysis and he said that it was not an easy case and " cannot be accurately reported."

The other two judges did not agree with the Master of the Rolls' wide formulation and it seems to have been generally agreed that it was too wide. In *Le Lievre* v. *Gould* [1893] 1 Q.B. 491 he recanted. In that case it was held that there was no liability for a negligent misstatement.

The preference of the common law was thus for a catalogue of particular duties of care. Although there are other reported cases in the period 1883 to 1932 they are illustrative of this latter approach.

Donoghue v. *Stevenson—The Broad and Narrow Approaches*

In 1932, however, we have the famous case of *Donoghue* v. *Stevenson* [1932] A.C. 562. This was a Scottish appeal to the House of Lords but the English and Scottish substantive law was assumed to be the same. The appellant drank ginger beer poured from a bottle of ginger beer manufactured by the respondent and purchased by a friend from a retailer. The bottle allegedly contained the decomposing remains of a snail which could not have been detected until most of the contents of the bottle had been consumed. As a consequence the appellant said she had contracted a serious illness and accordingly she sued the respondent. The House of Lords under a special Scottish procedure had to determine whether this disclosed a cause of action and they found for the appellant by a bare majority of 3 to 2. Of the majority Lord Atkin rested his judgment on the widest grounds and, while rejecting the formulation of Brett M.R. in *Heaven* v. *Pender* as too wide, set forth a new general principle or standard. Lords Thankerton and Macmillan were more cautious and found the duty to exist in the case of manufacture of food and drink for consumption by the public. The whole of Lord Atkin's judgment, which is reported at [1932] A.C. 578 onwards, is worth reading. The passages which I have italicised are particularly important for our purposes. He said

" It is remarkable how difficult it is to find in the English authorities statements of general application defining the relations between parties that give rise to the duty. *The Courts are concerned with the particular relations which come before them in actual litigation, and it is sufficient to say whether the duty exists in those circumstances. The result is that the Courts have been engaged upon an elaborate classification of duties as they exist in respect of property, whether real or personal, with further divisions as to ownership, occupation or control, and distinctions based on the particular relations of the one side or the other, whether manufacturer, salesman or landlord, customer, tenant, stranger, and so on. In this way it can be ascertained at any time whether the law recognizes a duty, but only where the case can be referred to some particular species which has been examined and classified. And yet the duty which is common to all the cases where liability is established must logically be based upon some element common to the cases where it is found to exist. To seek a complete logical definition of the general principle is probably to go beyond the function of the judge, for the more general the definition the more likely it is to omit essentials or to introduce non-essentials. The attempt was made by Brett M.R. in* Heaven *v.* Pender (11 Q.B.D. 530, 509), *in a definition to which I will later refer. As framed, it was demonstrably too wide, though it appears to me, if properly limited, to be capable of affording a valuable practical guide.*

At present I content myself with pointing out that in English law there must be, and is, some general conception of relations giving rise to a duty of care, of which the particular cases found in the books are but instances. The liability for negligence, whether you style it such or treat it as in other systems as a species of " culpa," is no doubt based upon a general public sentiment of moral wrongdoing for which the offender must pay. *But acts or omissions which any moral code would censure cannot in a practical world be treated so as to give a right to every person injured by them to demand relief.* In this way rules of law arise which limit the range of complainants and the extent of their remedy. *The rule that you are to love your neighbour becomes in law, you must not injure your neighbour; and the lawyer's question, Who is my neighbour? receives a restricted reply, You must take reasonable care to avoid acts or omissions which you can reasonably foresee would be likely to injure your neighbour. Who, then, in law is my neighbour? The answer seems to be—persons who are so closely and directly affected by my act that I ought reasonably to have them in contemplation as being so affected when I am directing my mind to the acts or omissions which are called in question. This appears to me to be the doctrine of* Heaven *v.* Pender (11 *Q.B.D.* 503, 509.) *as laid down by Lord Esher (then Brett M.R.) when it is limited by the notion of proximity introduced by Lord Esher himself and A. L. Smith L.J. in* Le Lievre *v.* Gould [1893] (1 *Q.B.* 491, 497, 504). Lord Esher says: ' That case established that, under certain circumstances, one man may owe a duty to another, even though there is no contract between them. If one man is near to another, or is near to the property of another, a duty lies upon him not to do that which may cause a personal injury to that other, or may injure his property.' So A. L. Smith L.J.: ' The decision of *Heaven* v. *Pender* (11 Q.B.D. 503, 509) was founded upon the principle, that a duty to take due care did arise when the person or property of one was in such proximity to the person or property of another that, if due care was not taken, damage might be done by the one to the other.' I think that this sufficiently states the truth if proximity be not confined to mere physical proximity, but be used, as I think it was intended, to extend to such close and direct relations that the act complained of directly affects a person whom the person alleged to be bound to take care would know would be directly affected by his careless act. That this is the sense in which nearness or ' proximity ' was intended by Lord Esher is obvious from his own illustration in *Heaven* v. *Pender* (11 Q.B.D. 503, 510) of the application of his doctrine to the sale of goods." [Lord Atkin cited Lord Esher and then continued:] " I draw particular attention to the fact that Lord Esher emphasizes the necessity of goods having to be 'used immediately' and 'used at once before a reasonable opportunity of inspection.' This is obviously to exclude the possibility of goods having their condition altered by lapse of time, and to call attention to the proximate relationship, which may be too remote where inspection even of the person using, certainly of an intermediate person, may reasonably be interposed. With this necessary qualification of proximate relationship as explained in *Le Lievre* v. *Gould* ([1893] 1 Q.B. 491), I think the judgment of Lord Esher expresses the law of England; without the qualification, I think the majority of the Court in *Heaven* v. *Pender* (11 Q.B.D. 503) were justified in thinking the principle was expressed in too general terms. There will no doubt arise cases where it will be difficult to determine whether the contemplated relationship is so close that the duty arises. But in the class of case now before the Court I cannot conceive any difficulty to arise. A manufacturer puts up an article of food in a container which he knows will be opened by the actual consumer. There can be no inspection by any purchaser and no reasonable preliminary inspection by the consumer. Negligently, in the course of preparation, he allows the contents to be mixed with poison. It is said that the law of England and Scotland is that the poisoned consumer has no remedy against the negligent manufacturer. If this were the result of the authorities, I should consider the result a grave defect in the law, and so contrary to principle that I should hesitate long before following any decision to that effect which had not the authority of this House. I would point out that, in the assumed state of the authorities, not only would the consumer have no remedy against the manufacturer, he would have none against any one else, for in the circumstances alleged there would be no evidence of negligence against any one other than the manufacturer; and, except in the case of a consumer who was also a purchaser, no contract and no warranty of fitness, and in the case of the purchase of a specific article under its patent or trade name, which might well be the case in the purchase of some articles of food or drink, no warranty protecting even the purchaser-consumer. There are other instances than of articles of food and drink where goods are sold intended to be used immediately by the customer, such as many forms of goods sold for cleaning purposes, where the same liability must exist. The doctrine supported by the decision below would not only deny a remedy to the consumer who was injured by consuming bottled beer or chocolates poisoned by the negligence of the manufacturer, but also to the user of what should be a harmless proprietary medicine, an ointment, a soap, a cleaning fluid or cleaning powder. I confine myself to articles of common household use, where every one, including the manufacturer, knows that the articles will be used by other persons than the actual ultimate purchaser—namely, by members of his family and his servants, and in some cases his guests. I do not think so ill of our jurisprudence as to suppose that its principles are so remote from the ordinary needs of civilized society and the ordinary claims it makes upon its members as to deny a legal remedy where there is obviously a social wrong."

He then considered the cases which might stand in the way of the appellant and found that all of them could be distinguished either because the relations between the parties were too remote or because the dicta went further than was necessary for the determination of the particular issues. He then concluded—

"*My Lords, if your Lordships accept the view that this pleading discloses a relevant cause of action you will be affirming the proposition that by Scots and English law alike a manufacturer of products, which he sells in such a form as to show that he intends them to reach the ultimate consumer in the form in which they left him with no reasonable possibility of intermediate examination, and with the knowledge that the absence of reasonable care in the preparation or putting up of the pro-*

ducts will result in an injury to the consumer's life or property, owes a duty to the consumer to take that reasonable care.

It is a proposition which I venture to say no one in Scotland or England who was not a lawyer would for one moment doubt. It will be an advantage to make it clear that the law in this matter, as in most others, is in accordance with sound common sense."

As can be seen Lord Atkin's formulation can be thought of in terms of two propositions—a wide one, the neighbour principle, and a narrow one, the liability of a manufacturer to the ultimate consumer of his products. The second is generally accepted but the status of his neighbour generalisation is still conjectural. It seems to be a principle or standard not a rule. It works fairly well when applied to negligent interference with physical interests. In *Home Office* v. *Dorset Yacht Co.* [1970] A.C. 1004, 1026H–1027D Lord Reid said—

" In later years there has been a steady trend towards regarding the law of negligence as depending on principle so that, when a new point emerges, one should ask not whether it is covered by authority but whether recognised principles apply to it. *Donoghue* v. *Stevenson* [1932] A.C. 562 may be regarded as a milestone, and *the well-known passage in Lord Atkin's speech should I think be regarded as a statement of principle. It is not to be treated as if it were a statutory definition.* It will require qualification in new circumstances. But I think that the time has come when we can and should say that it ought to apply unless there is some justification or valid explanation for its exclusion." (Italics supplied.)

Lord Diplock put the matter slightly differently at p. 1058F– 1060E (italics supplied)—

" The justification of the courts' role in giving the effect of law to the judges' conception of the public interest in the field of negligence is based upon the cumulative experience of the judiciary of the actual consequences of lack of care in particular instances. And *the judicial development of the law of negligence rightly proceeds by seeking first to identify the relevant characteristics that are common to the kinds of conduct and relationship between the parties which are involved in the case for decision and the kinds of conduct and relation-*

*ships which have been held in previous decisions of the courts
to give rise to a duty of care.*

*The method adopted at this stage of the process is analytical
and inductive. It starts with an analysis of the characteristics of
the conduct and relationship involved in each of the decided
cases. But the analyst must know what he is looking for, and
this involves his approaching his analysis with some general
conception of conduct and relationships which ought to give
rise to a duty of care. This analysis leads to a proposition which
can be stated in the form:*

> *'In all the decisions that have been analysed a duty of
> care has been held to exist wherever the conduct and the
> relationship possessed each of the characteristics A, B, C,
> D, etc. and has not so far been found to exist when any
> of these characteristics were absent.'*

*For the second stage, which is deductive and analytical, that
proposition is converted to: 'In all cases where the conduct
and relationship possess each of the characteristics A, B, C, D,
etc. a duty of care arises.' The conduct and relationship involved
in the case for decision is then analysed to ascertain whether
they possess each of these characteristics. If they do the conclusion follows that a duty of care does arise in the case for decision.*

But since *ex hypothesi* the kind of case which we are now
considering offers a choice *whether or not to extend the kinds*
of conduct or relationships which give rise to a duty of care,
*the conduct or relationship which is involved in it will lack at
least one of the characteristics A, B, C or D, etc. And the
choice is exercised by making a policy decision as to whether
or not a duty or care ought to exist if the characteristic which
is lacking were absent or redefined in terms broad enough to
include the case under consideration. The policy decision will
be influenced by the same general conception of what ought
to give rise to a duty of care as was used in approaching the
analysis. The choice to extend is given effect to by redefining
the characteristics in more general terms so as to exclude the
necessity to conform to limitations imposed by the former definition which are considered to be inessential.* The cases which
are landmarks in the common law, such as *Lickbarrow* v.
Mason (1787) 2 Term Rep. 63, *Rylands* v. *Fletcher* (1868) L.R.

3 H.L. 330, *Indermaur* v. *Dames* (1866) L.R. 1 C.P. 274, *Donoghue* v. *Stevenson* [1932] A.C. 562, to mention but a few, are instances of cases where the cumulative experience of judges has led to a restatement in wide general terms of characteristics of conduct and relationships which give rise to legal liability.

Inherent in this methodology, however, is a practical limitation which is imposed by the sheer volume of reported cases. The initial selection of previous cases to be analysed will itself eliminate from the analysis those in which the conduct or relationship involved possessed characteristics which are obviously absent in the case for decision. *The proposition used in the deductive stage is not a true universal. It needs to be qualified so as to read*:

> ' In all cases where the conduct and relationship possess each of the characteristics A, B, C and D, etc. but do not possess any of the characteristics Z, Y or X etc. which were present in the cases eliminated from the analysis, a duty of care arises.'

But this qualification, being irrelevant to the decision of the particular case is generally left unexpressed.

This was the reason for the warning by Lord Atkin in *Donoghue* v. *Stevenson* [1932] A.C. 562, itself when he said, at pp. 583–584:

> ' . . . in the branch of the law which deals with civil wrongs, dependent in England at any rate entirely upon the application by judges of general principles also formulated by judges, it is of particular importance to guard against the danger of stating propositions of law in wider terms than is necessary, lest essential factors be omitted in the wider survey and the inherent adaptability of English law be unduly restricted. For this reason it is very necessary in considering reported cases in the law of torts that the actual decision alone should carry authority, proper weight, of course, being given to the dicta of the judges.'

The plaintiff's argument in the present appeal disregards this warning. It seeks to treat as a universal not the specific proposition of law in *Donoghue* v. *Stevenson* which was about a manufacturer's liability for damage caused by his dangerous

products but the well-known aphorism used by Lord Atkin to
describe a ' general conception of relations giving rise to a duty
of care ' [1932] A.C. 562, 580 :

> ' You must take reasonable care to avoid acts or omissions
> which you can reasonably foresee would be likely to injure
> your neighbour. Who, then, in law is my neighbour? The
> answer seems to be—persons who are so closely and
> directly affected by my act that I ought reasonably to have
> them in contemplation as being so affected when I am
> directing my mind to the acts or omissions which are
> called in question.'

*Used as a guide to characteristics which will be found to exist
in conduct and relationships which give rise to a legal duty of
care this aphorism marks a milestone in the modern development of the law of negligence. But misused as a universal it is
manifestly false.*"

Qualifications to the Neighbour Principle

It should be noted that Lord Atkin's general principle is in any
event subject to qualifications in the following areas :

1. *Omissions*. There is still no general duty to act positively for
the benefit of another but the courts are inclined to treat nonfea-
sance as misfeasance—see further H. Street, *The Law of Torts* (6th
ed.), p. 111, and *Winfield and Jolowicz on Tort* (10th ed.) by W. V.
H. Rogers, p. 49.

2. *Negligent Misstatements*. The strong *obiter dicta* of the House
of Lords in *Hedley Byrne & Co. Ltd.* v. *Heller & Partners Ltd.*
[1964] A.C. 465 state that mere foreseeability of loss is not enough
and that a " special relationship " between the parties must exist.
See further Street, *op. cit.* pp. 207 *et seq.* and Winfield and Jolowicz,
op. cit. p. 51.

3. *Economic loss* (in cases other than negligent misstatement).
The courts are reluctant to hold that there is a duty to avoid incur-
ring economic loss however easily foreseeable—see further Street,
op. cit. p. 112 and Winfield and Jolowicz, *op. cit.* p. 51.

4. *Occupiers' liability*. The duty is now a statutory duty under the
Occupiers' Liability Act 1957. It does not, however, extend to
trespassers who are still governed by the common law.

5. *Land law.* Here the test was thought to have no application because the law was well settled before *Donoghue* v. *Stevenson.* Statute law, however, is now making some inroads into the old law and in *Dutton* v. *Bognor Regis U.D.C.* [1972] 1 Q.B. 373, Lord Denning M.R. and Sachs L.J. thought the old cases no longer bound the court.

An Epilogue

The development of negligence is an interesting example of the case law process at work. It reflects all the crucial aspects of that process—analogy, induction, deduction, shifting categorisation, rules, principles, standards and policy. Recently there has been some indication that some judges at least wish to treat some of the matters such as the duty of care as straightforward issues of policy. Thus in *Dutton* v. *Bognor Regis U.D.C.* [1972] I Q.B. 373 Lord Denning M.R. referred to the speeches of Lords Reid, Pearson and Diplock in the *Dorset Yacht* case and said

" It seems to me that it is a question of policy which we, as judges, have to decide. The time has come when, in cases of new import, we should decide them according to the reason of the thing.

In previous times, when faced with a new problem, the judges have not openly asked themselves the question: what is the best policy for the law to adopt? But the question has always been in the background. It has been concealed behind such questions as: Was the defendant under any duty to the plaintiff.... In short, we look to the relationship of the parties, and then say, as a matter of policy, on whom the loss should fall."

Again in *Spartan Steel and Alloys, Ltd.* v. *Martin & Co. (Contractors) Ltd.* [1973] 1 Q.B. 27 Lord Denning M.R. said

" *The more I think about these cases, the more difficult I find it to put care into its proper pigeon hole. Sometimes I say: 'There was no duty.' In others I say: 'The damage was too remote.' So much so that I think the time has come to discard those tests which have proved so elusive. It seems to me better to consider the particular relationship in hand, and see whether or not, as a matter of policy, economic loss should be recoverable.*" (Italics supplied.)

His Lordship was talking in both cases immediately about economic loss and his views on the larger question have not yet gained acceptance although there are signs of growing disenchantment with Lord Atkin's general principle. Legal policy, as we saw in Chapter 13, can be regarded as an interaction of three sets of variables—interests, legal values and a range of practical factors such as convenience and cost. To say that the general principle of Lord Atkin should be discarded for an open avowal of policy is perhaps not to say much at the end of the day. It is inherently a very general kind of principle or standard. It is certainly too general to be a legal rule. Policy plays a key role in the formulation and application of principles and standards. Policy is relevant, as we have seen, to legal rules created and applied in an analogical fashion but it would be a mistake to equate those *rules* with policy or to discard them for policy. Law needs some predictable formal rationality to exist as law. Without it, it is power politics administered by a legal system. Judges need to be political animals but they should not become politicians.

Notes
1 *An Introduction to Legal Reasoning*, pp. 8–9.

BIBLIOGRAPHY OF FURTHER READING

IN addition to the materials specifically cited, the following are of general relevance to the matters discussed in the various chapters.

Preface

The Report of the Committee on Legal Education (the Ormrod Report) Cmnd. 4595.

William Twining, "Pericles and the Plumber" (1967) 83 L.Q.R. 396.

Chapter 1

H. L. A. Hart, *The Concept of Law*.

Dennis Lloyd, *The Idea of Law*.

Edwin M. Schur, *Law and Society*.

M. D. A. Freeman, *The Legal Structure*.

G. Sawer, *Law in Society*.

Karl Llewellyn, *The Bramble Bush*.

Robert S. Summers, *Law: Its Nature, Functions and Limits* (2nd ed.).

E. A. Hoebel, *The Law of Primitive Man*.

R. Dworkin, "Is Law a System of Rules?" in *Essays in Legal Philosophy* (ed. R. S. Summers), p. 25; "Social Rules and Legal Theory," 81 Yale L.J. 855 (1972).

J. Raz, "Legal Principles and the Limits of Law," 81 Yale L.J. 823 (1972).

Chapter 2

Walker and Walker, *The English Legal System* (4th ed.).

R. M. Jackson, *The Machinery of Justice in England* (6th ed.).

D. M. Walker, *The Scottish Legal System* (4th ed.).

J. A. Jolowicz (ed.), *The Division and Classification of the Law*.

Chapter 3

Robert S. Summers, "*The Technique Element in Law*," 59 California L.R. 733 (1971); *Law: Its Nature, Functions and Limits* 2nd ed.).

Chapter 4

Bishin and Stone, *Law, Language and Ethics*.
Walter Probert, *Law, Language and Communication*.

Chapter 5

D. Lloyd, " Reason and Logic in the Law " (1948) 64 L.Q.R. 468.
A. G. Guest, " Logic in the Law " in *Oxford Essays in Jurisprudence* (ed. Guest), p. 176.
Edward Levi, *Introduction to Legal Reasoning*.

Chapter 6

F. W. Maitland, *Equity*.
G. W. Keeton and L. A. Sheridan, *Equity* (2nd ed.).
Hanbury's *Modern Equity* (10th ed.) by R. Maudsley.
P. H. Pettit, *Equity and the Law of Trusts* (3rd ed.).

Chapter 7

See materials under Chapter 5.
Sir Carleton Allen, *Law in the Making* (7th ed.).
Sir Rupert Cross, *Precedent in English Law* (2nd ed.).
Salmond on Jurisprudence (12th ed.) by P. J. Fitzgerald.
R. W. M. Dias, *Jurisprudence* (4th ed.).
Julius Stone, *Legal Systems and Lawyers' Reasonings*.

Chapter 8

S. A. Walkland, *The Legislative Process in Great Britain*.
H. L. A. Hart, *The Concept of Law*.
Sir Carleton Allen, *Law in the Making* (7th ed.).
The Law Commissions' Report on Interpretation of Statutes (Law Com. 21) and see the literature listed there.
J. H. Farrar, *Law Reform and the Law Commission*.
Odgers, *Construction of Deeds and Statutes*.
Maxwell on the Interpretation of Statutes.
Craies, *Statute Law*.
C. Tapper, *Computers and the Law*.
The Report of the Committee on the Preparation of Legislation.
Sir Rupert Cross, *Statutory Interpretation*.

Chapter 9

Glanville Williams (ed.), *The Reform of the Law*, Chap. 1.
G. Gardiner and A. Martin (ed.), *Law Reform Now*, Chap. 1.
J. H. Farrar, *Law Reform and the Law Commission*, Chap. 5, and the materials there cited.

Chapter 10

O. Hood Phillips, *First Book of English Law* (6th ed.), Chap. 14.
Sir W. Holdsworth, *Some Makers of English Law*.
D. L. Carey Miller, " Legal Writings as a Source of English Law " (1975) 8 C.I.L.S.A. 236.

Chapter 11

D. Lasok and J. W. Bridge, *Introduction to the Law of the EEC* (2nd ed.).
K. Lipstein, *The Law of the EEC*.

Chapter 12

W. Friedmann, *Law in a Changing Society*.
Stuart S. Nagel (ed.), *Law and Social Change*.

Chapter 13

R. Pound, " The Limits of Effective Legal Action " (1917) 27 *Ethics* 150.
Harry W. Jones, *The Efficacy of Law*.
R. S. Summers, *Law: Its Nature, Functions and Limits* (2nd ed.).

Chapter 14

R. W. M. Dias, *Jurisprudence* (4th ed.), Chap. 9.
P. Stein and J. Shand, *Legal Values in Western Society*.
L. Fuller, *The Morality of Law*.
R. S. Summers, " Evaluating and Improving Legal Processes—A Plea for Process Values," 60 Cornell L.R. 1 (1974).

NAME INDEX

SUBJECT INDEX
(including Statutes)

Supplementary Benefits Appeals Tri-
bunal, 33
Supplementary Benefits Commission, 33
Supply of Goods (Implied Terms) Act
1973...142
Supreme Court of Judicature, 59
Supreme Court of Judicature (Consolida-
tion) Act 1925...59
Supreme Court (U.S.), 135, 136
Syllogism, 49

Table of Government Orders, App. 2
Tax, 32
Textual amendment, 102
Theft Act 1968...108
Times Law Reports, App. 2
Tort, 26, 65, 142
Trade, Department of, 31
Trade Descriptions Act 1968...29
Travaux preparatoires, 97, 126
Treaty of Rome, Chap. 11
Truisms about human nature, 3, 4
Trust, 30, 57
Truth, 39 *et seq.*

United States of America, Apps. 2 & 3
Utilitarianism, 6, 139, 167

Vagueness, 90
Values, 157 *et seq.*, Chap. 14
legal, 157, 158
process, 162
(legal administration), 161 *et seq.*
(legislative), 161 *et seq.*
(judicial), 161 *et seq.*

Wales; 12
Weekly Law Reports, App. 2
Weekly Notes, App. 2
Welfare state, 7
White Papers, 97
Women, 141

Year Books, App. 2
Yurok Indians, 5